VICTOR S. SY, CPA, MBA
2606 GREENFIELD AVENUE
ARCADIA, CA 91006
(626) 433-5150

MW01046743

HOW TO AVOID
IRS AUDITS

(OR SURVIVE ONE)

A COMPILATION OF
TAX TIPS ARTICLES

BY

VICTOR S. SY, CPA, MBA

© 2016, VICTOR S. SY, CPA MBA, ALL RIGHTS RESERVED

Text copyright © 2016, Victor S. Sy, CPA MBA

All Rights Reserved. No part of this book may be reproduced or utilized in any form or by any means, electronic or mechanical, including photocopying, recording, or by any information storage and retrieval system, without permission in writing from the publisher.

Asian Journal Publications, Inc.

USA
1210 South Brand Boulevard,
Glendale, California 91204

Philippines
2nd Floor, Fort Palm Spring Towers, 30th Street & 1st Avenue
Bonifacio Global City, Taguig, Philippines
Visit our Web site at *www.AsianJournal.com* and *www.BalikbayanMagazine.com*

Additional Research: Louie Gajardo of Sy Accountancy Corporation
Editorial Assistance: Malou Aguilar Bledsoe of Asian Journal

Layout & Design: Allana Santos
Cover Design: Kenno Samulde

ISBN:1530746477

DEDICATION

This book is lovingly dedicated to

My wife, *Marissa Espiritu-Sy.*
Our children *Karen, Byron, Jonathan, and Abigail.*
Our grandchildren *Kirsten, Tyler, and Emily.*
My siblings *Josephine, John, Sol, Te, and Butch.*
Our parents *Sy Pek Tat and Juliana Santos Sy.*

Appreciation is due to my mentors

Bal Endriga, CPA of SGV/Ernst & Young.
Frank Chan, CPA of SGV & KPMG.
Gary Kuwada, CPA, Tax Lawyer.
Gil Vasquez, CPA of Vasquez & Company LLP.

Huge thank you to my main staff

Esthela Espin Fernandez
Theresa Simbol, Bert Dalmacio
Louie Gajardo, Kikuko Martin
Myh Espiritu, Sanny Tan, Gladys
Susan, Joann, Lea, Rod, Deedee
Cecille, Sandy, Alyn, Cora, Rosan

V ictory in the trenches...

That's where I've been—in the trenches—for a hundred times. I have fought wars with IRS auditors over several decades. My writings are based on actual battles with the IRS. My tales are born of experience, my tips from actual dealings with the IRS.

I spent 50 years working as a Certified Public Accountant (CPA), 39 running my own firm.
I held licenses for the states of California, Hawaii, and Illinois performing tax, accounting, systems, consulting, and audit jobs for the then big eight international accounting firms—Ernst & Ernst, SGV (SyCip Gorres Velayo)/Arthur Andersen, and Andersen Consulting. Some years were boring, some interesting.

During this half-century career as a CPA and tax consultant, I enjoyed IRS audits the most. Accounting is not the most exciting job; fighting the IRS is. I developed a passion for both fighting and working with IRS auditors. Defending taxpayers before the IRS is the love of my life, next only to my family. I like it. I enjoy it. I feel at home at the IRS. And for good reasons—I win. This may not be a common element, but somehow I like the challenge, face-to-face, eyeball to eyeball incidents with auditors, struggles, and handshake at the end of the chess match.

In my earlier years, I was intimidated by older IRS veterans. I hoped to be matched against younger auditors, greenhorns. Little did I know that years later, I'd wish for older auditors and dread neophyte auditors who are out to impress their supervisors and managers.

I'm so proud of our string of victories in income tax audits. I lost a few, of course. But of the few losses, I brought most to the Appeals Division and won them all. I consider myself lucky at Appeals where I never lost a case. This is one of the reasons I compiled my tax articles for this book—victory in the trenches!

A popular win ends with a "no-change" result where the IRS accepts what you filed. No tax due. Paying much less mulla than the assessed amount is also a win. So is a successful damage control plan that limits exposure.For example, I may have given up seven of 10 issues, but the three that I won packed more $$. I may have lost most issues but there was an 11th issue that I protected, a rather delicate one. Keeping you out of Criminal Investigation Division (CID) with threats of jail is definitely a huge victory.

Here are the secrets of my success: meticulous planning and preparation, having efficient staff like Louie who worked with me for 13 years, psychology, and humility. Braggadocio does not win cases; humility does. My ultimate weapon: credibility. But humor got me there. So did a penchant to work with agents—as a team! Can you believe working with the agent in your own team? This may sound strange to you, but this is how I managed to be so adept at winning my battles.It's called the art of tax representation by my buddy, noted tax attorney Gary Kuwada. Yes, knowledge of tax law is vital, but humor, humility, timing, and willingness to compromise and settle are all ingredients to victory.

Dealing with the IRS requires you to understand the Agency's culture:
Shoot first, ask later.
You are guilty until proven innocent
You must prove that the IRS is wrong; the IRS does not have to prove itself right.
All income are taxable unless you prove that they're not.
All deductions are not allowed unless you can prove that they are.

All these, you have to overcome. It's an uphill battle. To win a battle against the IRS, you must unlock its secrets. To unlock its secrets, you must have been in the trenches to see what tactics work and what don't. I have been there. Done that.

If you retain a Certified Public Accountant (CPA), Enrolled Agent (EA), or tax attorney to represent you as your Power of Attorney (POA), open up. Open your closet to your rep. Show the good, the bad, and the ugly. You really don't want your own rep learning of skeletons in your closet from the auditor.Keep your rep more informed than the auditor so he can defend and counter attack as needed. Keeping dirty secrets from your rep can make life miserable for you.

Upon seeing me score wins, my wife Marissa encouraged me to write a book on IRS audits. Roger Oriel, publisher of Asian Journal and Balikbayan Magazine, who has seen me prepare, go to war, and win encouraged and helped me publish this book. His son, Raphael John "RJ" Oriel gave me a boost to proceed with his youth and optimism. I just retired so this is the perfect time to compile my articles into a book.

My book is a compilation of articles that I wrote over five decades. Bear with me if some phrases appear similar or repetitive as these were penned for Asian Journal, California Examiner, Apartment Association of Greater Los Angeles, Foothill Apartment Association, and other newspapers and magazines all over the country over different periods of time.

I hope you will like reading my book, learn tips, and enjoy some humor along the way.

My promise to you: it's not boring.

Vic Sy

Victor S. Sy, CPA, MBA

Education:	BBA Bachelor of Science in Business Administration – University of the East, Cum Laude.
	MBA Masters in Business Administration – Indiana State University.
CPA Licenses:	State of California.
	State of Illinois.
	State of Hawaii.
Work Experience:	SGV SyCip, Gorres, & Velayo/Andersen Consulting, Manila.
	Ernst & Young, Indiana, USA
	Sy Accountancy Corporation, California, USA
Years Of Practice:	50 years as CPA.
	39 years in private practice as President of Sy Accountancy Corporation.
Areas of Practice:	Audits and appeals before the IRS, Franchise Tax Board, Employment Development Department, Board of Equalization, Department of Labor.
	Offers in Compromise & Installment agreements with the IRS, FTB, EDD.
	Tax & Accounting Services for LLC, Corporation, Partnerships, Individuals.
	Real estate taxation, asset protection planning, tax planning.
Memberships:	American Institute of CPAs, California Society of CPAs
	Tau Alpha Sigma Fraternity, Philippine American Society of CPAs
Commissions:	Commissioner, Legal Advisory Council, State of California.
	Commissioner, Code Enforcement Commission, City of Pasadena.
	Commissioner, Cultural Heritage Commission, City of Los Angeles.
	Member, Committee on Productivity, City of Los Angeles.
	Commissioner, Arcadia Beautiful Commission, City of Arcadia.
Awards:	Outstanding CPA in Public Practice, PICPA.
	Outstanding CPA award, PASCPA.
	Top 66 Graduate Award, University of the East.
	Outstanding Alumni Award, University of the East.
	Exceptional Achievement Award, University of the East.
	Certificate of Commendation, Mayor Tom Bradley, City of Los Angeles.
	Certificate of Commendation, Mayor Antonio Villaraigosa, City of Los Angeles.
	Businessman of the Year, National Republican Business Advisory Council.
	Top 10 Ernst & Young Midwest Conference.
Publications:	Tax columnist for Asian Journal, California Examiner
	AAGLA Apartment Assn of Los Angeles, Apartment Age, Foothill Apartment Reporter.
	Author, How to Avoid IRS Audits (Or Survive One).
Charity:	Benefactor of teachers and schools in Jones, Isabela, Philippines.
	Volunteer for CHP California Highway Patrol.

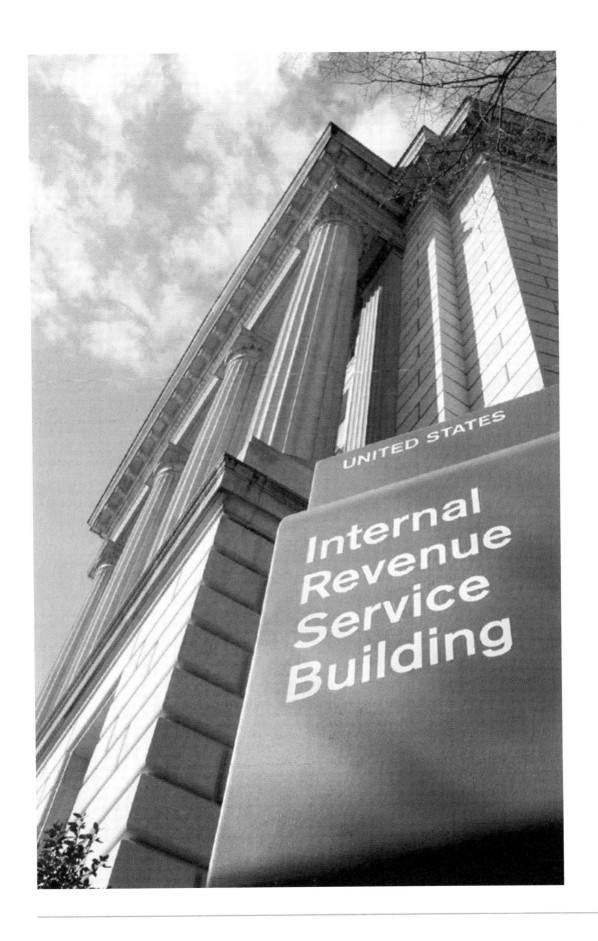

"My corporation and I were special guests of honor at annual IRS audit events. You took care of our audit with a victory and took off our names from the IRS hit list! We have not had any IRS problem since. Thank you!"
— NM

"Despite our IRS audits and other serious tax problems, our meeting last Friday was a breath of fresh air. You took care of the audit and found a solution to our tax debts with an offer in compromise. Your brotherly advice was indeed very rejuvenating. Again, thank you so much for caring. Best regards to you and your family."
— AD, for RD, MD

"Dear Vic, Thank you for cleansing our tax returns of red flags. You're terrific! If we make the same mistake again next year, we deserve some punishment. Thanks again."
— MJ

"Of course it's very useful. Of all your newsletters, this edition on "Should you attend your own IRS audit?" is the most scary but also the funniest. I don't want to attend my own funeral....ha...ha...ha...Thanks for making me laugh today."
— YD

"Dear Vic, I really admire your efficiency and the quality of your work products. It was very nice working with you. I learned so much in so short a time. More power to your firm!"
— Gratefully, ME, Accountant

"Indiana State University certainly produced an outstanding alumnus in Victor Sy, CPA, MBA. I had anxiety attacks from IRS audits and serious tax problems that threatened me and my son. He calmly took charge and solved our IRS problems. That was 25 years ago. I have been so impressed by his terrific professionalism, honesty, and integrity since then. You don't have to search any further to solve your anxiety from IRS audits. I found the perfect CPA and a most trustworthy friend!"
— JM, R.N.

"Victor, This is the second tax seminar of yours that I attended. You were brief, understandable, and to-the-point. The IRS website is a maze and hard to understand. Your wonderful handouts in bullet forms are brief, easy to understand, and answered questions precisely. What I like the most is your use of bullet form. I encountered my first 1031 real estate tax deferred exchange as a real estate broker. I called the IRS. Responses were confusing. You described 1031 in a clear way that was easily understood by the audience. I conduct my own seminars and find yours to be informative, effective, and enjoyable with lots of humor."
— LJ, Realtor

"My wife and I know several experienced accountants. However, it's rare to hear an expert with Victor's background and knowledge. He has an impressive education and his professional experience covers almost every possible tax and accounting subject. It's indeed rare to find an accountant so well versed through the most complex subjects from 1031 tax deferred exchange, and IRS audits. Victor at his tax seminar made us understand complex issues and put us at ease with his humor and wit. We happy to find an accountant with his humility and professionalism.."
— Atty WB

"Sooner or later, you and I knew this day will come. You will be missed. Yes, you and I have been through both good and challenging times, but in the end, I have always landed on my feet with a smile, all because of you. Your advice, your guidance, your caring and comforting words have always given me support and assurance.
Again, I will miss you dearly, but I'm so happy for you—you have paid your dues." Enjoy, old friend..."
— IW, Bank Sr VP and COO.

"Hi Victor: I was so glad to see you at the office the last time I was there. You gave me good advice to stop our 1031 exchange and to use the money to enjoy our retirement, while my husband is still with us, regardless of his stroke. We will miss you, since you have taken good care of us."
— CW, LLC, Landlord

"Thank you SO much Victor for ALL of your hard work and service. Thank you from our family for your kindness and competence! Hugs!" —
JK of JPL in Pasadena, California

"Dear Victor, *It's hard for to grasp that you are gone. You have helped me in my greatest time of need, I WISH YOU WELL and may God keep you and your family happy."*
— Your friend, VR, Real estate Investor

I have known Vic since the '80s when we worked on income tax compliance cases. He was already writing tax tips columns for newspapers and magazines then. I'm pleased to see him compile his Tax Tips into a book.

I have not seen a book that dives this deep with practical tips into IRS audits and appeals. It's very informative.It serves as a valuable resource for taxpayers undergoing audit or trying to avoid one. It's loaded with tips on Offers in Compromise and Installment Plans to avoid financial hardships. The list of banks that report depositors to IRS should be of interest to those who have not been reporting their cash and financial assets abroad.

I identify with this book because I used to work for the IRS as a field Revenue Agent and Appeals Officer. I was a full-time college instructor at California State University and have been teaching Federal Income Taxation at UCLA (University of California in Los Angeles) for 32 years. His published tax columns are easy to read which is why I used them for my own classrooms. I've been a tax attorney for 40 years and have dealt with various tax professionals. Vic stands out with his efficiency via systems and procedures in dealing with IRS auditors. For example, we had a case of a celebrity client who had major issues and had not filed for 10 years. Vic took over the case and methodically prepared delinquent returns in a professional manner. What could not be done in 10 years, he did in less than a year, which I found rather noteworthy. I'm sure you'll learn valuable lessons from this seasoned veteran. You may also find his humor quite entertaining.

Morton D. Rosenthal, Esq.

**EX-IRS FIELD INTERNAL REVENUE AGENT
AND APPEALS REFEREE**

HOW TO AVOID IRS AUDITS
(OR SURVIVE ONE IF YOU ARE CHOSEN)

TABLE OF CONTENTS

HOW IRS REVIEWS, SCORES, AND CHOOSE TAX RETURNS FOR AUDIT

The Internal Revenue Service (IRS) goes back to the Civil War when President Lincoln and Congress enacted an income tax law to pay war expenses in 1862. In the 1950s, the agency was reorganized to replace a patronage system with career, professional employees. The Bureau of Internal Revenue name was changed to the Internal Revenue Service. It's a bureau of the Department of the Treasury and is responsible for collecting taxes.

The mission of the IRS is to provide America's taxpayers with top quality service by helping them understand and meet their tax responsibilities and by applying the tax law with integrity and fairness to all. The agency has been perceived as a police force to collect taxes. President George Bush changed that image to a "kinder and gentler" IRS. However, the pendulum has swung back to audit and collection.

We have a voluntary tax system that allows us to compute our taxes and file our own tax returns. An IRS audit is a review of tax returns to ensure that they are properly reported. The word "audit" is scary for most of us as it involves visits to an IRS office or even worse visits from revenue agents to our homes and businesses.

The first chapters of this book deals with such audits — how to avoid and survive IRS audits. We start this chapter by discussing how the IRS verifies tax returns that you file, stores them into master files, and scores them for audit. Chapter one also discusses the life cycle of tax returns — from filing to storing, sorting, selection, audit, and appeals.

And by the way, IRS uses the "examination" and "review" for what we commonly refer to as audits.

HOW IRS SCORES YOUR INCOME TAX RETURNS FOR AUDIT
(Part 1 – Verification, Validation, and Review for Accuracy)

Have you ever been audited by the IRS? Did you ever wonder how they picked you? Here's a three-part series on how tax returns are received, stored, and chosen for audit:
1. How e-filed and paper-filed tax returns are *verified, validated, and reviewed* for accuracy.
2. How tax returns are *stored* into master files.
3. How IRS *scores* your tax returns for audit.

Let's explore the first part in this series – verification, validation, and review for accuracy.

UPON RECEIVING YOUR INCOME TAX RETURN, THE IRS CAN:
- Question any entry on your return,
- Request an explanation of income that does not match Form W-2, 1099 and other data from 3rd parties,
- Audit your return, or
- Collect tax due on the return.

HOW E-FILED RETURNS ARE VERIFIED, VALIDATED, AND ACCEPTED:
- Electronic tax return data are transmitted to a designated Submission Processing Center.
- Coding and correcting errors are sharply reduced with the elimination of manual chores.
- Tax softwares assign a unique 14-digit Declaration Control Number to each return.
- A unique Filing Location Code shown as the first two digits distinguishes returns as e-filed.
- An electronic Management System provides data verification, data translation, and delivery.
- Federal return is validated and accepted.
- Any attached state return is transferred to a State Retrieval Subsystem.
- State returns are then made available for retrieval by participating state revenue agencies.
- This explains how state tax agencies learn of your IRS audit.
- This also explains how the State Board of Equalization learns of undeclared sales tax.

HOW PAPER-FILED RETURNS ARE SORTED, NUMBERED, AND REVIEWED FOR ACCURACY:
- Tax returns are sorted upon arrival at a Service Center.
- Payments included with the returns are removed and deposited.
- Return and checks are assigned Document Locator Numbers for identification.
- Different numbers may be assigned to the same taxpayer (all tied together by your social security number).
- Business returns are tied by employer identification numbers.
- Each return is reviewed for completeness and mathematical accuracy.
- Service Center personnel look for gross or obvious errors and fill in incomplete items
- A computerized version is forwarded to the computing center in Martinsburg, WV.
- Martinsburg generates refunds and notices.
- It also notifies Service Centers if any other action is required to settle your account.
- Any discrepancy between data on the return and information on your account is classified as unpostable and returned to Service Centers for resolution.

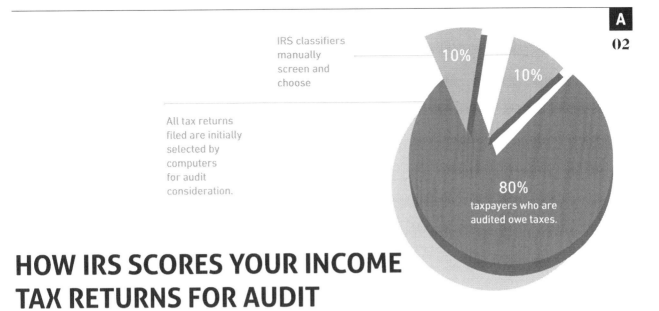

IRS classifiers manually screen and choose

All tax returns filed are initially selected by computers for audit consideration.

10%

10%

80%
taxpayers who are audited owe taxes.

HOW IRS SCORES YOUR INCOME TAX RETURNS FOR AUDIT

(Part 2 - Master Files)

In the prior article, we discussed how tax returns are received, verified, and reviewed for completeness. **Let's now discuss the second part that deals with how your tax returns are stored into master files.**

After receiving your tax return, the IRS enters your tax data into an IRS master file. The master file is separated into Individual Master File, Business Master File, and Non-Master Files.

1. **Individual Master File** is a magnetic tape record of all individual income tax filers in social security number sequence. All tax data and related information pertaining to each individual income tax filer are posted to this file. It's continuously updated as a current record of each taxpayer's account.

2. **Business Master File** is a magnetic tape record of all business taxpayers with employer identification numbers. Taxes processed include corporate, partnership, LLC, employment, excise, fiduciary, estate, gift, and tax-exempt organizations with investment income.

   Each taxpayer's account is divided into tax modules (tax years) reflecting current status, balance, and transactions applicable to each tax year. This information includes tax return data, assessments, and changes made to return as filed. A transcript of taxpayer's account is a printout of tax module information.

3. **Non-Master File** is a smaller database that controls returns not processed on the master files. This includes assessments, adjustments, and refunds that are performed manually at the Service Centers. Master files are not efficient because of manual processing required to obtain accurate balances from other files. The IRS hopes this problem to disappear with the introduction of a modern data engine called CADE (see below).

4. **There's a new kid in town—CADE** that stands for Customer Account Data Engine. It's replacing the aging Master File System. This is a modern data storage management and accessing system that is designed to provide real-time access to taxpayer accounts, up-to-the-minute data, and easy access by authorized IRS personnel. CADE handles returns with Schedules C, E, and F and those claiming Earned Income Tax Credit (EITC) and Dependent Care Credit. A newer version called CADE 2 updates taxpayer account information on a daily basis. This speeds up responses to taxpayer inquiries, reduce the number of out-of-date notices, and allow a shorter refund cycling time.

HOW IRS SCORES YOUR INCOME TAX RETURNS FOR AUDIT

(Part 3 – Audit Scores)

Let's now discuss the last article: **How the IRS scores tax returns for audit.** The *higher the score, the more likelihood that you'll be chosen for audit.*

1. **Scoring System:** The IRS uses a Discriminant Function System (DIF) to determine returns that are most likely to generate additional revenue for the government. Although the scoring is secret, it's based on two factors: Total Positive Income and Total Gross Receipts. A return with a high DIF score is more likely to be audited, since such a score indicates a greater probability that additional revenue will be generated. The DIF score is based on statistical profiles developed through the National Research Program (NRP).

2. **National Research Program (NRP):** The IRS developed a new NRP to replace the old Taxpayer Compliance Measurement Program (TCMP). NRP developed new audit criteria from a stratified sample of approximately 50,000 individual audits. Data obtained from the NRP audits are being used to score returns for audit.

3. **Exceeding National Averages Attract Audits:** Taking deductions that exceed national averages increases your audit score. TIP: If you exceed the averages, *opt out* of e-file. Instead, *paper file and attach explanation of unusual amounts such as big donations or large medical bills.*

4. **Other Sources of Audits:** Audits also come from matching programs, return preparer programs, claims for refund, or separate related-party audits.

5. **Employment Tax Audits:** The main goal is to secure statistically valid information for determining the most noncompliant employment tax areas (home care industry for example). The IRS selected 2,000 taxpayers each year for the last three years to focus on worker classification issues—independent contractors versus employees (1099 versus W2).

6. **Nation's Tax Gap:** The IRS estimated the nation's annual gross tax gap (meaning the difference between what taxpayers should pay and what they actually pay) at $450 billion 10 years ago. The Treasury Inspector General for Tax Administration (TIGTA) indicated that the tax gap is even wider since the IRS formulas are outdated and unable to include much of the underground economy (workers paid under the table and purchases paid by cash).

7. **Tax Gap –** Statistics Show That:
   - Failure to report income accounts for 80% of the total gap.
   - Nonfiling and underpayment account for 10% each.
   - More than 80% of individual underreporting comes from understated income.
   - Most of understated income comes from business activities.
   - Individual income tax is the largest source of the gap, accounting for 60% of the total gap.
   - Underreporting is lowest where there is third-party reporting or withholding (W2 and 1099).

FUTURE AUDITS: The IRS Commissioner and the Treasury Inspector General for Tax Administration (TIGTA) have indicated that closing the tax gap has become a higher priority with increased document matching prograams, expanded information reporting programs, examination of high income individuals and Schedule C's with a history of losses. All these factors lead to more IRS audits in the coming years.

IRS EXPANDS AUDITS TO PRIOR YEAR & SUBSEQUENT YEARS

The Treasury Inspector General for Tax Administration (TIGTA, an agency that oversees the IRS) instructed the IRS to *expand audits to prior and subsequent years.* While this was already a standard operating procedure, the new instruction reiterates that agents obey this instruction to get you for three years. If the IRS audits your income tax return for 2015, they must expand the audit to your 2014 and 2016 as well. Ouch!

The Treasury Department conducted its own audit of the IRS (yes, they also get audited!) to determine whether tax compliance officers conducted required filing checks in accordance with IRS policies and procedures.

TIGTA stated that IRS must make every effort to ensure that audits are expanded to prior year returns, as well as subsequent year returns, when "substantial" taxes may be involved.

TIGTA evaluated single-year audits of individual returns for which the taxpayers understated their tax liabilities by more than $4,400. Auditors scrutinized 100 of such sample cases. Although similar tax issues may have existed on prior and/or subsequent year returns, the audits were not expanded to those returns in 48 of the 100 sample cases. As a consequence, opportunities may have been missed to address the noncompliance that contributes to the tax gap and promote tax system fairness among the vast majority of taxpayers who properly report and pay their taxes year in and year out.

IRS has estimated that $197 billion of the $345 billion tax gap is attributable to individuals underreporting their income tax liabilities.

TIGTA IDENTIFIED TWO FACTORS WHY THE IRS MAY NOT HAVE EXPANDED AUDITS:
1. The agency strives to keep its audit inventories free of old tax year returns.
2. Tax compliance officers do not take advantage of available internal sources of information.

LIFE CYCLE OF AN AUDIT

While audit penetration has substantially decreased over the last few years, courtesy of budget constraints and personnel reductions, the quality of audits has improved. Auditors undergo specialization training. They conduct economic reality audits that involve looking at issues beyond your tax returns into how you survive with the amount of income that you report. This intrusion into the lifestyle of taxpayers has become disturbing. Read on to analyze the life cycle of an audit to prepare for your next audit:

1. Returns are filed on April 15 of each year with the extensions through October 15 for individual returns. Upon arrival at the Service Center, the tax returns are sorted and assigned a document locator number (DLN), a control number that serves as the identification for the particular item. Although different DLNs may be assigned to the same taxpayer, the taxpayer's Social Security number ties all together.

2. After each return is sorted, returns are reviewed for completeness. Selected items are entered into computers and returns are checked for mathematical accuracy. Paper returns are filed and computerized versions are forwarded to the National Record Center in West Virginia.

3. After returns are received at the National Records Center, information is then entered into a master file, an online file of all known taxpayers. Returns are classified into individual master files (IMF) and business master files (BMF). The IMF is a magnetic tape record of all individual income tax filers arranged by Social Security numbers. All of tax data and related information pertaining to an individual are posted to this IMF and is continuously updated. The BMF is arranged by employer identification numbers (EIN) and is maintained for corporations, partnerships, payrolls, fiduciaries and gift taxes.

4. At the National Records Center, the returns are scored with a discriminant function system (DIF) to determine which of you will be reviewed for audits. The DIF function is a statistical scoring of each return based on information developed by the taxpayer compliance measurement program (TCMP). The scoring is based on total positive income and total gross receipts. Once scored, the returns are sent back to the Service Center (in your case, the Fresno Service Center) for audit consideration. The returns are selected for audit based on the DIF score and other criteria such as failure to report all W2s and 1099s.
    Development: *The TCMP is old and outdated and was replaced by National Research Program (NRP). A new scoring system has been generated as a result of the recent audit of 50,000 tax returns.*

5. The selected returns are then scheduled for audit—internal audit, correspondence audit, office audit, or field audit. Returns with specific questions or easily verifiable information such as missing W2s and 1099s undergo correspondence audits. Office audits require you to visit an IRS office where you will be examined by an office auditor. The more complex returns are assigned to Revenue agents in field audits.

6. The first notice that you receive, one that will stick in your mind for a while, is a contact letter advising you that your return has been selected for examination. It spells out the preliminary areas for audit. You are required to contact the IRS office within 10 days. An appointment is made and you or your rep proceeds to the nearest IRS office. In field audit, the Revenue agent visits your place of business.

7. At the conclusion of the audit, the auditor issues an RAR (Revenue Agent Report) detailing the proposed adjustments. At this time, you have two choices: pay up or file an appeal.

8. If you disagree with the findings, file an appeal. The mission of the Appeals Office is to resolve tax controversies on a fair and impartial basis. It is designed to enhance voluntary compliance and improve public confidence in the integrity and efficiency of the IRS. The purpose of the Appeals process is to provide an administrative procedure for

taxpayers to resolve their disagreements with the IRS without resorting to legal action. You may file a formal written protest, a brief written statement, or an oral request, depending on the amount of taxes. Most cases referred to Appeals are settled. In my personal experience and those of my colleagues, the Appeals is a wonderful arena for taxpayers. The Appeals officer is neutral as opposed to being at the examination level where the office auditor or Revenue agent is, of course, pro-government. *(Caveat: Be careful in signing Form 870, waiver of the statute of limitations)*. If your case is not settled in Appeals, tax is assessed and a statutory notice (90-day letter) is issued.

9. You then have 90 days to file a Tax Court petition. If you fail to file that petition, you lose the case. It is equivalent to losing by default in a civil lawsuit. At that juncture, you have no alternative but to pay. You may then file a suit for refund in a Court of Federal Claims or Federal District Court. In the meantime, the IRS is prohibited from collecting the tax and harassing you until the Tax Court has rendered a final decision.

10. The *collection* phase starts as soon as it is determined that you owe additional taxes. At this time, you then find out that what was supposed to be a kinder, gentler IRS has become a leaner and meaner IRS. The Service assesses the tax and your account is forwarded to the Collection Division for further action. The Service Center issues the first series of collection notices (CP501 through CP504). These notices grow increasingly demanding and forceful in tone and eventually result, if unanswered, in levies and seizures of property.

11. If the Fresno Service Center fails to collect the taxes at that time, the case is referred to the Automated Collection System (ACS). The ACS is a nameless, faceless computerized collection system that utilizes the telephone. IRS personnel at various "call sites" have little authority to help you by way of compromise or installment but have great authority to harm you. If I may suggest, do not be rude to them of as they could easily levy your bank accounts by simply pushing buttons in their computer terminals.

12. If ACS fails, your case is then assigned for collection to a Revenue officer who contacts and visits you at your residence or place of business. It is at this time that you really have to be represented by a CPA, enrolled agent, or tax lawyer. This is serious, folks. I do not relish Revenue officers visiting my clients at their homes where they can spot a Lexus or Mercedes in your driveway or in your place of business where there is much more activity than what you may have reported in your income tax returns. The Revenue officer interviews and asks you to complete a detailed collection information statement that gives him/her a road map to what you own. The Revenue officer then proceeds to collect by using several avenues: file a lien on your properties, levy your bank accounts, garnish your wages, sell your assets, or allow you to enter into an offer in compromise or installment arrangement.

13. When delinquent taxes are paid or an offer in compromise or installment agreement is in place, the collection matter is closed. If collection efforts fail, your liabilities are entered into your very own individual master file where it will remain for the next 10 years. Future refunds will be seized to offset your outstanding liabilities.

14. You may go to the Appellate Division of the IRS just after your return is examined (pre- assessment case) or after you are referred to the Collection Division (post-assessment case). About 10% of examined returns are brought to Appeals with only *less than 2% unresolved requiring litigation*. Invocation of Appeals Division jurisdiction to hear contested issues before a petition is filed in Tax Court is a non-docketed case. On the other hand, it becomes a docketed case after a petition is filed in Tax Court.

As you can see, going through an audit and subsequent collection can be nerve-wracking. It can be an exciting lesson if you seek adventure. Sure, it can be a vindication if you win. But this is not one adventure that you want to take. In the end, your win or loss will depend on the condition of your records, the mood of the auditor, and the expertise of your representative. One final thought: You may save funds by defending yourself but do not represent yourself when issues get tough. Do not save on representation fees and end up paying more expensive penalties and interests.

IRS AUDITS 50,000 TAX RETURNS FOR NRP

Remember the dreaded Taxpayer Compliance Measurement Program (TCMP) audits of yesteryears? These audits were dubbed "audits from hell" and rightly so. That TCMP is gone. It was replaced by National Research Program (NRP) (defined below) but it involves the same torture. It's even worse because the IRS updated their guidelines and honed up their skills. If you had the misfortune of getting selected for such audit, you would not forget it. You would not forget how the agent put you through a treadmill by questioning *every single* item in your return, instead of just focusing on red flags. The audit of 50,000 tax returns forms the foundation of NRP that will be used in choosing who gets amongst you get audited.

1. The IRS needs parameters in choosing which returns should be audited in the future.

2. Out goes TCMP—leaving the Service with no systematic way of selecting tax returns for audit.

3. In comes NRP (National Research Program)—taking the place of TCMP.

4. The new NRP is less intrusive and burdensome to taxpayers than the old TCMP.

5. The goal of NRP is the accurate measurement of tax compliance.

6. It allows the IRS to replace outdated audit formula.

7. It targets tax returns most likely to have errors.

8. In other words, NRP is expected to provide a road map for selecting returns for future audits.

9. It updates screening techniques for selecting returns for examination.

10. The big difference between the old intrusive TCMP and the new NRP is the shifting of more burdens to the IRS rather than the taxpayer.

11. The IRS audited about 50,000 tax returns to start the National Research Program.

12. About 8,000 returns were checked *internally* using available information at the IRS. In other words, there were no contacts with taxpayers.

13. About 9,000 returns were audited by *correspondence* (instead of the usual face-to-face exam).

14. About 30,000 returns underwent *partial* audits (information was gathered from available records while taxpayers will be asked for missing data).

15. The remaining 3,000 went through *calibration* audits—the most rigorous of this batch. If you are chosen for such audit, there are a few things you can do: prepare well, be organized, and read our articles on how to survive IRS audits. And, yes—pray. You'll need it.

10 GENERAL ISSUES COVERED AT IRS OFFICE AUDITS

> TIP: Auditors can raise additional questions. It is therefore advantageous for you and your rep to work with the agent in a respectful and professional manner to contain the issues (rather than fight, antagonize the auditor, and expand the issues beyond the pre-selected items). Good luck. ☺

There are three basic types of IRS audits: correspondence, office, and field examinations. *Correspondence* audits are generally used for specific questions that can easily be verified. *Office* audits are conducted at the various offices of the IRS and tend to be structured. *Field* audits are geared toward businesses whose books and records have to be verified. Let's discuss *10 issues that generally come up during office audits*:

1. ***Unreported Income:*** Did you report all W2s and 1099s? Do you have other income from any sources that were not reported?

2. ***Itemized Deductions:*** Can you support mortgages, property taxes, contributions, and other employment-related deductions. Do you have checks and thank you letters to support, say, donations of $4,000 when the national average is only $1,000? ☺

3. ***Miscellaneous Deductions:*** Did you claim excessive employee business expenses? Does it make sense, for example, for you to spend $10,000 of auto expenses, dues, subscriptions, uniforms and small tools when your income from such employment grossed you $18,000? Of course not. But when you get too aggressive on deducting phantom expenses, you are inviting an audit.

4. ***Dependency Exemptions:*** Are you entitled to dependents that you claimed? Do they have social security or individual tax identification numbers? Did you provide more than half of their support?

5. ***Head of Household:*** Are you entitled to claim this status? Did you provide more than half the support of a child if you are married (but living apart) or of another dependent if you are unmarried? If you are divorced, was the final decree issued by the end of that year?

6. ***Bad Debts:*** Are you entitled to a bad debt deduction for a worthless receivable? Is the borrower related or a close friend (or used to)? Is the gift more of a loan? Can you produce a cancelled check or promissory note? Did you take enough effort to collect? Were those steps oral or written? (Write at least three letters—a nice first letter, a demanding second letter, and a warning third letter). Use certified mail especially if your ex-close friend has moved out or simply vanished with no forwarding address. That letter stamped "return to sender" could come handy.

7. ***Income from Business or Profession:*** Did you report all your collections? (I have represented clients who hid some of their income by depositing collections to their personal accounts that are routinely verified by auditors!) Did you deduct 100% of a car that is used mostly for commuting (home to office and office to home)? Did you deduct personal as business expenses?

8. ***Rental Income:*** Did you report all rentals from tenants? Is any tenant your relative? If so, did you charge the going rate for the rental unit?

9. ***Partnerships, LLCs and S Corporations:*** Did you properly report K—1s from pass-through entities?

10. ***Capital Expenditures:*** Did you deduct as current expenses items that should have been capitalized and depreciated over a period of time?

HOW TO AVOID
AN IRS AUDIT

As some of you may have noticed, the pendulum has swung back from a "gentler and kinder IRS" to enforcement and compliance. Ouch!

Every year, the IRS National Office sets up an audit plan to decide the number of tax returns and types of returns to be audited. The objective is to identify returns that are most likely to contain errors and therefore result in increased tax liability. Tax returns are scored. The higher the score, the more likelihood that your return will be audited. It's really economics folks – The IRS audits returns that are most likely yield more revenues to the government.

Once a return is selected for audit, a decision is made as to type - correspondence audit, office audit at a local IRS office, or as a field audit at your home or place of business.

This chapter helps reduce your chance of getting picked up for examination. It gives you tips – lots of do's and don'ts – to avoid IRS audits.

20 DON'TS IN AN IRS AUDIT

1. Don't ignore the IRS.

2. Don't mess with the IRS.

3. Don't go to your appointment unprepared.

4. Don't be late for your appointment with the auditor.

5. Don't volunteer information.

6. Don't be condescending of education, experience, age, or gender.

7. Don't be arrogant, even if you clearly have an upper hand.

8. Don't flaunt your being a CPA or lawyer to an agent who may have fewer qualifications.

9. Don't insult.

10. Don't bully.

11. Don't raise your voice.

12. Don't fight the auditor. This is an agent's case assignment, not a personal attack against you.

13. Don't create distance between you and the agent.

14. Don't insist on indefensible positions. You'll lose it anyway.

15. Don't argue for the sake of arguing. You know who's going to lose. ☹

16. Don't expect to win on all issues. Settle.

17. Don't reject the agent's position without adequate analysis. It could be worse.

18. Don't be fixated in resolving the case with the agent. Go to Appeals.

19. Don't complain about bureaucracy. Instead, use bureaucracy to your advantage.

20. Lastly, if you're in a hole, stop digging!

And if you don't behave, plead the fifth.

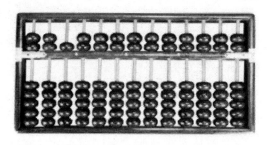

12 WAYS TO AVOID AN IRS AUDIT

1. Do not boast about how you got away with undeclared income or manufactured deductions. Ever heard of whistleblowers? They earn rewards of 15% to 30% of your assessments. If you have a tendency to be creative, keep it to yourself. Just shut up. Better yet, stop being creative. Remember the law of averages. Remember Murphy's Law.

2. Do not hide interest and dividend income from the IRS, even if your spouse may not be aware of some savings and stock brokerage accounts. Remember Murphy's Law—he/she will come to know about it at a worse time later when IRS sends notice of unreported income or notice of audit. Whew. L

3. Similarly, do not estimate income from interest, dividend, independent contract, partnerships, S-Corporations, or LLCs. Banks, stock brokers and entities send exact amounts of your income to IRS via form 1099s and K-1s. Estimates are bad. They generate mismatch - the main source of correspondence audits.

4. Do not estimate mortgage interest because lenders send exact amounts via form 1098 to IRS. TIP: Request copy of form 1098. Go online to lender website for interest paid.

5. Do not claim unsupported charitable contributions or use big round numbers that look like guesstimates.

6. Do not dump amounts into "miscellaneous" deductions that can accumulate and catch attention.

7. Do not exceed national averages for donations, mortgage interest, or taxes if you do not have documentation. IRS computers compare your deductions with others in your income bracket. Excess deductions could increase your DIF score, a secret IRS formula to select returns with the highest probability of helping reduce budget deficits via audits.

8. Do not be careless in organizing records and preparing tax returns if you belong to an industry that traditionally transacts in cash. Recent studies have identified small business owners and independent contractors that do not declare cash collections and therefore are inviting targets for IRS agents.

9. Do not be complacent about submitting Schedule C (Income from Business or Profession) with an attractive net loss. Avoid low gross receipts and few but unusually high expenses.

10. Do not consistently file late returns. It speaks of a taxpayer who disregards tax laws. It points to a taxpayer who is fair game for scrutiny.

11. Do not submit shoddy tax returns. A shoddy return speaks of a disorganized person who probably does not keep good records—a good catch for an IRS agent.

12. Do not go to unprofessional tax preparers who promise big refunds even if you have little withholding. You could be solving a tax dollar problem with bigger taxes, penalties, and interest. Mas problemas.

TWELVE TIPS TO KEEP THE IRS AWAY

The name of the game is keeping a low audit profile. It means getting lost in the crowd. It reduces the risk of audit. Here are 12 tips to keep the IRS from auditing your tax returns:

1. *File your returns on time.* Extensions are fine, but they also prolong your agonies. They also extend the Statute of Limitations during which IRS can audit you. Think about it—you may have an item that you don't want to be bothered but which can be exposed during the extended period. *Muy malo.*

2. Make sure that *social security numbers and names* that you use on your income tax match exactly what appear on your social security cards. An incorrect number or name could cause your e-file to be rejected and looked at. In the process, they may spot other interesting items on your tax return.

3. *Check your occupation.* A professional claiming employment or business expenses who takes a study leave and fills in "student" as an occupation could raise suspicion as to why business expenses show up in a student's return.

4. *Make sure that all 1099 income are reported.* This is a major cause of IRS notices. It's disheartening to miss a $50 interest income and be audited because the IRS just happened to notice other interesting deductions in your return. In this case, it is wiser to err on the side of reporting a little more than declaring a little less. Paying $1,000 in additional taxes and interest for failure to report a $50 interest income is not cool. But it happens.

5. Make sure that only *mortgage interests* covered by Form 1098s are reported on line 10 of Schedule A for itemized deductions. Report all other interest such as owner-carried mortgages or loans in the names of relatives or friends on line 11. This is important because IRS matches mortgage interests reported by banks with Form 1098 against line 10 of your tax returns. A mismatch generates an IRS correspondence.

6. The *same is true with K-1s from LLCs, S-corporations, and partnerships.* Double-check your entries from K-1s to your tax returns. IRS matches K-1s reported by partnerships with schedule E of your tax returns.

7. *Do not just fill in your changed name carelessly.* If you are a recently married woman, include your maiden name in the first year of filing a joint return to avoid receiving an IRS notice for not filing due to a mismatch between IRS and SSA (Social Security Administration) records.

8. Do not automatically *amend* your previous returns at the sight of an error or lure of a refund. Weigh the good with the bad, the good refund against the bad prospects of an audit. A 1040X may cause your original return to be pulled out from storage for a closer look. And an audit.

9. *Use IRS-approved software and forms.* The use of unauthorized forms from tax software that have not received IRS approval causes IRS personnel to pull out your return to manually transfer data to approved forms.

10. Depreciation schedule Form 4562 asks if you have evidence to *support business mileage on your car*. It follows this with a question asking if your evidence is in writing. To answer "no" is an invitation to an audit.

"Nice touch, but we don't have any openings in the auditing department."

11. And for those *make-believe Schedule Cs* (Income from Business or Profession), the days of reporting $100 of income and deducting $5,000 of expenses are over. Don't do it. Not anymore, anyway.

12. As for Rentals:
- Avoid large deductions. IRS agents are always looking for amounts that should be capitalized. A $1,000 repair is more attractive to audit than $316 electrical, $475 plumbing, $209 roofing expense.
- Avoid round solid numbers. Use $978 instead of $1,000 for carpentry.
- Never claim large travel expenses for rental purposes. If you insist, attach receipts and a good explanation.
- If your address is identical to your rental address, allocate non-deductible portion for owner-occupied space. If you don't, you could receive a letter that starts with "Your income tax return has been chosen for audit....."

HOW TO AVOID IRS AUDITS
(Part 1 – General Audit Guidelines)

As some of you may have noticed, the pendulum has swung back from a "gentler and kinder IRS" to *enforcement and compliance. Ouch!*

Let's identify audit triggers and get some help from this three-part series on avoiding audits:

*   How to Avoid IRS Audits – 10 General Tips.
*   How to Avoid IRS Audits – Income.
*   How to Avoid IRS Audits – Deductions.

LET'S START WITH ARTICLE ONE - 10 GENERAL TIPS TO AVOID AUDITS:

1. ***Get lost...,*** I mean, get lost in a crowd of taxpayers and disappear in a sea of returns. The idea of safe filing is to fit in with the crowd. You don't want red flags to jump out of your return and say "come and get me."

2. Make sure that your tax returns are ***complete and well-prepared.*** Make sure that numbers in your returns match IRS records. Any discrepancy in income or deductions can generate an IRS notice. Discrepancies bring attention, attention brings IRS notices, assessments, and possibly audits.

3. ***Respond promptly to IRS notices.*** To ignore notices draws even more attention to your tax return.

4. ***Avoid using round numbers.*** Your deduction may be legitimate but does not appear as such. Actually, it looks more like an estimate. And people who estimate can't usually provide documentation—a good catch for an agent, a good source of revenue for the government. Don't give the Service a reason to look at you as a source of funds.

5. Prepare your income tax in a ***professional manner.*** You may do it yourself, but hire a tax accountant if there are technical issues such as foreclosure, cancellation of debt, passive loss, 1031 exchange or net operating loss.

6. ***Don't brag*** how you got one over the IRS. Don't be loud-mouthed about your exploits—how you got away from paying taxes on undeclared income. There are rewards for informants, you know.

7. Make sure that the ***social security name and number*** that you use on your income tax match exactly what appear on your social security card. An incorrect number or name can also cause your e-file to be rejected. If you change your name, advise the Social Security Administration (SSA). If you don't, you'll receive a notice of mismatch from the IRS or SSA—another unwanted attention.

8. Check your ***occupation.*** A professional who takes a study leave and uses "student" as an occupation would raise suspicion as to why employee business expenses show up in a student's return. A waiter or cosmetologist without tips likewise generates curiosity—an ingredient of audits.

9. Keep ***penalties*** in mind when deciding to extend or miss deadlines. Remember that penalties for late filing are 5% per month while penalties for late payment are only ½ % per month. In other words, if you don't have funds, <u>file anyway</u>. It cuts down your penalties from 5% to ½% per month. Prompt filing also starts the running of the statute of limitations within which the IRS can audit you. The longer you extend, the more time the IRS has to get you. This is bad news if there are issues that you don't want disturbed.

10. If you have difficult issues, it may be wise to have a tax professional (CPA, EA, or tax attorney) represent you. IRS auditors can now access a Custom Comprehensive Report about you. It contains professional license, accidents, properties owned with addresses, type of neighborhood you live in, bankruptcies, liens, judgments, UCC filings, transactions with relatives, criminal records, and concealed weapons permit. Scary, isn't it?

HOW TO AVOID IRS AUDITS
(Part 2 – Income Issues)

Taxpayers who hide income solve problems with *problemas mas grande*—IRS audits. Dealing with the IRS is not amusing. It's a nightmare! Stress levels rise. Your otherwise comfortable world gets turned upside down. We discussed general tips to stay under IRS radar in our prior newsletter. Let's discuss *10 income issues* now and deductions next.

1. **Report all income.** IRS receives copies of 1099s and W2s from your work, bank, buyers, people who pay you. To miss a 1099 is flirting with IRS scrutiny.

2. If you are **missing a W-2** from an employer who moved or closed shop, **attach Form 4852**. Attach your last pay stub that shows year-to-date earnings and withholdings to complete Form 4852.

3. If you **misplace a 1099**, report your income anyway; otherwise, you'll get a notice of unreported income. It could start an examination if the Service finds more flags in your tax return. The trick to avoiding IRS notices for unreported income is to report all 1099s under your Social Security Number—right or wrong. If wrong, report the amount and back it out with an explanation. Failure to report it will generate IRS notice CP-2000 that can spell trouble if there are other "interesting" items on your return.

4. If you are **missing a 1099 for stock sale**s, request from your broker a year-end statement that summarizes your dividend income, interest income, and sales of stocks. Some brokers do not provide basis (cost) of stocks that you bought. Instead, they ask you to "consult your accountant"—a typical excuse for inefficient operations. They already have your cost in their data base files, but do not provide it to you until you complain. TIP: Do not forget to reduce your gains by dividends that were reinvested to buy more stocks or by stock splits and broker commissions. Every little thing helps save taxes.

5. Money that you receive **"under the table"** may not be as safe as you think. The payer may make a deal with you not to report the transaction, but what makes you think that his accountant will go along with that? I wouldn't. Company owners complain of paying too much taxes to accountants who make ways to save taxes—especially amounts paid "under the table" without regard to whatever promises may have been made to you.

6. Then there's the issue of **forgiven debt**—a sign of the times. If you owe $10,000 to MasterCard which agreed to accept $6,000, that $4,000 debt relief is income to you. The company will issue you a 1099-COD (Cancellation of Debt) which you must report as ordinary income with higher rates (not capital gain with lower rates).

7. **Forgiven debt on your main residence** is another issue. Please refer to a separate article on how to exclude debt relief from the foreclosure or short sale of your residence at my website of www.victorsycpa.com. Look for a newsletter on "Home Sale – Exclusion of Gain."

8. If you convert your **hobby** into a business, be careful about taking losses. Hobby losses are not deductible. You become a candidate for audit if you report this activity in Schedule C and become a prime candidate if you show losses. Read "Hobby Loss Rules" at www.victorsycpa.com.

9. If you are a small business owner who files **Schedule C** (Income from Business or Profession)—beware. You are at the top of the food chain for IRS consumption. Majority of audit cases that we handle come from Schedule Cs. Why? IRS studies point out that a big chunk of the "tax gap" can be traced to sole proprietors. The government's chances of collecting taxes, penalties, and interest from Schedule C audits are higher than the rest of the population, that's why.

10. Categories of cash-intensive businesses such as retailers and contractors lead the pack of candidates for audits.

HOW TO AVOID IRS AUDITS
(Part 3 – Deductions)

There's no substitute for conservatism when it comes to avoiding audits. Be aggressive and you increase your risk of IRS scrutiny. Play the odds and you invite an audit. The question then is—is it worth the risk? *No, it's not.* Saving a few dollars compared with what could be a disastrous experience of dealing with the IRS and paying tax, penalties and interest—for prior and subsequent years—is certainly not a rewarding proposition. This is the last of three articles on audits. The first two dealt with general guidelines and income. This one deals with *deductions.*

1. The first rule is to submit a return that *vanishes in a pack of returns.* To have a return pulled out for *improper deductions* increases your chances of an audit.

2. Present your return in a way that it does not become a candidate for IRS audit. If you take a legitimate but inappropriate-looking deduction, *explain and document* it satisfy agent curiosity.

3. Make sure that you*r tax return makes sense*. For example, it does not make sense to report a meager income and claim large deductions. It makes no sense to report business losses and drive expensive cars. How do you survive? Do not set up yourself for an *economic reality audit.*

4. Review your tax return to make sure that deductions are within *reasonable range*. Excessive amounts can get you into trouble. If you consistently surpass national averages, back it up. For example, a donation of $6,000 on an adjusted gross income of $40,000 is a red flag because the national average is only $2,100. If you are a Seventh Day Adventist, Mormon, or a Catholic who gives tithes, opt out of e-file and attach explanation and documentation. A few minutes of your time to back it up could save many days or weeks of defending an IRS examination. Check out our list of "*Average Personal Deductions.*"

5. Make sure that only *mortgage interests* covered by Form 1098s are reported on line 10 of Schedule A. Report mortgage interests that are not under your social security number (such as your house loan under somebody else's name) or those without 1098s (seller-financed or owner carried) on line 11. This is important because IRS *matches mortgage interests reported by banks* with Form 1098 against line 10 of Schedule A.

6. If you have *extra-ordinary expenses* such as big legal fees or huge donations toward a church building fund, *opt out of efile and send a conventional paper tax return with documentation.*

7. Office at home elicits emotions from taxpayers and interest from agents. Taxpayers swear that a portion of the home is used exclusively for business on a continuous basis. That's fine. We believe you. The problem is that IRS radar is locked into home office deductions. You have to be practical. *Weigh tax savings versus risk*. Most of the time, savings are so small that by the time you divide the square footage of a portion of the home used solely for business by the total area of your home and multiply that by your tax rate, the tax savings could be small but your audit profile has significantly increased. In other words, it's probably not worth it. The IRS recently promulgated simplified rules to reduce litigation in this area.

"He says you'll remember him from High-School where you once referred to him as an idiot."

8. For those of you who run a business, **be wary of deducting capital expenditures**. Some expenses benefit the current year and therefore can be expensed this year (telephone, supplies). Some benefit future years and therefore should be capitalized and depreciated over years (car, computer, machine). TIP: Use section 179 of the Internal Revenue Code to expense equipment—if you need deductions this year.
9. If you own rental properties, do **not deduct capital expenditures in the current year**. Agents are on the lookout for large "repairs" that are actually major renovations that benefit future years.

10. Start-up expenses for a new business are incurred prior to the time you actually open your doors to customers. Agents look for incorporation costs or market surveys that should be *capitalized*, not expensed.

HOW TO *ATTRACT*
AN IRS AUDIT

After all the coaching in prior chapters and you still have not caught on, perhaps there is a need to change our approach. How about offering tips to *invite* you in for an audit?

Attracting an audit is reverse psychology for taxpayers who do not listen when you tell them what not to do to escape audits; therefore, I wrote this section of tips to get you audited via directives outside the box. My goal is to reach those who do not listen to tax professionals...

12 RIDICULOUSLY EASY WAYS TO ATTRACT AN AUDIT

While there are no guarantees to avoid an audit, there are creative ways to attract one. Here are 12 ridiculously easy ways to help the IRS zero in on your tax return for audit: ☺

1. *Create a mismatch with IRS data base files by estimating income* from interest or independent contractor, instead of using exact numbers from forms 1099 and K1.

2. *Create another mismatch by estimating mortgage interests* instead of using numbers from form 1098.

3. Do *not report savings accounts* that you want to hide from your spouse..., I mean the IRS.

4. *Claim high and unsupported charitable contributions*. Claim casualty losses to increase your refund. While you are on a roll, claim high medical insurance and zero insurance reimbursement.

5. *Use big round numbers such as $1,000 or $5,000*. Better yet, dump them into "miscellaneous" deductions.

6. *Submit Schedule C Income from Business or Profession with an attractive net loss*. Report low gross receipts and deduct few but unusually high expenses. Make the schedule even more attractive by claiming deductions for *home office and 100% depreciation on a car* or home computer.

7. *Opt out of e-file and use a name different* from the one that appears on your social security card.

8. *Claim a number of dependents*—your mom, grandpa, aunt, cousins—and huge child care expenses.

9. *Claim a dependent relative without verifying with child's parents or guardians.* IRS computers automatically tract and identify *dependents who are claimed more than once.*

10. *Consistently file late* returns. Don't break tradition.

11. *Submit sloppy returns.* A sloppy return speaks of a sloppy person with shoddy supporting tax documents. You'd be a good catch for an auditor.

12. *Join a tax protest group. Join a Barter Club.* Stand up for your *constitutional rights*. The IRS loves people who fight for immunity from income taxes. They love you so much that they will even send you an invitation to visit them... for an audit.

DEVELOPMENT: IRS auditors can now access a Custom Comprehensive Report about you that contains:
- Birth date, professional license, driver's license, DMV registration, accidents.
- Properties owned & address, type of neighborhood you live in.
- Bankruptcies, liens, judgments, UCC filings.
- Number of people at work, possible associates, transactions with relatives.
- Criminal records, concealed weapons permit.

AVERAGE ITEMIZED DEDUCTIONS

For those of you who itemize, the table below should be of interest. For those of you who play the odds (you know what I mean), this table should be of special interest.

Having claimed too many exemptions at work to increase your take-home pay or failed to pay estimated taxes, you suddenly find yourself owing Uncle Sam. Before your creativity takes you over, keep your cool and check this table out. It could save you from visit the IRS.

The table shows the latest available average deductions taken by taxpayers in different groupings of Adjusted Gross Income (AGI). For example, a taxpayer with an Adjusted Gross Income (AGI) of $37,000 deducted an average of $7,192 of medical expenses, $3,950 of state and local taxes, $7,976 of interest, and $2,285 of contributions.

AVERAGE ITEMIZED DEDUCTIONS FOR VARIOUS INCOME LEVELS*				
Adjusted Gross INCOME RANGES	Medical EXPENSES	TAXES	INTEREST	CONTRIBUTIONS
15,000 to 30,000	7,590	3,271	7,976	2,285
30,000 to 50,000	7,192	3,950	7,976	2,285
50,000 to 100,000	7,312	6,111	9,320	2,815
100,000 to 200,000	9,932	10,860	12,093	3,857
200,000 to 250,000	19,850	18,078	16,450	5,824
250,000 or more	30,408	47,178	23,194	19,651

Based on latest available figures for 2013.

Note that these are averages for the whole United States. There are exceptions. Mortgage interests in California, Hawaii, and New York are much higher. Contributions by tithe-giving Catholics, members of the 7th Day Adventists, the Church of Jesus Christ of Latter-day Saints, Iglesia ni Cristo, and other faiths exceed these averages.

Again, these averages are for your guidance only. Do not claim these amount if you do not have documents to support your deductions.

IRS AUDITS SOLE PROPRIETORS' SCHEDULE C
(Income from Business or Profession)

In my experience of defending hundreds of taxpayers over five decades, IRS audits have been dominated by examination of Schedule C filed by taxpayers who conduct their businesses as sole proprietors (popularly referred to as "DBA" or doing business as) instead of corporations or LLCs. This includes professionals and independent contractors who receive 1099s as subcontractors (instead of W2s as employees). Sole proprietorships face a risk of about four times greater than wage earners.

Let's enumerate issues that generate the most dollar assessments & therefore draw the most attention from the IRS:

1. ***Unreported income:*** is checked by comparing reported revenues versus deposits. The Service adds all deposits to all your bank accounts and compares the totals with what you reported as gross revenues on your returns. If you deposited $70,000 but reported only $50,000, the IRS wants to know where that extra $20,000 came from. This undeclared excess amount could have come from non-taxable loans or bank transfers. It could also have come from business income that you chose to "hide" by depositing collections to personal or children's accounts. Remember that auditors are trained to catch these anomalies. They are professionals and will track down this rather basic scheme. Elementary, my dear Watson. They perform a BDA (business deposit analysis) on your business and personal accounts that can easily uncover unreported income.

2. ***Personal auto use:*** do not claim 100% of vehicle expenses. You do use that car for commuting to and from the office, buying groceries, or taking the kids to school, don't you? J

3. ***Personal insurance***: Business-related insurance such as fire and liability coverage on business properties are fine but coverages on personal auto, life, or home are not. Take time to allocate auto insurance among business and personal cars. It also enhances the most important criteria in an audit: credibility. This magic word makes a lot a difference when you are face to face with an agent.

4. ***Employees versus independent contractors:*** You have personnel who work under your supervision and control at your business location. You do not want to treat them as employees because you do not want to pay FICA, Medicare, or unemployment insurance. Your personnel also do not want you to withhold federal and state taxes. It is therefore quite tempting not to deduct taxes and therefore treat them as 1099 independent contractors instead of W2 employees. If the IRS or EDD determine that your staffs are indeed employees, you could be assessed for employer's share of payroll taxes as well as employees' taxes that you should have withheld.

5. ***Capital expenditures:*** Some expenses benefit the current year (telephone, supplies) and therefore can be expensed this year. Some expenses benefit future years (car, computers, roof) and therefore should be capitalized and depreciated over three, five, seven years or longer. Agents are on the lookout for equipment with a life of seven years but were expensed in one current year. (TIP: Use section 179 of the Internal Revenue Code to expense equipment—if you need deductions this year)

6. **Start-up expenses:** for a new business are incurred prior to the time you actually open your doors to customers. Agents look for incorporations costs or market surveys that should be capitalized.

7. **Loan applications:** if you submitted an "improved" version of your income tax to a bank for loan purposes, beware. The IRS has a program with banks and the SBA (Small Business Administration) by sampling returns that look cute compared to the universe of average returns. The banks can cooperate with the IRS because you signed an authorization (you may not even know it), along with other loan documents, for them to disclose your taxes to the IRS. Be careful. This is a no-win situation. If you stand behind the improved bank version, it becomes an IRS fraud case. If you stand behind the IRS version, it becomes a bank fraud case. Either way, you lose. Don't do it.

HOW TO SURVIVE AN IRS AUDIT

Have you ever wondered why IRS picks some but ignores most returns for audit? Your chance of getting chosen is quite low and has fallen to about 1% over the last few years. But let me you some give tips on how to behave during an audit if you do get picked up.

This chapter offers more tactics to stay alive during an audit. It also includes a choice of being organized or messy as you naturally are, or whether field audits should be done at your home or business. It gives you an idea how auditors are trained to grill... I mean to interview you. Hopefully, these tactics will help you prepare for your big day at the IRS.

12 DO's IN IRS AUDITS

Yes, I know, audits are serious stuff. But they do funny stuff to people who are under stress. I have seen clients pretend to be cool when they are actually scared. My advice is for you to act naturally; otherwise, the auditor may think that the return is also a fake. Here are 10 tips to pull you through an audit—alive.

1. Bring *credibility* to the audit—Aaahhh... credibility, the most critical factor in an audit.

2. Bring the right *attitude* with you. It makes a lot of difference.

3. *Dress modestly*. This is not the ideal time for you to wear expensive jewelry. Your tax returns could be showing losses for successive years. The auditor will probably wonder how poor you have been surviving all these lean years. Then you walk in with jewelry galore.

4. *Be on time*. Some auditors get irritated with taxpayers who come in late for an appointment.

5. *Bring in only what is asked for*. You might be inclined to give documents that are not under question if the auditor goes fishing. You might just innocently bring the fish that she wants.

6. *Respect the auditor*. She's is a human being. Treat her like one.

7. *Address auditors as Mr. Smith or Ms. Jones* (not as John or Ann).

8. *Listen to the questions carefully*. Respond carefully. Innocent questions on how you earn or spend have meanings behind them.

9. *Identify embarrassingly out-of-line deductions* and ask the auditor to disallow them. You heard me: disallow (he'll disallow them anyway). Use reverse psychology. Apologize. In the meantime, you recapture lost credibility.

10. *Point out obvious mistakes early on*, the ones that the auditor will surely find out.

11. *Get a tax professional to represent you*. Sure, you can take care of simple questions about simple issues. But when the going gets rough, hire a CPA, Tax Lawyer or Enrolled Agent who can save whatever fees you pay her.

12. *Ask your representative to go without you*. You pay him not only to represent you but also to give you *peace of mind*. Let him worry about it while you sleep. Bear in mind that he can negotiate better without you in the room. Most auditors are rigid, formal, and righteous in your presence. Two professionals have a better chance of reaching a settlement *without you* in the room. I can work my magic *when left alone with an agent*.

SHOULD YOU BE ORGANIZED OR MESSY WHEN YOU FACE IRS AUDITOR?

There are two different approaches to prepare for an audit: organized and shoebox. Organized means systematically arranging your records. Shoebox means simply being you—naturally disorganized. Let's discuss each method so you can determine which one is best for your next audit.

WHY YOU SHOULD BE ORGANIZED:

1. This methodical approach of presenting data in a logical and structured fashion has worked well for me in five decades of defending taxpayers audited by the IRS. It may work for you too.

2. It calls for organizing disbursements by *category* (interests, taxes, donations, rental, advertising, business promotion) and by *periods* (January through December). It calls for preparing lead sheets with checks and receipts clipped behind Excel spreadsheets. Auditor gets impressed and may let you off the hook on gray matters.

3. This method speeds up the audit. It cuts down on your period of anxiety.

4. You send a subtle message to the agent that you want to work together. I have observed agents' relieved (and happy) faces when they see neatly filed records. They always appreciate your assistance to decrease their inventory of open cases (including yours, *especially yours*) before the end of the month. This is what it's all about—working *with* instead of working against the agent.

5. You may also end up finding documents that should not be there in your pile of records.

6. In other words, I recommend this organized approach. It has worked well for me and my clients.

WHY YOU SHOULD BE DISORGANIZED:

1. The shoebox approach calls for simply presenting records in a jumbled manner. It's like being yourself. The rationale: There is less time available for the agent to dig deeper. You hope that he (includes she) spends his time sorting through your mess and not have time for examine problematic issues. You hope that the time pressure pushes the auditor to focus only on few issues rather than meticulously burrowing through more issues.

2. This paper bag approach damages your relationship with the auditor who will be less willing to compromise disputed issues.

3. While this is convenient for you (you don't have to do a lot work), the agent will certainly not appreciate this style (he has to do much more work). You are merely transferring workload to him. Are hiding something?

4. When tax data are hard to find or not produced even after another information document request, the agent may give up and be less inclined to raise new issues (good for you). On the other hand, the auditor may threaten to issue summons for the missing records (not so good for you, *malo*).

5. It may be more difficult to achieve a good settlement.

6. The auditor may discover new issues amongst higgledy-piggledy records that you failed to weed out.

7. In other words, I do not like this approach. Stay away from this method.

20 DON'TS DURING AN IRS AUDIT

1. Don't be late. It doesn't make a good first impression.

2. Don't walk in without records. Be cool, but don't be too cool.

3. Don't be a chatterbox. Taxpayers are scared to talk before introductions and then become relaxed and chatty upon observing that the auditor is not a mean dude after all. This is why I *never* bring my clients to IRS audits. I strictly forbid my clients from talking with and writing to the IRS. If a client breaks this rule, I disengage.

4. Don't volunteer information. Be informed that a typical agent is a low-key, friendly agent. *They get your guard down by playing a nice guy role.* Don't be deceived by it. Remember that he is *not* on your side. He may appear to be, but he is *not*. Don't get fooled by a relaxed atmosphere. If you start talking or singing, you are indeed a fool.

5. Don't dump a paper bag in the auditor's face. Don't have him (includes her) wade through paper bags of messy documents. A happy auditor may not necessarily favor you but an angry auditor certainly will not help you.

6. Don't fight the auditor. Don't tell him to go after the Mob instead of small fish like you. Remember: he did not choose to audit you. Somebody else did. He was given a case file to work on and he is just doing his job. He could make life more difficult for you, you know.

7. Don't ever bribe an auditor. Don't even think about it. If you think you have a problem now, wait until you offer a bribe. Your case <u>will</u> be referred to the Criminal Investigation Division (CID). Jail time. *Malo.*

8. Don't underestimate the skills of the auditor. The agent is a professional. He does this kind of thing for a living. Compared to his skills, you're an amateur.

9. Don't attack the auditor's intelligence or competence; instead, be subtle and use words such as "oversight" instead of "blunder."

10. Don't be overconfident especially if you know something about taxes and audits. This is not the time for an ego trip.

11. Don't represent yourself if there are difficult issues at hand. What you are trying to save could cost you a lot more. This is not the time to save a penny for a buck.

12. Stay away from referring to the IRS as Nazi, Gestapo or ISIS.

13. We understand that this experience can be nerve-wracking, but don't be overly nervous. You must be hiding something.

14. If you want to end your misery, don't make it so obvious that you want to rush, rush, rush. The auditor must have missed a major issue.

15. Don't bring up a new deduction until after the auditor has decided on all adjustments. If you bring this up too early, auditor can look harder for offsetting adjustment.

16. Don't attract attention to your return by going out of character such as a waiter with no tips or a 70-year-old taxpayer with five minor dependent children. True, you may even have 10 so opt out of e-file to explain the wonders of Viagra.

17. Don't use big round numbers. These are dead giveaways that you are guesstimating.

18. Don't file tax return during an audit. That return is likely to be audited as well. Consider not filing. Instead, pay taxes owed to minimize penalties. Prepare a clean return, one devoid of current mistakes. Personally, I have promised to review and clean out return prepared by another accountant and actually showed the new clean return to agent. It worked every time. Subsequent year returns were never audited. Nada.

19. Don't lie. The auditor may already have the answer and is just testing your credibility. For example, you may say "no" to a question if you have a stock brokerage account while auditor stares at a dividend income 1099 in his files.

20. Don't react negatively to an office auditor who may not respond positively to your friendly gesture. Office technicians have a tight schedule—four per day for wage earners and two for small business. They also have to prepare their report in between.

"I'm sorry, but if I let you in, it wouldn't be Heaven."

10 TIPS TO HANDLE *FIELD* AUDIT AT YOUR PLACE OF BUSINESS

There are three basic types of audits: correspondence, office, and field examinations. Correspondence audits are the simplest ones – W2s, 1099s and other items that can be easily resolved by mail. Office audits are more complicated and involve small businesses and individuals with difficult issues. The exams are conducted at IRS offices (not your office). **Let's now discuss Field Audits—the most complex of the three.**

Field audits are more problematical and are conducted at your place of business. The audits are done by Revenue Agents who have many years of experience and hold advanced degrees. Many are CPAs and attorneys. Revenue Agents are the elite of the crop. They undergo intensive audit training to act as detectives looking for clues.

Field audits are different from correspondence and office audits and should be monitored closer because this type of audit is done right at your home or place of business—office, store, shop, or warehouse. You have to be more careful because you have employees and possibly customers in your premises. It gives the agent a chance to see and feel how you operate your business. With this in mind, let me give you *10 tips on how to handle field audits.*

1. Plan the engagement with your representative—CPA, Enrolled Agent, or Attorney (don't attempt to handle field audits yourself). It is far too complicated for you. You are no match for a Revenue Agent.

2. Designate a contact person to act as a liaison between you, your rep, and the auditor to assemble and regulate the flow of information with the IRS. The contact person should review all information before it is turned over to the IRS and be present during tours and interviews of employees. This setup will increase the likelihood that the information provided to the IRS is organized, complete, and focused.

3. The agent should deal only with this one person. The agent should not be allowed to chat with employees or request any document from anybody. Everything should be coursed through this contact person.

4. The agent should not be allowed to conduct a tour of the facilities without your CPA, enrolled agent, or lawyer. This should be done at the beginning of the audit with your rep.

5. Designate a room for the agent. Clean up all files beforehand. Keep the door closed so the agent cannot overhear business discussions. This room therefore should be as far as possible from financial areas.

6. If no room is available, place the agent far from sensitive areas. Tell workers not to discuss business issues within hearing distance of the agent. Instruct workers to remind each other of the agent's presence.

7. If you think of placing the agent with the contact person for convenience and monitoring, don't. This will create an atmosphere for talking. And when they talk, you could have problemas mas grande.

8. Provide only data that are requested. Not more.

9. The contact person should notify your rep if additional issues arise.

10. Make sure that the contact person understands his/her role: a contact person with no authority to argue issues or settle things with the agent.

And most important, tell employees to treat the agent with the courtesy and respect.
No IRS jokes, *por favor.*

REMEMBER:
- Field audits are more rigorous than correspondence or office audits.
- About 15% of all audits are field audits and about 90% result in an assessment. This is high.
- Revenue agents encourage you to talk, especially about yourself, your vacations, your lifestyle, listening for clues of undeclared income. Don't fall for it.
- The Internal Revenue Manual requires the officer to tour your place of business or home.
- They look for time cards (worker reclassification audit), calendars on walls (3rd party verifications), or vending machines (unreported income). I always conduct a trial run before the tour to remove expensive works of art such as paintings or photos of cruises and lavish parties. I also observe workplaces where a vengeful employee can utter a remark to spark a fire.

HOW IRS AGENTS INTERVIEW TAXPAYERS DURING AN AUDIT

While my audit tips usually focus on how you—the taxpayer—should conduct yourself, let's look at how IRS agents conduct themselves when they interview you. Let's change roles and learn how they work you over, I mean, work with you—from the *agent's perspective.*

IRS AUDITORS ARE TRAINED TO:

1. Establish rapport with the taxpayer.

2. Maintain a friendly and professional demeanor.

3. Maintain control of the interview. Establish pace and direction. Continually assess whether the taxpayer is giving relevant information or merely stalling and rambling.

4. Look for pertinent leads. Follow up any answer that is not complete or to the point.

5. Concentrate more on the answer than on the next question.

6. Ask questions that require narrative answers. Avoid "yes" and "no" questions whenever possible.

7. Avoid leading questions.

8. Recognize that an IRS audit is often once-in-a-lifetime experience for the taxpayer who may be may be tense. Give some latitude. Don't think that the taxpayer is nervous because he/she is "hiding" something.

9. Use an outline. Remember though that an outline should not keep you from spontaneous questioning. Provide enough leeway to cope with unexpected situations that may occur.

10. Develop leads that may arise—leads for more issues and *mas dinero* for the government.

There you are. This is how IRS head office trains their agents to interview you. Keep these 10 tips handy for your next audit.....

SHOULD YOU BE PRESENT AT *YOUR OWN* IRS AUDIT?

Should you attend your IRS audit? Yes, I mean, you—your own audit. Well, you don't have to. This is always a strategic question that should be discussed at the early planning stage of an audit. Of course, you do not want to go. As your power of attorney, I do not want you to go either. So why go?

Let's discuss the benefits and drawbacks of attending your own funeral..., I mean, your audit. ☺

WHY YOU SHOULD NOT ATTEND:

1. You won't enjoy it, before, during, or after the examination. It is normal to get rattled. It is normal to be affected in some way, including the way you eat, sleep, or work. You might get testy and may even pick a fight with your mate. Personally, my philosophy has always been: sign a power of attorney, pay your accountant to handle this whole thing, and go on with your life - normal life.

2. If you attend, your demeanor may convey fear that may be misconstrued by the auditor that you are hiding something. I have dealt with auditors who ask me why my client is afraid if he/she is not hiding anything. Some auditors act naïve or have been on this job for so long that they have become cold and insensitive.

3. You can be emotional (and should be) about issues raised by the agent. This can create animosity that raises the temperature in the room, one that can work against you.

4. Some taxpayers tend to be chatterboxes when they get nervous. Others appear cool from our coaching but talk-a-talk as soon as they get comfortable. They volunteer more than what is asked for. This could only mean trouble: more issues, mas problemas.

And just between you and me, I cannot work my magic when you are around. The auditor tends to be formal. I tend to be formal. I dare not trade issues when you are there. Your presence is a hindrance to my effectiveness, an obstacle to the agent's willingness "to work it out." So why attend?

WHY YOU SHOULD ATTEND:

1. You are a convincing witness.

2. You present yourself rather well even in times of adversity.

3. You are a convincing fellow.

4. You are a credible witness.

5. Your presence helps win the case.

6. You exude an aura of your trustworthiness.

7. Your presence is crucial to win the battle.

Evidence has been lost and your oral testimony can sway the auditor to believe that such evidence truly existed.

If you are this type of person, consider attending. But in my five decades of IRS work, you are indeed a rare creature that comes around once in a blue moon. My advice is, unless you are that rare breed, sign that power of attorney and leave it to the professionals. Try to be "normal" at this time of your life, even if you are not most of the time. Good luck!

12 TACTICS TO SURVIVE AN IRS AUDIT

You have just received an invitation to visit an office of the Internal Revenue Service to examine (meaning audit) your tax returns. Don't panic. You have stashed funds for a rainy day, and this is it – a gathering storm. Take a minute to compose yourself, then read these tactics to shelter you from the storm.

You have just received an invitation to an office of the Internal Revenue Service. They want to examine your return. Don't panic. All these years, you have stashed funds for a rainy day. This is a rainy day. A gathering storm. Compose yourself. Then go to battle. Don't be over confident though. I am just boosting your morale. Read these tactics to shelter you from the storm:

1. *Prepare.* This is your best line of defense against the IRS. If they want to verify your contributions, bring canceled checks and statements from charitable organizations.

2. *Schedule* the audit to your advantage. Do not be bullied by their ten-day letter. Schedule your appointment just before a three-day weekend when they are eager to go out on vacation. Schedule it near the end of the month when auditors are under pressure to close their inventory of open caseloads. Postponing an October or November examination to the holidays is not bad idea either. These tactics worked for me in 50 years of tax practice.

3. *Schedule your appointment early in the morning or late in the afternoon.* An early morning appointment could get you an auditor who is still fresh and probably in a good frame of mind. In a late afternoon appointment, the auditor may want to leave the office before traffic builds up.

4. *Don't be afraid to go to Appeals.* Your chances of winning there are better than the examination level.

5. *Don't bring unnecessary documents.* This is not the time to come extra prepared. I have seen taxpayers bring documents for travel & entertainment when all that is being verified are interests and contributions. If the auditor decides to go on a fishing trip, you will be tempted to show excess bait that you just happen to bring along.

6. *Auditors always request tax returns for the previous and succeeding years.* That's standard operating procedure. But that doesn't mean that you should provide what you cannot find right away. Stall to give you time to evaluate those returns with your tax accountant.

7. If you do get the (mis)fortune of being confronted by an *unreasonable auditor,* do not be afraid to intimidate back. Request for a change of auditor even of it will probably be rejected. Most employees of the IRS are reasonable and professional. Treat them nicely. They are likely to reciprocate. But be wary of agents who are still trying to impress their superiors or are on a mission to pay back an oppressive and cruel world. Personally, I have had my best wins with veteran auditors. I have had my most terrible moments with young, minority auditors who carry police badges. (This is merely my own personal experience of dealing with the IRS for fifty years and may not reflect yours).

8. If an agent goes to *your place of business* in a field audit, do not feel sorry for placing the auditor in a small poorly ventilated room with stale air, if that happens to be the only available space. You cannot help it if the Revenue Agent feels so uncomfortable that he'll beg to wrap things up and go home. (Folks, there is no law that requires you to welcome them in an embassy suite).

9. If the issues are simple and the stakes are low, *you may represent yourself.* But if the issues are *unwieldy and problematic,* have a professional who is well versed in tax controversy represent you against the IRS.

10. If auditor is *replaced in midstream*, it's understandable to get upset especially if you have established rapport with the prior agent. Make lemonade out of lemon. Instead of complaining, use it to your advantage. Minimize major finds by prior auditor. Change tactics to skirt around problematic issues that were identified by the prior agent.

11. If you don't want an agent to see a *troublesome item,* vaguely promise to send it but you may just forget to. This is ideal for seniors with early signs…

12. *Learn when to observe, when to talk, when to shut up.* Your best answers are yes, no, I don't recall, or I'll check on that. If you cannot stand silence, don't talk to fill in the void. This is a dangerous reaction. You may blurt out something that opens a Pandora box.

Good luck.

WHERE SHOULD IRS CONDUCT *FIELD* AUDIT - YOUR HOME OR OFFICE?

Neither one, actually. You see, IRS conducts field audits where the books and records of a business are maintained. This, of course, is your home, office, warehouse, factory, or store. But I don't like any of these locations.

What I like is *my own accounting office*. After representing taxpayers in IRS disputes for decades, I prefer that your memorial services...I mean your audit, be conducted at my office—as your power of attorney. Let me tell you why:

1.   I do not want a Revenue Agent *snooping around your place of business.*
2.   I do not want the agent *interviewing your employees.*
3.   I do not want your customers or clients *noticing an IRS agent in the premises.*
4.   It's not good for business. It's not good for employee morale. It's not good for you.

HERE ARE TIPS TO MANAGE IRS FIELD AUDITS:

Establish an internal team before the IRS meeting. Assign a *"contact person"* to assemble and regulate the flow of information with the IRS. The contact person should review all information before it is turned over to the IRS and be present during tours and interviews of employees. This setup will increase the likelihood that the information provided to the IRS is organized, complete, and focused.

So how do we move the audit to our office? IRS regulations state that if conducting the audit at the place of business would essentially require the business to *close or would unduly disrupt business operations,* the agent can change the place of the exam to an IRS office, but this only my second choice.

My first choice is our own office. This shifts the audit venue from your office to mine. We do not have to worry about the agent overhearing employees talking or observing business operations. I can control the flow of information, the timing of interviews, and the general course of the audit at my office.

The agent will resist the change so we just have to be persistent. One way is to request for a site where the main books and records are located. The main books are sales journals, cash receipts journals, cash disbursements journals, general ledger, and trial balances that are all located in my office. Backup records such as receipts and invoices are at your place of business and can be produced as requested. It may not work but if you are persistent enough, the agent and his/her manager may permit the change of venue.

The agent will then request a "tour" (on-site inspection). That is fine. The Internal Revenue Manual (IRM) requires agents to do so. Here are a few tips:

1.   Ask your rep to visit your site to get it ready for the tour.
2.   Remove expensive collections including paintings or photos of cruises.
3.   Your representative should accompany the agent.
4.   Your presence will be requested, but make it brief.
5.   The tour should be brief and general, no looking in every room or closet, no thumbing through files.
6.   Look out for any vengeful employee who may take this opportunity to blurt out a comment that can start a fire.

Lastly, make sure that requested invoices, receipts, bank statements and other documents are at my office; otherwise, the rationale for the change of venue is blown. This would be embarrassing. In the meantime, conduct your business as usual and let me take care of your audit at my office. Under my supervision. Under my control. Good day.

10 TIPS TO HANDLE IRS *CORRESPONDENCE* AUDIT

As you know, there are three basic types of IRS audits: correspondence, office, and field examinations. Today's topic deals with correspondence audits, the simplest of the three. Here are 10 tips for your next correspondence audit:

1. Read the exam notice. I have seen taxpayers come to me with unopened mail, unopened certified mails even. In many cases, the 30-day letter or 90-day letter (Stationary Notice of Deficiency) has already expired! Case was lost by default in Tax Court due to non-appearance. *Por Diyos, Por Santo!*

2. *Respond promptly.* You have 30 days to call or write back.

3. If you cannot, *request for an extension of time* in writing before the expiration of that 30-day period.

4. Be *convincing and persuasive in your first response*. Make it your last response. You do not want a second request or a telephone call that could elicit more audit questions and prolong your agony.

5. *Address each issue separately.* Back it up with logical explanations and supporting documents.

6. Provide *schedules to reconcile* differences of unreported income and questioned deductions.

7. *Gather documentation.* Create manila folders for each issue & place checks & invoices inside each folder.

8. *Be organized.* This is a time when you need to be orderly in gathering and filing. Remember, you will not be there to explain when the agent goes through your stuff. It is therefore critical that the documents be filed in an orderly fashion to facilitate communication.

9. *Include a copy of the immediately notice* to help the IRS personnel match your response with your case files.

10. *Send by certified mail* with return receipt and tracking number, especially when responding on the 30th day (some folks find it more exciting to wait for the last minute).

If the audit doesn't go your way and problems start to unravel, consider getting help from a tax pro for damage control. You probably should have done this in the first place. Remember that a tax practitioner can help you sidestep landmines and save you enough tax, penalties, and interests to pay for his fees. Good luck!

RIGHTS OF TAXPAYERS UNDER AUDIT

(PART 1)

In answer to complaints from taxpayers, Congress enacted the Taxpayer Bill of Rights to level the playing field between auditors and taxpayers. The goal: prevent intimidation and abuse. Here are 10 selected provisions of that bill to protect you from audits by the Internal Revenue Service:

1. ***The right not to be interviewed:*** You can refuse to be interviewed if you have appointed an authorized representative. If you attend an interview unrepresented, the examiner must suspend the interview at your request. This is an inalienable right (unless your rep causes unreasonable delays or an administrative demand has been issued).

2. ***The right to be represented***: You don't have to deal directly with the auditor. Hire a CPA, enrolled agent, or attorney to represent you during an audit. The agent must deal with your POA (Power of attorney or representative instead of you. This is an important tip to preserve your way of life, including your sanity, when there are complicated troublesome issues. Your representative will earn his/her fees anyway. So why do you have to do it yourself? Start the process by executing Power of Attorney Form 2848.

3. ***The right to an explanation of the audit process:*** The Service is required to furnish plain English, easy-to-understand information about the audit process, your appeal rights, and how to contact the taxpayer advocate. The agents are also instructed to explain these same rights again at the commencement of an audit including asking you whether you read the information, understood it, and have any questions.

4. ***The right to obtain IRS information about you:*** Yes, you. The IRS maintains master files of individuals and business, including you. You may request in writing such dossier about you. I do this when new clients that I represent have communicated directly (and wrongly) with the agent or when the case is inherited from a prior practitioner. I have to analyze the strengths and weaknesses of a case that may have been jeopardized by clients who may have innocently hurt themselves by spilling data unnecessarily.

5. ***The right to be notified of any third-party contacts:*** The IRS is required to give you advance notice when they intend to contact banks or vendors for missing bank statement or supplier invoices.

6. ***The right to have a closed audit closed:*** The IRS can examine your books and records only once per year. Unless fraud is involved, the Service also cannot reopen a case that has been closed to make an adjustment that is unfavorable to you.

7. *The right to appeal results of an audit:* You have the right to appeal any examination result that you think is incorrect or unfair. You do not have to pay their bill until after the appeal is heard (You have a better chance of winning in appeals anyway).

8. *The right to be free from repetitive audits:* This applies where the examination of a prior year resulted in no change. This also applies when the assessment is less than $1,000 (this exception does not apply to auto expenses, meals and entertainment).

9. *The right to abatement of penalties and interests:* If you rely on an erroneous advice from the IRS, you may have penalties and interests forgiven. This is also true when penalties are caused by unreasonable delays from agent transfers, illness, or extended training (They did have lots of training during the recent reorganization).

10. *The right to contact your taxpayer's advocate:* Use Form 911 Taxpayer Assistance Order (TAO) to contact your local advocate when you suffer significant hardships because of the way the agent is administering tax laws. The TAO may be used to stop aggressive audit tactics or oppressive collection tactics, expedite a claim for refund, and request the transfer of a case.

These are your rights. Discuss them with your tax adviser. Congress passed these taxpayers' bill of rights in three different years. They must be serious about protecting your rights. Use them.

RIGHTS OF TAXPAYERS UNDER AUDIT
(PART 2)

As you know, there was a lot of media coverage on IRS abuses that finally led to the enactment of the IRS Restructuring and Reform Act of 1998. To better understand this Act, we will adopt a new format wherein we will discuss the background of a particular provision, then follow this up with an explanation and how it affects you. Any commentary will immediately follow.

1. **Audit selection criteria:** The Internal Revenue Service (IRS) examines (or audits) Federal tax returns to ascertain whether Federal tax laws have been complied with. If we are subject to threats of audit, then, the IRS believes that we would be more likely to comply with tax laws. Their limited resources could not possibly audit all of us; accordingly, they select some returns with the greatest likelihood of collecting mulla.

   They use different methods of selecting which returns will be audited. One is a computerized classification system called DIF (Discriminant Function System), a closely guarded secret that selects returns for audit based on computer scores. The higher your score, the more likelihood that you'll be chosen for audit. The Service also uses computer-matching techniques to compare amounts that you report against returns filed by banks and other record keepers. The IRS also audits returns reported by informants. While this procedure is frowned upon by practitioners as sleazy, informants are paid up to 15% TO 30% of collected taxes. That's a lot of dough, enough to be persuasive to some. Whatever the source of the audit is, it is mysterious and puzzling to some taxpayers as to why they are chosen for examination.

   Reform Act: The IRS is instructed to include in their publications the criteria and procedures utilized by the IRS for selecting returns for audit in simple, non-technical terms. While they need to protect certain investigative strategies, the publication must specify the general procedures used in selecting taxpayers for examination.

2. **Financial status audits:** Prior to the new Act, any IRS agent who encountered a low gross income of a taxpayer who is living comfortably could ask financial-status questions to determine if there is any unreported income. While traditional audits focused on books and records, the new financial status audits focus on you, the taxpayer. Questions are asked about your lifestyle, standard of living, vacations, where your children go to school, and how much cash you have in your safety deposit box. The nagging question: How do you survive? How can you support a lavish lifestyle with meager income? This technique became quite controversial as many taxpayer advocates voiced concerns over their abuse of this technique. Overzealous IRS agents were using techniques to convert a conventional audit into a criminal-fraud inquiry. In addition, IRS agents insisted upon personal interviews, with the taxpayer often at the taxpayer's personal residence. The American Institute of CPAs viewed this tactic as overly intrusive and fought for taxpayers' rights.

   Reform Act: Congress determined that these financial status audits (formerly known as economic reality audits) are unreasonable and overly intrusive and should be limited to situations where there are indications of unreported income. This technique should not be used for everybody. This prohibition is now codified and violations give a taxpayer rights against the Federal government.

3. **Interview rights**: When IRS agents come knocking at your door for a person-to-person interview, you must be notified of your rights in audit and tax collection matters. If you inform the agents of your wish to consult with an

attorney, certified public accountant, or enrolled agent, the interview must be suspended immediately. This is not always the case. If you have been visited by IRS agents (especially a surprise visit), you probably could not think well and could keep on talking, nervously chattering. This is very dangerous as it will be very difficult for a representative to pull you out of a pothole of mud that you dug for yourself.

Reform Act: Congress instructed the IRS to rewrite Publication 1 (your rights as a taxpayer) to more clearly inform taxpayers that you can suspend the interview by informing the officers that you want to be represented by a lawyer, CPA, or enrolled agent.

4. ***Taxpayer assistance orders (TAOs)***: Under prior law, you could file for a taxpayer assistance order if you faced a significant hardship because of a completed or pending IRS action. In my experience of requesting TAOs through Forms 911s, they rarely worked. Requests were either ignored or acted upon so slowly that it would be useless by the time they contact you. I suspect that the meaning of the words "significant hardship" was too subjective. I believe that overworked IRS personnel who received these requests were exploiting their subjective meaning.

Reform Act: Congress puts more teeth into these TAOs by moving the Taxpayer Advocate Offices from the IRS to the Treasury Secretary. In other words, the Taxpayer Advocate who oversees TAOs is no longer under IRS control and now directly reports to the Treasury Secretary. With separate telephones and fax machines independent of the IRS, the Taxpayer Advocate can now perform its mission meaningfully in helping taxpayers.

"I assume you have documentation to back up these 27 light-years of business travel."

RIGHTS OF TAXPAYERS UNDER AUDIT
(PART 3)

We, taxpayers, have seen daylight from the days of dealing with a bureaucratic, abusive Internal Revenue Service. Read on and enjoy your rights as a taxpayer, courtesy of the IRS Restructuring and Reform Act ("Act"). This is the last of three articles on taxpayer rights.

1. ***Civil damages for unauthorized collection actions:*** Under prior law, a taxpayer could not recover damages because of the negligent disregard of the Internal Revenue Code in connection with a collection matter. Second, a taxpayer could not recover civil damages because of an IRS personnel's willful violation of the US Bankruptcy Code. Third, parties made subject to IRS collection actions could also not recover damages for unauthorized collection actions that affect such third parties.

   Act: There are three new provisions that extend the rights of taxpayers to sue the Federal government. First, any taxpayer may recover civil damages for an IRS employee's negligent disregard of the Code. Second, a third party can likewise sue the government for unauthorized IRS collection actions. Third, any taxpayer can sue for willful violations of certain Bankruptcy Codes with respect to the collection of Federal taxes. In effect, Congress caused a lower standard of liability for an aggrieved taxpayer to prevail in a negligence action against the IRS.

2. ***Audit threats to report tips:*** Employees who work in the entertainment, restaurant, and casino industries are required to report tips. A restaurant may enter into a Tip Reporting Alternative Commitment (TRAC) to help employees comply with reporting requirements. In return, the restaurant can receive an IRS promise that the IRS will agree to base the restaurant's liability for employment taxes solely on reported tips in the event of an IRS audit. There have been reports on those restaurants that failed to cooperate subsequently received threats of audit as an inducement to participate in this program.

   Act: The new law expressly prohibits IRS employees from using this audit threat to coerce establishments into joining TRAC. Agents can no longer twist arms of employers to force their employees to begin paying taxes at an agreed percentage of tips.

3. ***Audit influence by the executive branch:*** There have been allegations that high-level executive officers have caused their opponents to be audited by the IRS. While it is ethically wrong, the Internal Revenue Code did not explicitly prohibit such politically motivated practice. Even conservative tax-exempt organizations that, in the first place, are prohibited from intervening for political candidates, were subject to politically motivated audits.

   Act: The new law expressly prohibits "applicable persons" from requesting an IRS employee to conduct or terminate an audit.

4. ***Request to give up right to sue:*** Prior to the new Act, any officer or employee of the Federal government could use a position of authority to persuade, or even coerce an unknowing, unwitting, unrepresented taxpayer to waive rights to bring a civil action against the Federal government, its officers, or employees.

    Act: The new law has codified a prohibition on requests that taxpayers waive their rights to sue the IRS or any agency of the Federal government.

5. ***Confidentiality privilege extended to non-attorneys:*** As you know, certain communications and discussions between you and your attorney with respect to legal advice are privileged information and cannot be disclosed to third parties or hearings in a court of law. This privilege information was not enjoyed by Certified Public Accountants (CPAs) or enrolled agents (EAs).

    Act: The new law extends the confidentiality privilege to any federally authorized tax practitioner, meaning CPAs, enrolled agents, and enrolled actuaries. (This confidentiality privilege, however, does not apply to criminal tax proceedings in Federal court).

    Caveat: To circumvent this new provision, the IRS may then increase its criminal investigation since the confidentiality rules only apply to non-criminal proceedings. Note that this statute does not apply to State tax advice.

6. ***Service to record keepers:*** Under prior law, summons must be served by delivering an attested copy by hand to the taxpayer or by leaving a copy at the last place of abode.

    Act: The IRS now has the option of serving summons to third party record keepers either in person or by Certified or Registered Mail to the last known address. This is actually beneficial to both taxpayer and the Service. You really do not want an IRS officer visiting your residence or place of business. Just imagine an IRS agent coming through your door and serving you with a summons in front of your employees and customers. As for the IRS, they no longer have to spend time and effort in driving to your residence or place of business.

7. ***Taxpayer Pre-notification:*** Under prior law, the IRS may issue summons to any person who has information of records and then notify you of such summons within three days of the date of service. This notice of a summons is done after the fact. It can have a chilling effect on your reputation, as you were not given the opportunity to resolve such issues in place of the summons.

    Act: The IRS is now prohibited from third-party contacts without prior notification to taxpayers. The Service needs to provide reasonable notice in advance to you before contacting third persons. This gives you an opportunity to provide the information in some other way to prevent summons to third parties. The IRS is also required to periodically provide you with a record of persons contacted during certain periods.

"I thought we always had a deal."

HOW IRS AGENTS EVALUATE EVIDENCE

The IRS is back. In full force. Leaner. Stronger...well, maybe not as strong with all these budget cuts, but effective. After reeling from congressional hearings and keeping a low profile for many years, the IRS reorganized and is back. Their mission then *was* to protect taxpayers. The mission *now*: go raise some money. Rates of audit have declined over the last few years, but let's learn how agents evaluate evidence against you so you can pre-empt their next strike.

1. IRS agents are trained to gather facts, all available facts, on both sides of the issues. They gather evidence, not proof (evidence is something to prove a fact while proof is the result of such evidence).

2. The Internal Revenue Code requires all taxpayers to *keep adequate records*. There are times, however, when such records were lost or even never existed. This is when oral testimony comes into play. IRS agents need not accept oral testimony that must be verified from other sources of evidence.

3. In my 50 years of defending taxpayers against IRS audits, taxpayer *credibility* (or lack of it) is the single most critical factor in winning (or losing) an audit. It is this credibility that leads agents to accept or reject oral testimony or written evidence.

4. Agents keep a summary of conversations with taxpayers as documentation for their case files. This is why I get nervous when taxpayers talk directly with agents. I have one rigid rule that I keep for my clients: *never, never communicate with agents directly*. It makes our job of defending you really difficult. I remember a client who called and argued about the ownership of a rental property that was the main issue of their audit. He followed this up with several letters. Unfortunately, he was going the *wrong way*. He tried so hard to convince the agent of a position that was bad for his pocket. It took me quite a bit of subtle convincing, gentle persuasion, and lots of luck to turn the case around for an eventual win. But it is not something that I enjoyed. These are the sort of circumstances that make CPAs, Enrolled Agents and Tax Lawyers get nervous and wary.

5. When neither documentation nor oral testimony is available, you may use an *affidavit* to attest a statement (use Form 2311). The agent, on the other hand, could use that same affidavit to record your testimony as a witness or to prevent you from changing your testimony should the case go to trial.

6. Have you observed examiners (agents) preparing *worksheets* during the interview? These are work papers to documents facts and corroborate evidence and conclusions.

7. A secondary source of information is hearsay. It is what a witness says that another person was heard to say. The trustworthiness of this type of evidence lies on the reliability of source.

8. *Contemporaneous writings* made at the happening of an event have great value during audits because it shows what was in the mind of the taxpayer at that time. For example, auto mileage jotted down right after the trip has more significance than a logbook reconstructed three years later, just before an audit.

9. After facts have been gathered, the Internal Revenue Manual instructs auditors to arrive at a definite conclusion by a *balanced and impartial evaluation* of all evidence. If you have experienced an audit, you may feel otherwise, and for good reason, especially if you lost the audit.

10. The bottom line: If you want to win in a potential audit of your current tax return in the next two or three years, *prepare for it now*. Keep complete and accurate records. Do not take positions that could not be defended in an audit. For example, do not claim $2,000 of charitable contributions if you can only support $300. Do not claim business expenses of $8,000 on gross revenues of $3,000. Be sensible. Save taxes with proper planning and good tax advice, not from make-believe numbers that wave red flags. The personal demeanor and integrity of your tax accountant will win, or lose your audit. Good day.

"Now, remember, when we get in there, let me do all the talking."

HOW TO TAKE YOUR CASE TO APPEALS – AND WIN!

If you cannot resolve disputes at the examination level, you can either pay what you owe or pursue an administrative appeal. Of course, the IRS understands that many taxpayers will not agree with the findings of its auditors. Therefore, it has created a separate branch called the Office of Appeals.

The role of Appeals is to make an independent review of a tax dispute and to consider positions taken by both the taxpayer and the IRS. It strives to resolve tax disputes in a fair way and to remain impartial to both parties. From my personal experience, it really is.

Appeals officers were auditors themselves, at one time, but are now senior employees in the IRS system. They usually have legal or accounting experience. Their sole function is to review finished audit reports and provide an impartial platform for taxpayers to plead their cases to a higher power within the IRS. They attempt to avoid litigation by resolving tax disputes internally.

Personally, this is my favorite venue for resolving tax disputes. Your case gets a fresh look by experienced personnel. Appeals officers have greater authority and flexibility in deciding cases than auditors. Their performance is judged by how often they reach successful compromise with taxpayers – not by their willingness to back an auditor's findings. This is good. ☺

12 BASICS OF IRS APPEALS PROCESS

After an audit of your tax returns by the IRS, you have a choice of either ending your misery by paying up or by continuing to fight at the Appeals Office. The appeals process is an administrative means to resolve your problems without resorting to legal action. It's a *good way* to resolve disputes. It is *less strenuous* than the audit process and is *less costly* than Tax Court. You also have better odds of settling your case.

LET ME GIVE YOU 12 BASICS OF THE APPEALS PROCESS:

1. If an IRS *agent with an attitude had just put you through a treadmill*, go to appeals. If you feel that there were mistakes in handling your case or that you were not adequately represented in the audit, go to appeals. It is faster, cheaper, and more equitable. You go before an experienced Appeals Officer who has a better understanding and a broader mind than the agent who put you through a ringer.

2. You have a fairly good advantage. The Appeals Officer acts like a *mediator*. You have another advantage: your *opponent is not there*. It is just you and the Appeals Officer. It therefore frees your senses from adversarial feelings against the prior agent creating an atmosphere that is conducive to settlement.

3. Remember that *your objective is to settle*, not to triumph. Your goal is to rectify something wrong. And if a broadminded tax veteran can see it your way, your chance to settle increases.

4. Of course, bear in mind that this Appeals Officer is a CPA, lawyer, or both, who may *find critical issues that may have been overlooked* by the prior agent. If this is your case, *stay away from appeals*.

5. After the audit of your returns, you receive a notice from the exam division asking you to agree or disagree. They send a *30-day letter*. This is your *ticket to appeals.*

6. Your first step is to prepare a *written protest*. Be persuasive. Maximize issues in your favor. Counter arguments on issues that are not in your favor.

7. The protest will be forwarded to the original agent who will file a response. *Get a copy of that response* from either the Appeals Officer or through FOIA (Freedom of Information Act) so you can prepare for rebuttal.

8. *Prepare well for the conference*. Read our separate article that is loaded with tips on how to prepare for the conference. We also have tips on how to behave during the conference.

9. Again, the appeals conference is one of *negotiation*. It is not a place to bully your way into a win. If this is your attitude, skip it and go to court. (Up to this point, your forum has been an informal proceeding, one of mediation. It remains as a non-docketed case).

10. If a settlement cannot be reached, the Appeals Office sends a *Notice of Deficiency* (also referred to as a 90-day letter). Your case becomes a docketed case. The chief Counsel of the IRS becomes involved. It becomes more expensive to defend as your case moves from informal mediation to the formal jurisdiction of a court where lawyers and CPAs battle in trial before a judge.

REMEMBER:

- Less than 10% of audited taxpayers request appeals. 70% are settled in appeals.
- Appeals Officers are rated by the number of how many compromises they reach, not by how often they uphold auditors.
- Appeals officers are experienced tax pros, experienced negotiators.
- They are long time employees who rise from the ranks.
- Appeals officer and auditor may even know each other. ☺

11. If the deficiency is $50,000 or less, it is classified as *a small case and can remain in appeals*; otherwise, it will be forwarded to area counsel where it will be calendared for trial in Tax Court.

12. A word of caution: unless you know what you doing, do not represent yourself. With all due respect to your courage, you are no match for the experienced officers. You might be trying to save a few hundred dollars in fees only to lose thousands in potential savings of tax, penalties, and interests.

You can also use appeals for liens, levies, seizures, claims for refund, and rejections of OIC (offers in compromise) or installment agreements (payment plans) but not for fraud or bankruptcy cases. My recommendation: Go to appeals. Give it a try. Good luck.

SHOULD YOU GO TO IRS APPEALS?

After losing an audit to the IRS, you have the option of paying or appealing. Pay if you are happy with the results or don't want to extend the agony of dealing with the IRS. Appeal if you are not happy or feel that you have not been treated fairly. **Let's explore the advantages & disadvantages of going to the Appeals.**

ADVANTAGES OF GOING TO APPEALS:

1. The Appeals Officer is neutral.
2. The Appeals Officer is independent and does not communicate with exams at all. 2015 Update: The head of Appeals in Glendale, CA stated that they don't communicate at all with Exams - no telephone calls, no meetings. *Nada.*
3. The appeals process is quicker. The new IRS emphasizes the reduction of time to resolve tax cases by delegating more authority to frontline Appeals Officers to resolve cases quickly.
4. The Appeals Officer has a mission: to settle tax controversies without litigation.
5. The officer is more open-minded to the merits of your case to avoid hazards of litigation.
6. Your bargaining position is enhanced as you no longer have to deal with a combative agent who may have been locked into certain positions on unagreed issues.
7. It may force an unreasonable agent to rethink a position if you signify your plans to appeal.
8. The Appeals Officer is more open and candid than government attorneys during formal discovery procedures in a court of law.
9. The appeals process gives you more time to find out about the IRS' position.
10. It also buys you time to decide on which trial forum you eventually want to use - the Tax Court, Court of Federal Claims, or US District Court.
11. Tax, penalties, and interests need not be paid until the case is settled.
12. You may collect attorney's fees if a court determines that the IRS position was not justified.

DISADVANTAGES OF GOING TO APPEALS:

1. The Appeals Officer may raise new issues that were overlooked, ignored, or deemed irrelevant by the prior agent. If there are issues that are critical against you, stay away from appeals. Personally though, I have not dealt with an officer who opened new issues during the appeals process. For example, the head of Appeals in Glendale, California stated that his group does not raise additional issues.
2. Interest accrues as your case drags on.
3. The strain of an unsettled IRS audit may be too heavy for you. You may just prefer to pay.
4. There are additional fees for representation by an attorney, CPA, or enrolled agent. (These fees, however, may be offset by savings in reduced tax, penalties, and interest charges when you are adequately represented).
5. Non-docketed settlements with Appeals Office have less finality than docketed tax court rulings.

My Suggestion: *Go to appeals.* In my 50 years of dealing with government agencies, it is by far the *best forum* to settle tax controversies. The Appeals Officer is a mediator, *not* an opponent. Compared to office auditors and field revenue agents, Appeals Officers are a welcome sight. It is quite challenging sometimes to deal with young or overzealous examiners who wear police badges to enforce the law. It is quite expensive to litigate in tax court. I have found Appeals Officers (usually CPAs or attorneys with master's degrees) to be reasonable, level headed, and easier to deal with. They have more understanding, wider perspective on running a business. They understand how we survive to make ends meet. They are just more sensible to deal with in putting your case to rest. Good luck!

REMEMBER:
- Appeals officers are experienced tax pros and experienced negotiators.
- They are realists and are conscious of the hazards of litigation where a loss can create a bad precedent.
- For this reason, 70% are settled—a high percentage compared to audits and Tax Court.

10 TIPS TO PREPARE FOR IRS APPEALS CONFERENCE

You are still upset from losing an IRS audit. You can either pay or fight. If you choose peace and quiet—pay. If you choose to fight—go to appeals. Let me give you 10 tips on how to prepare for the appeals conference:t

1. *Be organized* in gathering and grouping records. An organized approach to gathering, filing and presenting documents makes it easier on you and the Appeals Officer. I have so many cases where the Appeals Officers are so impressed by my documentation that the whole complexion of the conference changes from a chore to a relaxed atmosphere-an ideal atmosphere to negotiate.

2. *Research t*he issues at hand. Read the most current cases to counter older cases that the agent may have cited against your side of an issue.

3. *Cite code sections*, revenue rulings, revenue procedures, and court cases to bolster your position. These citations not only prove technical aspects but also impress the Appeals Officer that you know what you are doing (assuming of course that you use the right citations).

4. *Prepare a persuasive written protest.* Draft the protest to maximize issues that are favorable to you and minimize issues that are unfavorable to you.

5. *Request access to your case files.* Take a look at any dossier they have on you. If the Appeals Officer resists, file a request through the Freedom of Information Act (FOIA).

6. *Your files* contain a statement of facts from the agent who previously examined you. *Counter the agent's statements.* Provide a different perspective to erode the agent's credibility to help sway the Appeals Officer in your favor.

7. *Ask around regarding the Appeals Officer* in charge of your case. Ask CPAs, enrolled agents, or tax lawyers about how the particular officer approaches and resolves a case.

8. *If you decide to represent yourself,* discuss your strategy and approach with a *coach* (CPA or lawyer). Present your documents for a trial run to see how persuasive you can be.

9. Instruct your *CPA or tax preparer to be available* in case you need help. And you probably will.   Bring your cell phone and ask your coach to be available for consultation during the conference.

10. *If discussions get technical and things don't look too good,* respectfully admit to the officer that you are, er, kind of overmatched and that you *need a representative*—a CPA, enrolled agent, or tax lawyer take over your case. You have done your best. Let the pros take over.

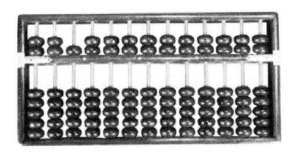

10 STRATEGIES AT APPEALS

Your case was closed unagreed and have decided to bring your case before the appeals office of the IRS. You have learned the basics of the appeals process and how to prepare for the conference from my prior articles.

LET ME NOW GIVE YOU 10 STRATEGIES AS YOU MEET FACE-TO-FACE WITH THE APPEALS OFFICER:

1. *Respect the Appeals Officer.* The appeals officer is *not the enemy.* The officer is here to *help settle your case.* The new IRS gives him/her even more new authority to resolve your case. Don't fight him (includes her).

2. *Be credible.* It is the *most important single element* in settling your case. Be honest and forthright with him. Even the best arguments, citations, and documentation won't be effective if you lose credibility during the conference.

3. *Be reasonable.* Heated arguments lead you nowhere. Threats or ultimatums backfire and merely lead you to more trouble. This is not the time to be bullheaded. This is not the forum to be combative.

4. *Be prepared to compromise.* Remember that the *purpose of the conference is to settle your case*—not to bully for a win.

5. *Be subtle as you control the tempo of the conference.* Suggest, not demand, the manner in which the conference is conducted. It is not in your best interest to be pushy.

6. *First address issues that are easiest to resolve* and hope to establish a pattern that will carry over to the rest of the conference. Again, your objective is a quick resolution. Starting with the most complicated issue may get you stuck, unable to move on, and diminish your chances for a good resolution.

7. *Present all your evidence that are in your favor.* Federal rules of evidence do not apply to appeals conferences.

8. *Analyze the strengths and weaknesses of the government's position.* This will guide you when to attack issues, when to step back, when to extend an olive branch. Hopefully, the end game will be peaceful.

9. *Help the Appeals Officer build your case* so he can help back you up in his written report to his superiors. In my experience, Appeals Officers feel for taxpayers but sometimes do not have tools to help deserving taxpayers. Submit persuasive documents such as cancelled checks and thank you letters to support donations, floor plans to support your office at home, or recent tax court cases to support your side of the issues.

10. *Learn how the appeals process works.* Learn how to gather, research, file, and prepare adequately. Get a coach to guide you through the survival process.

When things get tough, emphasize the hazards of litigation. You can lose all the issues if you proceed to court. So can the IRS. Good day!

"Mr. Reynolds, you can't count your litter box as a deduction just because you do your business there."

ADDITIONAL TIPS:
- Don't be fixated on resolving case at the examination level. Have an open mind for appeals.
- Appeals Officers are realists. They are conscious of hazards of litigation. Your case could set a bad precedent for future cases if they lose. They don't want that.
- Interject doubt in officer's mind that IRS could lose in court.
- Help the officer help you. Feed data to help justify arguments in your favor. Their work is reviewed by their managers so any assistance to build your case from you is welcome.
- If you owe less than $25,000, have your appeals treated as a small case for quicker disposition. Write "Small Case Request" on top of your protest letter. Small cases are often sent back to appeals for settlement even before sent to IRS lawyers (district counsels).
- Ask auditor for copy of notes and workpapers under Freedom of Information Act (FOIA).

SPECIAL AUDITS

This chapter touches on specialized topics such as how auditors target lawyers and consultants. It discusses a hot topic in today's business world - worker reclassification audits where both the IRS and state agencies go after companies for treating workers as independent contractors instead of employees. It also discusses the dangers of business owners who do not get sufficient salaries but instead borrow loans from their companies and allow such loans to accumulate and go unpaid. Loans are not inherently taxable while salaries are.

Most of all, it delves into the Criminal Investigation Division (CID) which is responsible for conducting investigations of taxpayers suspected of fraudulent conduct. It has special agents whose investigative jurisdiction includes tax, money laundering, and Bank Secrecy Act laws. The agency has recently turned its gun sights at foreign bank accounts and assets.

Many criminal tax cases begin with a routine office or field audit. It turns ugly when auditors identify badges of fraud. CID cases also come from investigations of narcotics trafficking, organized criminal activity, and currency transactions. Information can also come from an assortment of sources - tips from disgruntled employees, spouses, business competitors, and neighbors.

Although CID recommends prosecution of only a few thousand taxpayers annually, each case prosecuted generally results in a conviction.

HOW TO SPOT AN IRS FRAUD AUDIT

It started with a dreaded letter from the IRS. Your tax return has been selected for audit. Lately, the agent has been asking about cash transactions, safety deposit box, foreign bank accounts and even showed up with a second agent. At your doorsteps! Something is wrong. Does the agent suspect fraud? Are you being referred to *CID (Criminal Investigation Division)*? If so, you need help. It would be foolish not to set up an adequate defense. Pronto! Let me give you some indicators of a fraud audit and what should do about it.

WHAT ARE WARNING SIGNS THAT YOU MAY HAVE BEEN REFERRED TO CID?
1. The agent requests detailed information about your *life style and spending habits*.
2. The agent asks about *offshore bank accounts*.
3. The agent asks about *safety deposit boxes* and other bank deposits.
4. The agent performs a cash deposit analysis and finds that deposits materially exceed reported income.
5. The agent begins requesting copies of every document that you show him.
6. The agent begins to contact third parties regarding payments made to you or received from you.
7. The agent *insists on meeting with you* despite your having a representative.
8. The agent insists on meeting in your place of business or home instead of your representative's office.
9. Suddenly, it is difficult to communicate with the agent who stops working on your case.
10. You are visited by *two special agents* (the second agent's role is to provide corroborating testimony).

WHAT SHOULD YOU DO AT THIS TIME?
1. Verify the identity of any agent who comes to your premises. Get a business card.
2. Do *not* talk with or write to any IRS personnel anymore.
3. *Hire a CPA or criminal tax lawyer* to represent you.
4. Execute a POA (Power of Attorney) and an engagement letter with your rep immediately.
5. Keep a copy of both POA and engagement letter at home, your office, and with you at all times.
6. Refer all calls for documentation or explanation to your tax representative.
7. Do *not* provide any more documentation directly to the agents. Go through your rep.
8. Provide the good, the bad and the ugly to your rep so he can develop strategies to counter any threat.
9. Prepare *written memoranda* of all meetings, dates, people, questions and responses.
10. List and copy each page that you provide to the IRS.

WORD OF ADVICE: Do *not* take fraud cases lightly. As soon as one or a combination of these red flags appears, *hire a representative*—preferably a tax attorney or seasoned CPA. This is not the time to be cheap.

A WORD OF CAUTION: Do not innocently offer discounts for services or goods to an agent. Such discounts are considered *bribes*. IRS personnel are clean—the cleanest among civil servants. The Service has *zero* tolerance for bribery. An innocent offer can lead you to CID.

DEVELOPMENT: Beware—*Criminal investigations increased* 8% the other year. Over 90% of indictments resulted in convictions. Traditional tax evasion cases make up 50% of cases. IRS hopes to increase time spent on unreported income to 70%. Scary stuff.

A SIGH OF RELIEF: If you receive Form 4549 RAR (Revenue Agent Report), you can breathe a sigh of relief. It means that you were *not* referred to the CID.

ADDITIONAL TIPS:
Informant? You may have a nagging suspicion that you may have been referred by an informant—a vengeful employee, ex-husband, girlfriend, or jealous competitors. Auditors are reluctant to reveal this info but I've found a way to get a hint: when an auditor responds by saying that "I'll ask my manager," you have been referred. If auditor says "I can't tell you" you have been referred.

CAN YOU BE DEPORTED FOR FILING FALSE TAX RETURNS?

Yes, you can be. Terrible, but it happens. In a landmark case, the Supreme Court held that a conviction for willfully filing a false tax return *is a deportable offense under our immigration laws*. It reached the same conclusion with respect to a conviction for aiding and abetting in the preparation of a false return.

BACKGROUND:
- Tax evasion is a felony punishable by a maximum fine of $100,000, five years imprisonment, or both.
- A person who willfully makes and signs any return, statement, or other document verified by a written declaration that it is made under the penalties of perjury and which he (includes she) does not believe to be true and correct in every material matter is guilty of a felony.
- A person who willfully assists, counsels, or advises in the preparation or presentation of a return, affidavit, claim or other document, which is fraudulent or is false as to any material matter is guilty of a felony.

FACTS:
- Akio and Fusako Kawashima, both Japanese citizens, are lawful permanent residents of the U.S.
- Mr. Kawashima pleaded guilty to one count of willfully filing a false tax return.
- Mrs. Kawashima pleaded guilty to one count of aiding and assisting in the preparation of a false tax return.
- Following their convictions, the Immigration and Naturalization Service charged the Kawashimas with being deportable from the U.S. as aliens who had been convicted of an aggravated felony.
- Aggravated felony is an offense that involves fraud or deceit in which the loss to the victim exceeds $10,000.
- In this case, the victim is the U.S. government and the loss exceeded $10,000.
- Therefore, their conviction was considered as aggravated felony.
- At their deportation hearing, taxpayers argued that their convictions did not qualify as aggravated felonies.
- The Immigration Judge disagreed and ordered their deportation.
- They appealed to the Board of Immigration Appeals, which affirmed the Immigration Judge's decision.
- In short, the taxpayers lost their case.

SUPREME COURT AFFIRMS. The case went up all the way to the Supreme Court which agreed with the Ninth Circuit that convictions in which the Government's revenue loss exceeds $10,000 qualify as aggravated felonies.
- The Supreme Court rejected the Kawashimas' argument that they could not be deported for the commission of an "aggravated felony" because their crimes did not involve fraud or deceit.
- The Court stated that the taxpayers involved in deceitful conduct when they knowingly and willfully submitted a tax return that was false as to a material matter.
- Mrs. Kawashima committed a felony involving deceit by knowingly and willfully assisting her husband's filing of a materially false return.
- Their tax evasion case was therefore a deportable offense. Ouch.

Citation: *Kawashima v. Holder, Attorney General, (S Ct 2/21/2012) No. 10-577.*

HOW IRS AUDITS ATTORNEYS

If you are a lawyer, you may find this article interesting. IRS agents are equipped with audit techniques unique to attorneys. Here's an insider info on how IRS instructs its agents to probe into the following areas:

- Unreported income, deferral of income.
- Advanced client costs.
- Bartering.
- Constructive receipts.
- Personal service corporations.
- Worker Reclassification – were employees misclassified as independent contractors?
- Were Form 1099s issued to independent contractors for payments from a trust account?
- Were Form 8300s issued for receipts of cash of $10,000 or more?

UNREPORTED INCOME: Generally, attorneys deposit settlement and award proceeds to their trust accounts. Settlement and award checks are usually made out to both attorney and client. After depositing the funds to their trust accounts, attorneys must distribute the proceeds. However, the attorney will draw a portion of these funds to cover their fees and case costs for fees on a contingency basis. IRS tells auditors to determine *if fees were included in income at the proper time*. Some attorneys may *cash checks or deposit them directly into personal or investment accounts*. Inspect endorsements on checks written to the attorney from trust accounts. Pay special attention to all checks that either are cashed or deposited into other accounts.

DEFERRAL OF INCOME: After a case is settled, an attorney may attempt to defer earned income by allowing fees to *remain in the trust account* until the following year. Once the settlement is received, the attorney's fee is both determinable and available and therefore *should be included in income*. Analyze the source of funds remaining in the trust account at year-end, particularly if there is a large ending balance.

ADVANCED CLIENT COSTS: Attorneys who take cases on a contingency fee basis commonly advance litigation expenses on behalf of clients and recover the costs out of the settlement or award. These attorneys generally use a cash basis of accounting and may deduct those expenses when paid, and include the recovered costs in income when received. However, this causes a distortion of income since it can take years to resolve these cases. Courts have determined that costs paid on behalf of a client are loans for tax purposes and are *not deductible* as current costs. The costs are the client's and not the attorney's since there is an expectation of reimbursement. However, a bad debt deduction may be taken in the year that any costs are determined to be uncollectible.

BARTERING: Auditors are told to verify client subsidiary ledgers that may lead to *exchange of legal services for other services that do not hit the books.* For example, an attorney may borrow money from a corporate client and pay it off by performing legal services. The income from legal services is not declared and no income tax is paid on it.

CONSTRUCTIVE RECEIPT: Income earned under the constructive receipt doctrine is an exception to the general rule that cash basis taxpayers must have actual receipt of income to be taxable. Income is constructively received if it's subject to demand and there are *no substantial limitations or conditions on the right to receive it*. For example, a criminal defense attorney acting as a public defender bills the county on a monthly basis. At the end of the year, a Form 1099 is issued to the attorney for the income that was actually paid. To defer income, the attorney may *not* bill the county for services that have been rendered. In this case, the attorney's gross income is understated.

PERSONAL SERVICE CORPORATIONS: Attorneys doing business as regular C corporations are classified as *Personal Service Corporations* (PSC) and are *taxed at a higher rate*. They do not get to use the lower graduated rates that start at 15% and 25%; instead, they are taxed at a high flat rate of 35%. Check if entity is properly classified as PSC and if taxes are computed at the higher tax bracket.

HOT TIP: Elect S status to avoid the high 35% rate and enjoy a zero federal rate at the corporate level. Some states including tax breaks as well. For example, California have ridiculously low rate of 1 ½% (instead of high rates that apply to C corporations).

HOW IRS AUDITS CONSULTANTS

The IRS developed a guide for its agents in auditing consultants to focus on:

- Travel and meals,
- Bartering,
- Independent contractor 1099 versus employee W2,
- Shifting or assignment of income by a taxpayer to a related entity,
- Personal service corporation, and
- Internal controls, books and records, electronic software, and use of the Internet.

TRAVEL: The nature of consulting business requires extensive travel inside and outside the U.S. Many consultants have a specialized niche and a wide geographical client base. Auditors are told to look for *spousal and family travel and personal travel,* particularly out of country.

MEALS AND ENTERTAINMENT: Given the considerable travel usually required in the consulting industry, auditors are alerted that there may be sizeable expenses for meals and entertainment. Check deductions for personal meals and entertainment.

BARTERING: Auditors are told to verify client subsidiary ledger cards that may *lead to exchange of consulting services for other services that were not booked.* For example, a consultant may borrow a large sum of money from a corporate client and then pay it off by performing legal services. The income from legal services is not declared and no income tax is paid on it.

INDEPENDENT CONTRACTOR VS. EMPLOYEE: IRS has observed that the independent contractor versus employee issue is prevalent in the consulting industry. Potential areas of concern include a former employee coming back to a company as an independent consultant with a minimal break in service. This issue has evolved due to the downsizing taking place in the business world over the past decade. Many employers, in an effort to lower costs, have terminated specialized employees and then *hired them back as independent consultants.* This allows the employer to lower their costs in payroll and employee benefits.

SHIFTING OR THE ASSIGNMENT OF INCOME/SUBSTANCE VS. FORM: Auditors are informed that closely-held or one-person personal services corporations may have *shifted income from themselves to another entity in order to reduce their income and self-employment taxes.* The taxpayer may shift income earned by one entity to a related entity in order to offset net operating losses of a related entity. Subsequent to this shifting of income, the taxpayer may take a relatively small salary from the entity that received the assigned income in relationship to the amount of income shifted. Examiners are told to review the taxpayer's consulting agreements/contracts and to look for certain information. For example, auditors should look at whether the taxpayer is an S corporation or a partnership and yet the contract requires the services of a particular employee/owner.

PERSONAL SERVICE CORPORATIONS: Consultants doing business as regular C corporations are at tax disadvantage because they are classified as *personal service corporations (PSC) and must use a higher rate.* Check if the entity is using low tax brackets that start at 15% and 25% instead of the high flat rate of 35% that applies to PSCs.

HOT TIP: Elect S status to get out of this unfortunate tax situation. Not only do you avoid the high 35% rate, you also elect to pay zero federal income tax. You also get a bonus in California: a very low rate of 1 ½ % instead of the regular rate of about 9% for C corporations.

IRS AUDITS CORPORATE SHAREHOLDER LOANS

(Part 1 – The Problem)

Loans to shareholders attract IRS attention—*unwanted attention*. These are amounts borrowed by shareholders of corporations. And left unpaid. They borrow funds from closely held businesses and fail to make repayments. This matter is even worse when a shareholder/employee gets little or no salary. The issue that started to attract renewed IRS scrutiny is the conversion of those loans to constructive receipts of dividends. Constructive dividends are not distributions that are planned or declared by the business but instead arise as a result of an IRS examination (audit). Dividends, as you know, are not deductible as expense but have to be declared as income by the recipient shareholder. *Malo.*

It is indeed tempting for shareholders to borrow money from their own businesses as they please, as they need, without thinking of repaying them. The situation grows from bad to worse when these loans accumulate to a point where repayment has become impossible. Worst, it becomes a glaring item in the corporate tax returns. If the IRS audits the tax returns, it becomes an issue, a bad one. The loans can be *re-characterized as dividends that cannot be deducted* by the business but have to be taxed on the owners' individual tax returns. The loans can also be characterized as wages—resulting in payroll taxes that should have been withheld from the employee and taxes that should have been paid for employer's share. IRS auditors are now equipped with a whole section devoted to loans to and from shareholders in their audit techniques under MSSP (Market Segment Specialization Program).

How can one avoid shareholder loan problems? According to IRS regulations, a genuine debt occurs only when there is a legally valid and enforceable obligation. It has to be reasonable. There should be a reasonable expectation of repaying on the part of the shareholder and a reasonable expectation of enforcing the collection on the part of the corporation.

THE TAX COURT VIEWS THE FOLLOWING FACTORS TO HELP PROVE BONA FIDE DEBTOR-CREDITOR RELATIONSHIP:
1. A promissory note or other written note of the debt is prepared and signed
2. Interest is charged
3. There is a fixed schedule of repayment
4. Repayments are actually made
5. The loan is secured by collateral
6. Borrowers were solvent at the time of the loan
7. The loan was approved by the board of directors
8. The loan is substantiated with corporate minutes
9. The loan is recorded on the corporate books of account as a loan
10. If the debt becomes past due, a demand for repayment is made

The shareholder loan issue invites a closer scrutiny if the lender is a closely held corporation. Because of the absolute control exercised by the shareholder, courts have considered these additional criteria:
1. The taxpayer's degree of control over the corporation,
2. The existence of external restrictions such as bank covenants on the amounts of disbursements to shareholders, the corporation's earnings and dividend history, the ability of the shareholders to repay the loans, the shareholders' intention and attempt to repay the loan.

IRS AUDITS CORPORATE SHAREHOLDER LOANS

(Part 2 – The Solution)

Shareholder loans accumulate over time and become red flags for IRS audits. Left unchecked, they grow to sums that are hard to repay. Worse, they are hard to defend. Cookie jar variety. We discussed problems in the first article. Let's discuss *solutions* with this second article.

HERE ARE TIPS TO ALLEVIATE THIS PROBLEM: Make some payments, even a small amount from time to time. This indicates the existence of a true loan. Successful defenses on IRS audits have identified the key to winning on this issue: Repaying the loans in full occasionally. Use a credit line, borrow from your credit card, and raise funds from anywhere to pay-off at the end of the year. I have personally found out through audits (that I have defended) that some repayments and a subsequent valid effort to enforce repayment have saved the day for some seemingly lost cases. I also had to contend with a typical IRS approach to loans to family members as a two-step transaction: First, as a dividend distribution from this corporation to the shareholder and, second, as a loan from the shareholder to the family member. The shareholder, not the corporation, is stuck with a non-business bad debt and has to pick up dividend income. The IRS may also argue that if it is a non-business bad debt at the corporate level, there is no corporate deduction for the loss because it is not an ordinary and necessary business loss.

HERE'S THE SOLUTION: Clean up your books by formalizing the transaction and substantiating the loan arrangement by preparing promissory notes, demand letters. Create a regular and systematic repayment schedule of outstanding loans. If you have the funds, *pay off the loan balances at the end of the year.* If you do not have the resources, borrow, pay it off and after some reasonable period of time, re-borrow and pay back your sources. Sit down with your tax adviser and plan to clean up before the IRS comes calling. Do not forget to include such borrowings in your corporate minutes. Good Luck.

IN CONCLUSION, shareholder loans become an issue on IRS audits when they are converted to constructive dividends. This problem is caused by shareholders getting loans and failing to conduct these transactions at arm's length. The *lack of formality* in dealing with these loans is the usual culprits for losses at IRS audits. It is not so bad when the loans are *converted to salaries* because such wages are deductible by the corporation and, therefore, offset the tax effect of picking up the income on your individual income tax returns.

Development 1: IRS has stepped up scrutiny of shareholder loans and compensation. Compensated corporate officers are statutory employees for federal income tax withholding, FICA, and FUTA. This means that the only way to compensate a corporate officer is as an employee. IRS agents examine all payments to officers—loans, dividends, draws, and distributions.

Development 2: EDD (Employment Development Department of California) is also on the lookout for S corporation shareholders who take little or no salary. California conforms to federal law that payments to shareholders who perform services for the corporation but do not receive a salary for services—are wages, not distribution of earnings and profits that could qualify for the special 15% rate on dividends.

HOW TO PROTECT YOUR BUSINESS FROM WORKER RECLASSIFICATION AUDITS

Employment tax audit to reclassify independent contractors to employees is the hottest topic in today's audit priorities. Often times, business establishments classify workers as 1099 independent contractors instead of W-2 employees. There is a myriad of reasons for this (mis)classification. You see, contractors are not subject to payroll taxes; employees are. Payroll taxes cost money—badly needed resource to run your business. IRS and state agencies have been conducting reclass audits for some time, but they have been tightening the screws for the last few years. I know this because I've been defending these audits for decades. I can tell you from first-hand experience that it's been getting more difficult to score wins. The taxation theatre is changing, my friends—for the worse. So are the courts that hear these cases. IRS and state agencies are stepping up these audits with the main goal of collecting payroll taxes.

If you operate a business that classifies workers as independent contractors, you may want to read these tips. Here we go:

1. Have independent contractors fill out and sign W-9s as a source of full name, social security or federal identification number, and address—before paying their first bill. Try getting this at the end of the year.

2. Use a *written agreement* with independent contractors.

3. *File all Form 1099-Misc on a timely basis*. Consistent and timely filing of 1099 forms is key to both Section 530 relief and access to the Classification Settlement Program.

4. Require independent contractors to submit *invoices*, not time cards or time sheets.

5. Require independent contractors to submit *competitive bids*.

6. Encourage independent contractors to carry their *own workers' comp* coverage.

7. Do not add independent contractors to *company benefits* such as medical insurances.

8. Avoid making *advances or loans* to independent contractors.

9. Keep vendor records *separate* from employee records.

10. Maintain *vendor files* that contain:
    *   Form W-9.
    *   Contracts and bids.
    *   City license and county fictitious business name (DBA).
    *   Workers' compensation insurance certificate.
    *   Documented times when work was turned down by the worker.
    *   Invoices from the worker.

STATUTE OF LIMITATIONS

Statute of limitations provides final dates after which neither you nor the IRS can be disturbed by the other. From an IRS perspective, the agency can no longer audit your tax return or collect what you owe. From your perspective, you can no longer claim a refund for overpaid tax.

When the statute expires, you either breathe a sigh of relief or have blown a chance to receive refunds.

BASICS OF STATUTE OF LIMITATIONS

Background:
When is your return free from IRS audit? From your point of view, statute of limitations prevents the IRS from collecting a deficiency in tax or beginning a civil or criminal case. Statute of limitations provides a date of finality after which the IRS or the taxpayer can take no further actions. We can breathe a little easier when we know that our returns are out of the line of fire.

Three-year Statute of Limitations:
Normally, the IRS must assess tax, or file suit against the taxpayer to collect the tax, within three years after the return is filed. The three-year period of limitation on assessment also applies to penalties. The statute increased to four years if you omit 25% of your gross income. There is no statute for fraudulent returns. The statute never runs out and you can be audited anytime.

When the Statute Runs:
The statute of limitations on assessment begins to run on the day after you file your return. Thus, the day of filing is excluded from the computation of the three-year period. For example, taxpayers who filed their 2015 Form 1040 on 4/15/16 are free and clear after 4/15/19 as the IRS can't assess a deficiency after that date. A return filed early is considered filed on the due date of the return. A return filed after the original due date, is considered filed on the date the return is actually received by the IRS. Extending the due date of the return does not shorten the assessment period.

Example 1: Statute of limitations for individual income tax Form 1040:
If you filed your 2015 Form 1040 return on 3/5/16, the return was deemed filed on 4/15/16, and thus, the IRS can't assess a tax deficiency after 4/15/19. If the return was extended to 10/15/16, and was filed on that date, the period of assessment would run from 10/15/16 to 10/15/19. If you filed your 2013 Form 1040 return on 4/15/14, the federal statute runs out on 4/15/17. Add two years if you omitted 25% of your income. California has a 4-year stature so the state has until 4/15/18 to audit your 2013 tax return.

Example 2: Statute of limitations for quarterly federal payroll tax returns:
If your corporation timely filed its quarterly federal payroll tax return Form 941s for the four quarters of 2015 on 4/30/15, 7/31/15, 10/31/15, and 1/31/15, all four returns were deemed filed on 4/17/16, which means that the IRS has until 4/15/19, to assess a tax deficiency for any of the four quarters.

Example3: Statute of limitations for unemployment tax return (FUTA) Form 940:
Employer's annual federal unemployment tax return (FUTA) Form 940 doesn't fall under this rule even though it is an employment tax return. The statute of limitations for a 2015 return expires three years after the filing deadline on 1/31/16, not 4/15/16.

Caveat: The countdown never starts if a return is not filed.

TIPS:
* The usual "out" for a taxpayer under stress is to close the audit fast.
* You want to end your misery by closing the audit ASAP.
* But consider going the opposite way: slow down the process.
* Time can be in your favor. The IRS is not a model of efficiency.
* Auditors get sick, go for medical checkups, and take care of their kids just like the rest of us.
* They are promoted, transferred, or fired. In the meantime, the statute can run out.
* They have only 36 months from the time you file to the time they close the audit.
* IRS Manual instructs them to finish audit within 28 months.
* They only have eight months to close your audit, a narrow window for complicated cases.
* The strategy: speed up or slow down depending on the issues of your case.

HOW LONG SHOULD YOU KEEP RECORDS?

How long do you have to keep tax records? How long can the IRS audit your tax returns?
Let's discuss **15 TIPS ON STATUTE OF LIMITATIONS** so you can clean your garage this weekend.

1. The general statute to audit you is *three years* after the return is filed.
2. The statute is extended to *six years if you omit 25% of your gross income.*
3. The statute to collect what has been established to be your tax liability is *10 years*.
4. A personal tax return that is filed earlier than the deadline of April 15 is considered filed on that deadline. For example, a 2012 return filed on February 15, 2013, is considered filed on April 15, 2013 with a statute expiration of April 15, 2016.
5. A personal tax return that was extended and filed on October 15, 2013 is considered filed on that date with statute expiring on October 15, 2016. (TIP: If you have some sensitive issues that you don't want disturbed, file on time so as not to give the IRS and extra six months to snoop around).
6. There is *no statute if you do not file a return.* They can audit you anytime—even after three or six years after filing deadline. The three years starts only after a timely filing.
7. There is *no* protection from the statute if the IRS does *not receive your tax return.* There is no protection even if you filed a return but the IRS did not receive or claims not to have received your return!
8. Mail via certified or register mail especially if your return contains some critical income or deductions.
9. There is *no* statute for false or *fraudulent returns. Nada.*
10. If you want statutes to protect you but are not ready to file, file anyway. File a processable return that bears your signature. Provide sufficient data for the IRS to ascertain and assess your tax liability. Remember that your return does not need to be perfect. Just show an honest and genuine attempt to comply with the law. This is my message to non-filers who have not filed because of incomplete records.
11. If the IRS identifies you as a non-filer and you do not file after their demands, they can file a substitute return for you. Believe me, that return will be estimated on the high side; pardon me, on the very high side, resulting on a tax due approaching 200% of what you actually owe. Add penalties and interests and, Houston, you have a problem.
12. Filing a gift tax return is advisable even if not required. It starts the running of the statute of limitations.
13. An estate or decedent's estate may also request for a prompt assessment within 18 months.
14. The executor of an estate can also request for discharge from personal liability within nine months after the request is filed. It does not shorten the 3-year statute but relieves the executor of personal liability.
15. What if you are under examination and the agent wants you to extend the statute? Should you extend or not? Well, if you do, you are just giving the IRS more time to get you. If you don't, they will bypass appeals (by not issuing a 30-day letter) and go straight to Tax Court with a notice of deficiency. This could get expensive. Here is my recommendation: Unless there are unusual circumstances, agree to the extension especially if you have good chance at settling in appeals. You will be asked to sign either Form 872 or Form 872-A. Go with **Form 872 that expires at a specific future date**. *Avoid 872-A which is open-ended and has no expiration period.*

This concludes your Statute of Limitations Course 102. Good day.

REMEMBER:
*   Keep records for 2012, 2013, 2014, 2015 (OK to dispose most records for prior years).
*   But keep an additional 2 years if you may have omitted 25% of your income.
*   Keep an extra year for California and other states.

HOW LONG MUST EMPLOYERS KEEP RECORDS?

Some of us are file rats, keeping every document every year for every conceivable transaction. On the other hand, some of us hate paper files and throw every receipt, invoice, or paper. There must be some sense, some balance between minimizing paper files and retaining some records for future use in case government agencies come knocking at your door. Scanning is a good solution.

LET'S REVIEW 10 RULES FOR EMPLOYERS AND BUSINESS OWNERS:

1. **Internal Revenue Service** – three to four years after the payment, deduction of taxes, or due dates of returns. This includes any record relating to payments to employees, employer tax reports, and deposits - covering federal income tax withholding, social security, Medicare, and FUTA taxes.

2. **U.S. Department of Labor (Fair Labor Standards Act)** – three years from date of last entry. Records must be kept on all employees including name, home address, date of birth if under 19, gender, and occupation, rate of pay, hours worked, earnings, dates of payment, and periods covered.

3. **Immigration Reform and Control Act** – three years from date of hire and one year from date of termination. This includes INS Form I-9 (Employment Eligibility Verification Form).

4. **Employment Retirement Income Security Act (ERISA)** – six years from filing date of documents. This includes plan documents, reports, resolutions, vouchers, and worksheets.

5. **Occupational Safety and Health Act (OSHA)** – five years after end of year to which records relate. Keep log and summary of occupational injuries and illnesses with brief descriptions of injury and illness, extent and outcome of each incident, and summary totals for each calendar year.

6. **Age Discrimination in Employment Act** – three years. Keep payroll and other records of employee name, address, date of birth, occupation, rate of pay, and compensation per week.

7. **Americans With Disabilities Act** – one year after the date record was made or personnel action taken, whichever is later. Keep application forms and records concerning hiring, promotion, demotion, transfer, layoff, termination, rates of pay or other terms of compensation, and selection for training or apprenticeship.

8. **State Unemployment Insurance for California** – four years. Keep employee's name, address, social security number, dates of hire, separation, rehire, payments dates for cash or non-cash wages, dates and hours worked.

9. **State Income Tax Records for California** – four years from the date taxes are filed, paid, or due, whichever is later. You may maintain records on magnetic tape, microfilm, diskettes, drum, or DVD instead of bulky space-consuming paper files. Note that the average state requires records to be kept for four years. Some states require three years (Hawaii, Idaho, Indiana, etc.) or five years (Alabama, Iowa, Montana, New Jersey, etc). The longest is eight years for Minnesota.

10. **CONCLUSION:** If you want to be safe, keep records for at least the number of years indicated above. If in doubt - keep. Better yet, consult with your accountant, enrolled agent, CPA, or lawyer.

12 RECORD RETENTION RULES

I have clients who throw away everything instantly. Can't stand records. I also have clients who keep records forever. Rat packs. There must be some balance in between. Unfortunately, there is limited guidance from the IRS. Fortunately, there are relevant statutes of limitation to guide us on the period when you can amend a tax return or the IRS can assess additional tax.

LET'S DISCUSS 12 RULES ON RECORD RETENTION:

1. Federal statute of limitations remains at *three years*.

2. Statute for most states, including California, is four years.

3. For example, if you file your 2015 tax return on April 17, 2016, keep your tax records until April 15, 2019. If you file that return early in January, the statute is still April 15, 2019. If you wait until your favorite deadline of October 15, the authorities have until October 15, 2019 to get you.

4. Tax returns with substantial understatemen t of income are six years for federal, seven years for state.

5. It is more prudent to add a year to these periods.

6. There is no limit if tax return is not filed. In other words, if you do not file a tax return, the IRS has forever to audit you. If you have some issues that bother you, file. And pray. If you are not audited within the statute period, you are fine, thank goodness.

7. There is no limit for fraudulent tax returns either.

8. Bad debts and worthless securities should be kept for seven years.

9. There are some records that should be kept longer such as invoices and checks to buy property that could be sold (house, rental units) or depreciated (furniture, equipment).

10. Some records such as tax returns, audit results, and financial statements, should be kept indefinitely.

11. Then there are non-tax reasons for keeping some records longer such as insurance policies, leases, real estate escrow closing statements.

12. A revenue procedure allows you to convert paper documents to electronic images or transfer computerized records into electronic storage media such as CDs or DVDs. You may then destroy the original hard copies or delete original computerized records.

HERE ARE SOME FILING TIPS:

- **FIRST TIP:** Consider storing each year in a *separate box* that you can easily dispose as each statute year expires. There no need to refile. Simply throw away each box as it matures over statute of limitation.
- **SECOND TIP:** use filing cabinets to divide your files into two categories
  A. *Permanent file* for tax returns, contracts, escrows, deeds, life insurance policies.
  B. *Annual files* for paid invoices for deductible expenses, groceries, supplies for each year.
- **THIRD TIP:** go clean your attic this weekend.

HOW TO PAY YOUR IRS DEBTS – OIC
(OFFER IN COMPROMISE)

If you are unable pay what you owe the IRS, you can apply for either an Offer in Compromise (OIC) or Installment agreement (payment plan). For example, if you owe $10,000, you can submit an OIC of $4,000 or so. If the offer is rejected, you may negotiate or request a payment plan to pay the $10,000 in monthly installments of say $500 over 21 months.

The OIC program makes sense for both sides because it provides a way for you to resolve your tax liability and for the IRS to collect funds that may not be collected through other means. If the IRS accepts your offer, you pay a lesser amount in full satisfaction of an unpaid tax liability, including interest, and penalties.

The IRS will accept an OIC when it is unlikely that the tax liability can be collected in full and the amount offered reasonably reflects collection potential. The OIC allows the government to obtain what is reasonably collectible at the earliest possible time at the least cost, while providing you with a fresh start.

IRS has authority to compromise taxes when there is a legitimate dispute as to what you owe (doubt as to liability) or when it is unlikely that the IRS can collect your tax liability in full (doubt as to collectability) or to promote effective tax administration.

I OWE THE IRS – WHAT CAN I DO?

HERE ARE 10 TIPS IF YOU CANNOT IMMEDIATELY PAY YOUR LIABILITIES TO THE IRS:

1. **Pay What You Can:** Pay promptly to stop additional penalties and interest from accruing. If you are unable to pay, consider getting a loan to pay the bill in full rather than make installment payments to the IRS.

2. **Additional Time to Pay:** If you are unable to pay, request for a payment plan.

3. **Installment Agreement:** You may request an installment agreement but you have to be current with filing and paying requirements. File all required returns for the past years and pay estimated taxes for the current year.

4. **Form 9465:** Complete and mail an IRS Form 9465 (Installment Agreement Request) along with your tax return or bill (use return envelope supplied by the IRS).

5. **Collection Information Statement:** If you owe more than $50,000, you will be required to complete Form 433-F (Collection Information Statement).

6. **Online Payment Agreement:** If you owe $50,000 or less in combined taxes, penalties and interest, you can request an installment agreement using the Online Payment Agreement application at www.irs.gov.

7. **Credit Card Payments:** You can pay your bill with a credit card. The interest rate on a credit card may be lower than the combination of interest and penalties imposed by the Internal Revenue Code. Contact one of the following processing companies: Link2Gov, www.pay1040.com, RBS WorldPay, Inc, www.payUSAtax.com, or Official Payments Corporation, www.officialpayments.com/fed.

8. **Electronic Funds Transfer:** Use the Electronic Federal Tax Payment System by either calling 800-555-4477 or using the online access at www.eftps.gov.

9. **User fees:** If an installment agreement is approved, a one-time user fee is charged.

10. **Reduce the Number of Withholding Exemptions at Work:** If you want to prevent future nightmares, reduce your exemptions at work. Submit a new W-4 (Employee's Withholding Allowance Certificate) to accounting. Example: Go from M-2 (married with two dependents) to M-0 or even S-0 (Single with no dependent). Your employer will withhold a little more each payday but this will alleviate your tax problems when you file. You don't claim your dependents at work but you'll deduct exemptions for all dependents when you file. Result is either less tax due or more refunds. Try it.

SHOULD YOU SUBMIT AN
OFFER IN COMPROMISE (OIC)?

If you are unable pay all your taxes owed to the IRS, you may make an offer to pay a smaller sum to fully pay all taxes, penalties, and interests. This is called Offer in Compromise (OIC for short). Let's discuss the pros and cons of OIC.

ADVANTAGES:

If the offer is accepted, you will be left alone; tax liens will be removed and enforced collection avoided. The IRS, through a policy statement, declared that they will accept an offer in compromise when it is unlikely that the tax liability can be collected in full and that the amount offered "reasonably reflects collection potential." The goal is to achieve collection of what is potentially collectable at the earliest possible time and at the least cost to the government. The ultimate goal is to arrive at the compromise that is in the best interests of both the taxpayer and the IRS. Acceptance of an adequate offer relieves you of a financial burden and gives you a fresh start toward compliance with your future filing and payment requirements.

DISADVANTAGES:

1. You must list all your assets. In the process, you are giving them a roadmap to seize and sell your assets if the offer is not accepted and nothing else works.
2. Offers have been tough to get approved. However, IRS demonstrated some humanitarian aid:
   - Acceptance rate increased from 16% to 39%.
   - Rejections decreased from 21% to 17%
3. The statute of limitations for the assessment and collection is suspended during the period plus another year thereafter.
4. One missed payment results in a default that gives the IRS the right to resume collection.
5. You must comply with all provisions relating to the timely filing of returns and payment of taxes due for the next five years.

Of course, if things do not work out, you can always consider the alternatives of installment agreements and bankruptcy. In the meantime, there is a hold in the collection process that in itself is an accomplishment as you straighten out your financial affairs. I suggest that you use an enrolled agent, CPA, or tax lawyer to prepare it for you. If you cannot afford their fees, prepare it yourself and just pay a professional to review your offer before submitting it to the IRS.

National Taxpayer Advocate Criticizes IRS's Collection Practices

In her annual report to Congress, former National Taxpayer Advocate Nina Olson noted her "continuing concern that IRS collection practices inflict unnecessary harm on financially struggling taxpayers and fail to achieve the IRS's overriding objective of increasing long-term voluntary compliance with the tax laws." By filing a lien against a taxpayer with no money and no assets, "the IRS often collects nothing, yet it inflicts long-term harm on the taxpayer by making it harder for him to get back on his feet when he does get a job," she said. A filed tax lien on a credit report can render someone unemployable, unable to obtain housing (owned or rented), and unable to obtain car insurance or a credit card, at least at reasonable rates. A tax lien can be particularly devastating to small businesses, as it often cuts off their access to credit.

TIPS:
If you file for bankruptcy, timing is critical. The IRS cannot and will not entertain your OIC after you file bankruptcy.

ECONOMIC HARDSHIP FOR OFFER IN COMPROMISE (OIC)

(PART A)

Media coverage on IRS abuses and subsequent tax laws put pressure on the Service to revamp the Offer in Compromise (OIC) program for taxpayers who could not pay their tax liabilities. The IRS proposed regulations which provide relief if present collection activities create economic hardships.

Previously, the IRS could accept offers only if there was doubt as to liability and collectability. Now, there's a third criterion: economic hardship.

HOW DOES THE IRS DETERMINE ECONOMIC HARDSHIP?
HERE ARE SOME FACTORS TO SUPPORT YOUR CASE:
1. You are incapable of earning a living because of a medical condition, long-term illness, or disability and that providing for your care and support will exhaust your financial resources,
2. Although you have certain assets, liquidating them to pay outstanding taxes will render you unable to meet *basic living expenses*, and
3. Despite owning certain assets, you cannot borrow against your equity and that disposition by seizure or sale of the assets would have sufficient *adverse consequences* that would make forced collection unlikely to be successful.

HERE ARE EXAMPLES OF ECONOMIC HARDSHIPS:
1. You are incapable of earning a living due to *medical condition, long-term illness, or disability and the taxpayer's resources are reasonably foreseen to be depleted.*
2. Your dependent has long-term illness that requires the taxpayer to use assets for basic living expenses and medical care.
3. Liquidation of assets would render you *unable to meet basic living expenses.*

To expand access to the OIC program, the IRS also instituted a new review process for rejected offers, revised OIC Form 656, and modified its handbook for IRS agents. OIC specialists are advised to look for *"exceptional circumstances"* whereby collection would be *detrimental to voluntary compliance*. The new Form 656-A, Additional Basis for Compromise, is to be used in cases where acceptance of the offer would *promote effective tax administration* and would not undermine tax compliance.

To qualify, you must have a clean history of filing and paying their taxes. Businesses must have timely filed and paid all quarterly federal taxes for the two preceding quarters and must have timely made all federal tax deposits in the current quarter in which they submit an offer. You cannot be in bankruptcy at that time.

The procedures require that you submit the traditional Form 656 and the new Form 656-A that contains a full page of "explanation of circumstances."

While these new regulations open the door for taxpayers who could not qualify under traditional remedies, the IRS stresses that these regulations should not be viewed as an invitation to avoid paying taxes. Commissioner Rossitti describes the program as a "new way for the IRS to help some people who are trapped in severe hardship."

ECONOMIC HARDSHIP FOR OFFER IN COMPROMISE (OIC)

(PART B)

HERE'S A GOODIE:
Telephone calls, notices, and visits by agents of the IRS stop when you file an OIC. It brings temporary relief while your OIC proposal is being reviewed. Good luck.

Congress mandated the IRS to improve its Offer In Compromise (OIC) program as part of the IRS Restructuring and Reform Act. Prior laws dictated the IRS to accept your offer in compromise only when there was a doubt as to (1) whether the debt was actually owed, (2) whether it could ever be collected from you. New regulations require the IRS to add a third situation: **ECONOMIC HARDSHIP** and *advance effective tax administration to settle the liability.*

Under the new provisions, you are eligible to make an offer in compromise of your tax liability if such a compromise will not undermine compliance with tax laws and either collection of the entire tax liability would create economic hardships or exceptional circumstances exist where collection of the entire liability would be detrimental to our voluntary tax compliance system regardless of your financial circumstances.

How does one determine that your offer would not undermine compliance with tax laws?
The following factors help:
1.   You do not have a history of non-compliance with both filing and paying your taxes,
2.   You have not taken deliberate action to avoid paying taxes, and
3.   You have not encouraged others to refuse to comply with tax laws.

Let me cite a few examples of taxpayers going through economic hardships:
1.   You have developed a *serious illness* that resulted in almost continuous hospitalization for a number of years. Your medical condition is such that you have been unable to manage your financial affairs. You did not file your tax returns for years. The IRS therefore prepared a substitute return and assessed you with taxes, penalties and interests. The bill had grown to more than three times its original size. If you used to have a good history of complying with tax laws, you qualify for an offer in compromise based on exceptional circumstances.

2.   You provide time, care and assistance to your *child who has a serious long-term illness*. Although you have sufficient assets to pay taxes, you will need the equity in your assets to provide basic living expenses and medical care for your child. Before your child got sick, you filed and paid your taxes on time. Based on these facts, you should qualify for an offer in compromise because of an economic hardship.

3.   You are *disabled and live on a fixed income* that will not permit full payment of your taxes after allowing for basic living expenses. You own a house that has been especially equipped to accommodate your disability. Because of your disability and limited earning potential, you have not been able to refinance your mortgage. A forced sale of your house would create severe consequences making such a sale unreasonable. Assuming that you have a good history of complying with tax laws, you should be able to qualify for an offer in compromise based on economic hardship.

4.   You are retired and your only income is from a meager pension. While your retirement account has enough funds to pay off your taxes, doing so would leave you without adequate means to provide for your basic living expenses. You have filed and paid your taxes faithfully before these current problems. Based on these facts, you should be able to qualify for an offer because of economic hardship.

Use the new application Form 656-A in addition to the standard Form 656.

12 TIPS IN PREPARING YOUR OFFER IN COMPROMISE (OIC)

An Offer In Compromise (OIC) allows you to settle assessments for tax, penalties, and interests at *less than the assessed amounts.* You can apply for an OIC if there is doubt as to liability or as to collectability. Let me give you a dozen tips in **PREPARING AN OIC APPLICATION.**

1. If the tax due is a joint assessment, both husband and wife must submit the offer.

2. The offer must reasonably reflect your ability to pay.

3. The amount of the offer should be equal to or greater than the amount that the IRS will be able to recover through normal collection procedures including garnishments, levies, and seizures.

4. Your source of funds could be loans from relatives and friends or loans against your assets. The offer must be generally paid in full upon acceptance. There are few cases when short-term payments are allowed. Any deferred payment must specify the total amount of the offer and specific timeframes for the balance. (Example: "amount offered for $5,000, terms for $1,000 to be paid now and $4,000 to be paid within 30 days of acceptance").

5. Use Form 656. There have been several revisions so use the most current one.

6. Forms 656 must have original signatures (Copies and fax not acceptable).

7. State why the offer is being submitted (Doubt as to collectability).

8. On offers based on doubt as to liability, attach documentation as to why you do not owe the tax. This is important because the degree of doubt influences the amount of your offer.

9. On offers based on doubt as to collectability, explain why the IRS cannot collect more from your current assets, present and future income. Document your living expenses, current income, the value of assets owned and the related encumbrances such as mortgages and car loans.

10. In valuing your properties, use "distressed sale" value. Do not use fair market values. Value your house, cars and other properties at about 75 to 85% of fair market value. That is what you would receive anyway if you were to make a quick forced sale.

11. Do not forget to claim exempt properties such as:
    *   Furniture or personal effects in your household,
    *   Tools of your trade or profession.

12. The government also looks at your future income by calculating the present value of a stream of income for the next five years at a current fair market rate of interest. In doing so, they consider your education, trade or profession, age and experience, health, and past and present income. (This is presently based on a factor of 49.64 times net monthly cash flow). Generally, you are no longer required to enter into a collateral agreement (except when there are strong indications of available funds as in the case of fluctuating income).

"FRESH START" INITIATIVE FOR OFFER IN COMPROMISE (OIC)

The Internal Revenue Service (IRS) announced its "Fresh Start" initiative by offering more flexible terms to its Offer in Compromise (OIC) program. This enables financially distressed taxpayers to clear up tax problems quicker. Former IRS Commissioner Doug Shulman stated that this effort helps taxpayers who are still struggling to make ends meet as we recover from the last recession. This initiative focuses on financial analysis used to determine which taxpayers qualify for OIC.

If you are unable to pay your tax debts in full, you have two choices:
- Offer in Compromise (OIC) or
- Installment Agreement (payment plan).

WHICH ONE WORKS FOR YOU?

OIC works if you have enough funds to pay off a reduced balance.

Installment agreement works if you don't have funds to pay it off and what you need is *time*—extended time to pay your tax debts. **LET'S DISCUSS OIC TODAY** and payment plan in our next article.

BACKGROUND OF OIC (OFFER IN COMPROMISE):

OIC allows you to *pay less than what you owe.* Tax debts are a pain. They weigh you down. They wear you out. Dealing with the IRS takes over your financial life, sometimes life itself for some of us. It impedes your recovery from the recession. You may have plans to move forward but can't because of this heavy burden on your shoulders. So, after being bombarded by aggressive radio and TV advertisers, you decide to make an offer. If you get lucky, IRS accepts your offer to pay a lesser amount. The beauty of this deal is that the accepted OIC becomes an agreement between you and the IRS to settle your tax liabilities for less than the full amount owed. This is great!

Caveat 1: An OIC is generally not accepted if the IRS believes that you can pay in full or over a period of time. The IRS looks at your income and assets to determine if and when they can collect from you.

Caveat 2: Be wary of advertisers who promise "guarantees." Have an honest tax professional first evaluate if you are a good candidate; otherwise, it's a waste of time, energy, and money if you don't qualify in the first place.

THE NEW *"FRESH START"* INITIATIVE:

The IRS recognizes that many taxpayers are still struggling to pay their bills, so the agency started working on common-sense changes to the OIC program to reflect real-world economics. When the IRS calculates a taxpayer's reasonable collection potential, it will now look at:
- *Only one year* (instead of four years) of future income for offers paid in five or fewer months and
- *Two years* (instead of five years) of future income for offers paid in 6 to 24 months.

All offers must be *fully paid within 24 months* of the date the offer is accepted.

THE CHANGES INCLUDE:

- Allowing you to repay student loans.
- Allowing you to pay delinquent state and local taxes.
- Revising the calculation of your future income.
- Expanding the Allowable Living Expense allowance category and amount.
- Expanding the National Standard "miscellaneous allowance" to include additional items such as Credit card payments, bank fees, and bank charges.
- Payments for delinquent state and local taxes may be allowed based on percentage owed to the state & IRS.

OFFER IN COMPROMISE (OIC) UPDATES FROM THE IRS

If you cannot pay all your taxes owed to the IRS, you may make an offer to pay a smaller sum to fully pay all taxes, penalties, and interests. This is called Offer in Compromise (OIC). Let's discuss developments in this area of tax collection.

Update 1: The IRS published an electronic bulletin warning of *scams* enticing delinquent taxpayers to settle delinquencies for *"pennies to a dollar."* The IRS also asked practitioners to be vigilant and to report such scams to protect taxpayers already in need of help.

Update 2: Offers are becoming tougher. The National Taxpayer Advocate disclosed that the number of offers *returned* (not even considered) increased from 39 to 57%, the number of offers accepted decreased from 34% to 16%, while the numbers those rejected increased from 12% to 21%. L

Update 3: Taxpayers submitting lump-sum offers must make a *20% nonrefundable, up-front payment* to IRS. Similarly, taxpayers submitting a periodic-payment OIC must make nonrefundable, up-front payments while IRS evaluates the offer.

Update 4: IRS to be More Flexible with OICs from *Unemployed* Taxpayers – The IRS announced that its employees will be permitted to consider a taxpayer's current income and potential for future income when negotiating an offer in compromise. Normally, the standard practice is to judge an offer amount on a taxpayer's earnings in prior years. This new step provides greater flexibility when considering offers in compromise from the unemployed. The IRS may also require that a taxpayer entering into such an offer in compromise agree to pay more if the taxpayer's financial situation improves significantly.

Update 5: *Streamlined* OIC Program Announced – IRS announced a "streamlined" OIC program that allows taxpayers' with annual household income up to $100,000 to participate, provided their tax liability is less than $50,000, and the taxpayer is a wage earner, unemployed, or self-employed with no employees and gross receipts under $500,000. Benefits of the streamlined OIC program include (1) fewer requests for additional financial information, (2) when required; requests for additional information will be by phone instead of mail, and (3) greater flexibility when considering the taxpayer's ability to pay.

Update 6: Taxpayer Advocate Criticizes IRS Handling of *Financially Hard-Up Taxpayers* – In her annual report to Congress, former National Taxpayer Advocate Nina Olson noted her "continuing concern that IRS collection practices inflict unnecessary harm on financially struggling taxpayers and fail to achieve the IRS's overriding objective of increasing long-term voluntary compliance with the tax laws." By filing a lien against a taxpayer with no money and no assets, "the IRS often collects nothing, yet it inflicts long-term harm on the taxpayer by making it harder for him to get back on his feet when he does get a job," she said. A filed tax lien on a credit report can render someone unemployable, unable to obtain housing (owned or rented), and unable to obtain car insurance or a credit card, at least at reasonable rates. A tax lien can be particularly devastating to small businesses, as it often cuts off their access to credit.

HOW TO PAY YOUR IRS DEBTS –
INSTALLMENT AGREEMENT
(PAYMENT PLAN)

If you cannot pay your tax debt immediately, you can make monthly payments through an installment agreement. An installment plan allows you to pay your taxes over time while avoiding garnishments, levies or other collection actions. You'll still owe penalties and interest for paying late, but it buys you time. It helps make the payments more affordable. The minimum monthly payment for your plan depends on how much you owe and how much you earn.

GUARANTEED INSTALLMENT AGREEMENT WITH THE IRS

Guaranteed? Too good to be true? Read on.

The IRS cannot deny your application if you satisfy all of the following requirements:
1. The tax is not more than $10,000.
2. You timely filed and paid all income tax returns for the past five years.
3. You did not enter into any installment agreement.
4. The IRS determines that you cannot pay the taxes in full.
5. You provide any information needed to make that determination.
6. You agree to pay the full amount owed within three years and to comply with all tax laws while the agreement is in effect.

Now, let me give you 10 tips on how to successfully maintain your payment plan:
1. You will be charged interest at the current rate.
2. The late payment penalty of .5% per month is reduced in half to .25%.
3. If you pay by manual checks, the IRS will send you a letter of the balance after each payment.
4. If you pay by automatic bank withdrawal, the bank statement becomes your record of payment. The IRS provides a statement at the beginning of each year of all payments made during the prior year.
5. Any future refunds will be applied against your balance due.
6. The installment defaults if you miss one payment.
7. It also defaults if you fail to file a return or fail to pay taxes on such tax return.
8. File form 9465 with your income tax.
9. File form 9465 separately if you already filed your income tax.
10. Use form 3567 for California requests.

Observation 1: IRS charges a higher fee for new installment agreements that are not paid through direct debits from a taxpayer's account. Those unwilling or unable to use a direct debit arrangement will pay more than twice as much for a new installment agreement than those using a direct debit.

Observation 2: The new fees will also apply to installment agreements made using the Online Payment Agreement application.

12 TIPS TO KEEP YOUR PAYMENT PLAN CURRENT WITH THE IRS

1. Mail your payments to be *received on time.* The monthly due date is the date of *receipt* at the IRS Service Center, not the date of mailing.

2. Use *certified mail* with return receipt. Get a tracking number.

3. Do *not* skip one payment and double up on the next payment. One skipped payment causes the entire installment agreement to default. The doubled payment does not cure this default.

4. Make each payment in the *exact amount* of the agreement. Things are confusing enough.

5. If you have to pay a different amount, pay more but not less. Pay an extra whole installment, not just a few dollars that would just add to confusion. Paying less is equivalent to a missed installment that is in violation of the agreement and therefore will also cause the entire agreement to default.

6. *Enclose a reminder notice* from the IRS with your payment. If you do not receive a notice to pay (especially in the first month or two), attach a copy of Form 9465, 433-D Installment Agreement, or acceptance letter with your check.

7. *Write your Social Security Number* (or Federal I.D. number for business) on top of your check (preferably in red).

8. *Write "Installment #1"*, then "Installment #2" on the lower left-hand corner of your check. This helps both you and the IRS keep track of your payments.

9. Make your check payable to the *Department of Treasury* and mail that check and notice to the IRS address written in Form 433-D (Do not rely on old addresses. The recent reorganization transferred mailing addresses to different service centers).

10. Mail a copy of your check and the notice to your accountant and *scan or file a copy* to a manila folder labeled "IRS Installment Agreement."

11. If you have an agreement approved by telephone, keep bugging them for a *formal agreement* (a signed one). You do not realize how valuable that written agreement is until you need proof of such agreement and the IRS personnel assigned to your case had already been transferred or reassigned.

12. Follow these tips to keep an approved agreement in place. It keeps the government at bay from garnishing your wages, seizing your bank accounts and other properties. Do not blow it by missing a payment, sending late payments, paying the wrong amount, or using the wrong address. Good Luck.

TIP 1: If you pay by automatic debit (the preferred method), make sure that you have enough funds in your bank account as payments become due each month for the for the duration of the agreement.
TIP 2: Create a new account for the sole purpose of installment arrangement. Add "Installment Account" on the second line of your bank account name. This simple tip could save you hassles and headaches if your payments plan defaults (cancels) because of insufficient funds.
TIP 3: Behave.

IRS ANNOUNCES "FRESH START" INITIATIVE FOR PAYMENT PLANS

The Internal Revenue Service (IRS) announced a major expansion of its "Fresh Start" initiative to help struggling taxpayers by providing:

1. Offer in Compromise (OIC) – more flexible guidelines for collection potential.
2. Payment plans – more taxpayers can apply without financial statements.

We discussed OIC in a prior article. Let's now discuss installment agreements (payment plans):

1. An installment agreement is an option if you cannot pay all of your tax debts at their due dates.
2. Fresh Start provisions allow you to use *streamlined* installment agreements to catch up on back taxes.
3. The threshold for using an installment agreement *without* having to supply the IRS with a financial statement has been raised from $25,000 to $50,000. As you know, the preparation of financials is a major chore that discourages taxpayers from applying. It involves a lot of work and a lot of costs.
4. Taxpayers who owe up to $50,000 in back taxes will now be able to enter into a streamlined agreement with the IRS that stretches the payment out over a series of years.
5. The maximum term for streamlined installment agreements has been raised from 60 to *72 months.*
6. Individuals seeking installment agreements exceeding $50,000 will still need to supply Collection
7. Information Statement Form 433-A (Form 433-B for businesses).
8. If you owe more than $50,000, *pay it down to $50,000 to take advantage of this payment option. Penalties are reduced* (but interest continues to accrue on the outstanding balance).
9. You must agree to monthly *direct debit payments.*
10. You can go to the *On-line Payment Agreement* (OPA) page on IRS.gov to set up a payment plan.

As you can see, this initiative is designed to help individuals and businesses pay back taxes with fewer burdens. IRS also promised to issue fewer tax liens. These changes supplement a number of efforts to help struggling taxpayers. Former IRS Commissioner Doug Shulman stated that the goal is to help people meet their obligations and get back on their feet financially.

TIPS :
Here are my Personal Observations from Decades of Processing OIC and Payment Plans:
- If you are young, healthy, and have good earning potential, IRS will probably reject your offer.
- On the other hand, if you are retired, have a serious medical condition, do not have enough assets, or are merely surviving you have a better shot at an OIC.
- If in doubt, give it a try, even if you feel that your offer may be rejected.
- And when you give it try, take a dual approach—apply for both Offer in Compromise and Installment Agreement. If your OIC fails, move to plan B for an Installment agreement. J
- There's another advantage to this dual approach: you are shooting two birds with one stone. You prepare documents and forms *only once for both* OIC and payment plan. It saves time, energy, money, and aggravation as well as tax representation fees.
- Finally, convince the IRS that they are better off getting something from you now, rather than gambling for nothing when you go upstairs, high upstairs.

"There is no getting away from you guys."

HOW TO AVOID IDENTITY THEFT

An identity thief can use your Social Security Number (SSN) to file a false tax return early in the year. You may not be aware that you are a victim until you try to file your taxes and learn that one has already been filed using your SSN. The goal of thieves is to get your refund before you file. And they do.

The IRS has installed pre-refund filters to stop the vast majority of fraudulent returns. It stopped about 25 million suspicious returns and protected about $80 billion in fraudulent refunds from 2011 to 2015.To combat tax scams, the IRS recently limited the number of direct deposit refunds to a single financial account or pre-paid debit card to three.

The IRS is urging taxpayers to take a few easy steps to protect their personal, financial and tax data online and at home. This chapter lists what to do, what not to do, and offers tips on how to avoid scams of different varieties – email scams, telephone scams, and phishing.

12 TIPS TO PREVENT IDENTITY THEFT – WHAT TO DO

1. If you store passwords in your cell phone, use a *passcode* to open it. Do not store them as "passwords". Disguise characters of passwords. Use codes. Use a kill switch if cell phone is stolen.
2. *Use strong passwords*: at least six characters, including at least one symbol and number (no reference to your name, address, mother's maiden name, or pets).
3. Keep an inventory of everything in your wallet. *Physically copy the contents of your wallet.* Copy both sides of each license and credit cards. You will know what you had in your wallet and all of the account numbers and phone numbers when you call to cancel. Keep the photocopy in a safe place.
4. If you lose your credit cards, *file a police report immediately* in the jurisdiction where your credit cards were lost or stolen. This proves to lenders that you exercised due diligence.
5. Keep a *photocopy of your passport* when traveling abroad.
6. Put your mobile or *work (not home) phone number on your checks.*
7. Use a PO Box *or office address* on your checks.
8. *Back up your computer data* and store it to external hard, flash drive, or iCloud.
9. If you use wireless Internet access, make sure that you get help from someone who understands wireless security when you set up your access point or router.
10. If you are job hunting using resume web sites, don't apply unless the employer has a *verifiable address.*
11. *Keep your system and browser software up to date* and set to the highest security level you can tolerate. Install anti-virus, anti-spyware and firewall protection, and keep them up to date as well. When possible, use hardware firewalls that are available through your broadband connection router.
12. *Call the 3 national credit reporting organizations immediately to place a fraud alert on your name.* This alerts any company that checks your credit that your information was stolen, and they have to contact you by phone to authorize new credit.
    - **Equifax:** 800-525-6285
    - **Experian:** 888-397-3742
    - **TransUnion :** 800-680-7289

DEVELOPMENT: The IRS released a form for taxpayers who have experienced (or are at risk of harm from) identity theft. Use Form 14039, IRS Identity Theft Affidavit, to report identity theft to the IRS.

ADDITIONAL TIPS:
States have different procedures. For example, California State Franchise Tax Board does not have a similar form but has procedures to help victims who contact the FTB. If you receive an FTB notice (billing, refund reduction, e-file rejection) that you believe is attributable to identity theft, you are given priority handling. The State focuses on the following issues:
- Ensure the victim is held harmless, i.e., they get their full and correct refund.
- Minimize the burden on the victim in resolving their identity theft-related tax problem.
- Minimize the time to resolve the case (usually within two weeks to two months).
The State flags your account to block the automated processing of your account. Anything that comes in after are manually processed for verification.

12 TIPS TO PREVENT IDENTITY THEFT – WHAT <u>NOT</u> TO DO

1. *Don't sign the back of your credit cards.* Instead, write "Photo ID Required" with a permanent marker.

2. *Don't put the complete account number* on the memo line when writing checks to pay credit card accounts; instead, just put the last four numbers. The credit card company knows the rest of the number.

3. *Don't put your home address on your checks.*

4. *Don't print your Social Security number on your checks.*

5. *Don't keep your Social Security card in your wallet.*

6. *Don't store credit card numbers and other financial information on your cell phone.* If you do, use a passcode to open your mobile device and disguise the user names and passwords. But don't make it too complicated especially if you have early signs... J

7. *Don't send a user name or password via e-mail.*

8. *Don't open e-mails from strangers.* Malware can be hidden in embedded attachments and graphics files.

9. *Don't open attachments* unless you know who sent them and what they contain. Never open executable attachments. Configure Windows so that the file extensions of known file types are not hidden.

10. *Don't click on pop-ups.* Configure Windows on your Web browser to block them.

11. *Don't provide your credit card number online* unless you are making a purchase from a trusted website. Reputable sites always direct you to a secure page with an URL starting with https:// whenever you actually make purchases or are asked to provide confidential information.

12. *Don't neglect checking your charges, no matter the size.* Crooks usually start small to see if you'll notice. If you don't, they'll get bolder with larger amounts

12 IRS TIPS TO PROTECT YOURSELF FROM IDENTITY THEFT

1. If you receive a notice from the IRS and suspect that someone may have *fraudulently used your Social Security Number*, immediately respond to the telephone number on the IRS notice.

2. If you receive a letter from the IRS that *more than one tax return was filed for you*, this is a sign that your returns have been compromised – your SS number may have been used fraudulently by someone else.

3. Another sign that you may be the target of identity theft is an IRS letter indicating that you received *wages from an employer that you never worked for.*

4. The IRS has a department which deals specifically with identity theft issues - the *IRS Identity Protection Specialized Unit.*

5. You can contact this Unit by calling the *Identity Theft Hotline at 800-908-4490* Monday through Friday from 8:00 am to 8:00 pm local time.

6. Call this Unit if you *lose your purse or wallet or find a questionable activity on your credit card statement.*

7. Remember that *IRS never sends emails* to initiate communication with taxpayers about their tax accounts. If you receive a suspicious e-mail, forward it to the IRS at phishing@irs.gov.

8. If you find a website that you think is *pretending to be the IRS*, forward the link to the IRS at phishing@irs.gov.

9. You can find more resources about identity theft on the IRS Web site at www.IRS.gov where you can access information on how to report scams and bogus IRS Web sites. You can also visit an IRS resource page by typing "Identity Theft Resource Page" in the search box of the IRS.gov home page.

10. Websites such as IRS.com or IRS.net are bogus. The real sites end with "gov" as in IRS.gov.

11. The *Federal Trade Commission* can assist you with identity theft issues at 877-ID-THEFT (877-438-4338).

12. You may also get protection tips from the government and technology industry at a.gov.

IRS WARNS PUBLIC OF PHISHING SCAMS VIA EMAILS

There are many e-mail scams circulating that fraudulently use the Internal Revenue Service name or logo as a lure. The goal of the scam—known as phishing—is to trick you into revealing personal and financial information. The scammers can then use your personal information – such as your Social Security number, bank account or credit card numbers—to commit identity theft and steal your money.

HERE ARE FIVE THINGS THE IRS WANTS YOU TO KNOW ABOUT PHISHING SCAMS.

1. The *IRS does not send unsolicited e-mails* about a person's tax account or ask for detailed personal and financial information via e-mail.

2. The *IRS never asks taxpayers for their PIN numbers, passwords* or similar secret access information for their credit card, bank or other financial accounts.

3. If you receive an e-mail from someone claiming to be the IRS or directing you to an IRS site,
   - Do *not* reply to the message.
   - Do *not* open any attachments. Attachments may contain malicious code that will infect your computer.
   - Do *not* click on any links. If you clicked on links in a suspicious e-mail or phishing Web site and entered confidential information, visit IRS.gov and enter the search term 'identity theft' for more information and resources to help.

4. You can help shut down these schemes and prevent others from being victimized. If you receive a suspicious e-mail that claims to come from the IRS, you can forward that e-mail to a special IRS mailbox, ***phishing@irs.gov.*** You can forward the message as received or provide the Internet header of the e-mail. The Internet header has additional information to help us locate the sender.

5. Remember, the official IRS Web site is ***http://www.irs.gov/.*** Do not be confused or misled by sites claiming to be the IRS but end in .com, .net, .org or other designations instead of .gov.

DEVELOPMENT: The IRS doubled employees assigned to deal with identity theft. The Service also trained 35,000 employees to recognize theft indicators and help taxpayers victimized by identity thieves.

IRS ALERT 1 – IDENTITY THEFT

Many of my clients complained that their efiled tax returns were rejected because their tax returns have *already been filed.* It's quite shocking because they have not yet filed their tax returns. These poor taxpayers were victims of identity theft and did not even know it.

How did this happen? Well, thieves stole their social security numbers, passwords, PINs, mother's maiden names, and other personal information *to file bogus tax returns and claim your tax refunds.* When the real taxpayers filed, IRS rejected their returns that have already been filed. *Problema.*

SIGNS THAT YOUR IDENTITY HAS BEEN STOLEN – THE IRS NOTIFIES YOU THAT:

1. Someone has already filed tax returns using your information.
2. You filed more than one tax return.
3. You owe taxes for a year when you were not legally required to file.
4. You owe taxes for a year when you did not file.
5. You were paid wages from an employer that you did not work for.

HOW TO AVOID BECOMING AN IDENTITY THEFT VICTIM.

1. Guard your personal information from identity thieves who steal information that you provide to an unsecured website or in an unencrypted email.

2. Do not throw documents with your social security or bank information into your trash can.

3. Watch out for IRS impersonators. Be aware that the IRS does not initiate contact by email or social media channels to request personal or notify people of an audit, refund, or investigation.

4. Be aware that scammers use phone calls, faxes, websites or even in-person contacts. If you are suspicious that it's not really the IRS, don't respond. Visit the *IRS Report Phishing web page.*

5. Protect information on your computer. While preparing your tax return, protect it with a strong 5 password. After efiling your return, transfer data into a CD or flash drive and store in a safe place.

TIPS IF YOU ARE A VICTIM OF IDENTITY THEFT:

1. Respond quickly using the contact information in the letter you received from the IRS.

2. Contact the IRS Identity Protection Specialized Unit at 1-800-908-4490 if you lose a purse or wallet or if a questionable activity appears on your credit card or credit report.

3. Log on to the *Federal Trade Commission* for more helpful information about reporting identity theft.

4. File a complaint with the *Internet Crime Complaint Center* if you have information about the thief.

5. Visit the Identity Protection home page on *IRS.gov.* and click on the Identity Theft link.

IRS ALERT 2 – BEWARE OF SCAMS

Identity theft, phone scams and phishing continue to rise. Taxpayers have reported aggressive phone and email scams. Immigrants are frequently targeted. Potential victims are threatened with deportation, arrest, having their utilities shut off, or having their driver's licenses revoked. Callers are frequently insulting or hostile— apparently to scare potential victims who are told that they owe money that must be paid immediately to the IRS. If unsuccessful the first time, phone scammers call back with new strategy. Let's discuss what thieves do and what you can do to protect yourself.

1. IDENTITY THEFT:

What Thieves Do: Thieves steal personal and financial information to commit fraud. This can include your Social Security number or bank information. An identity thief may file a phony tax return to claim a fraudulent refund.

What You Should Do: Learn how to reduce your risk. Go the IRS.gov and click on a special identity protection page. It has many resources you can use to reduce your risk of becoming a victim. The page guides you with steps to take including contacting the IRS Identity Protection Specialized Unit.

2. PHONE SCAMS:

What Scammers Do: Scammers pose as agents of the IRS and call victims with one goal in mind: to steal your money. Callers will tell you that you owe taxes and demand immediate payment. They will tell you that you must pay the bogus tax bill with a pre-loaded debit card or wire transfer. The callers are often abusive and threaten arrest or deportation. They may know the last four digits of your Social Security number. They also rig your caller ID to falsely show that the call is from the IRS.

What You Should Do: Learn that IRS will first contact you by mail, not by phone if you owe taxes. The IRS does not ask for payment with a pre-paid debit card or wire transfer. If you owe, or think you might owe federal taxes and you get one of these calls, hang up. Call the IRS at 800-829-1040 (be patient though, it could a long wait). The IRS will work with you to pay what you owe. If you don't owe taxes, call and report the incident to the Treasury Inspector General for Tax Administration at 800-366-4484.

3. PHISHING SCAMS:

What Criminals Do: Criminals use the IRS as bait in a phishing scam. Scammers send emails that purport to come from the IRS. They lure their targets with a false promise of a refund or the threat of an audit. They set up a phony website that looks like the real IRS.gov. These phony sites have the IRS seal and realistic graphics to make them appear official. Their goal is to get their victim to reveal personal and financial information. They use the information to steal identities and commit fraud.

What You Should Do: Realize that the IRS does not contact people by email about their tax account. Nor does the agency use email, social media, texting or fax to initiate contact or ask for personal or financial information. If you get an email like this, do not click on a link or open any attachments. You should instead forward it to the IRS at *phishing@irs.gov.* Visit *IRS.gov* and select the *'Reporting Phishing'* link at the bottom of the page.

IRS ALERT 3 – PROTECT YOURSELF FROM *EMAIL* SCAMS

Tax scams via email have become widespread over the last few years. Thieves have become bolder. Their bogus IRS website has improved graphics and looks so real that even a veteran IRS auditor that I worked against unwittingly logged into. If he can be duped into this bogus website, what about ordinary folks like you and me?

The IRS is again warning the public about scams that continue to claim victims all across the country. Scammers send emails to lure victims to give up their personal and financial information. The crooks use this information to file tax returns in your name or steal your money. The thieves demand payment on a pre-paid debit card or by wire transfer. Here are IRS tips to protect you from scammers and thieves.

WHAT TO DO IF YOU RECEIVE A PHISHING EMAIL:

1. Don't reply to message.
2. Don't open attachments.
3. Don't click on any links.
4. Forward the email to your tax accountant and to *phishing@irs.gov*.
5. Then delete it.

HOW TO PROTECT YOURSELF AGAINST SCAMS AND IDENTITY THEFT:

1. Don't give personal information over the phone, through the mail or internet unless you initiated the contact and are sure of the recipient.
2. Protect your personal computers by using firewalls.
3. Use anti-spam, anti-virus software.
4. Update security patches periodically.
5. Change passwords for internet accounts periodically.
6. Don't carry your Social Security card or documents that include your Social Security number.
7. Don't give a business your SSN or ITIN just because they ask. Give it only when required.
8. Check your credit report every year.
9. Do not trash old tax returns, bank statements, or other records with sensitive data.
10. Shred records with your social security number, bank account, and credit card numbers.

REMEMBER THAT THE IRS WILL *NEVER:*

1. Call you about taxes you owe without first mailing you an official notice.
2. Demand that you pay taxes without giving you the opportunity to question or appeal what you owe.
3. Require you to use a specific payment method for your taxes, such as a prepaid debit card.
4. Ask for credit or debit card numbers over the phone.
5. Threaten to bring in local police or other law-enforcement groups to have you arrested for not paying.

IRS ALERT 4 – PROTECT YOURSELF FROM *TELEPHONE* SCAMS

About a dozen of my clients have complained of receiving threatening phone calls from the "IRS" to pay up or be subject to criminal investigation. This is a problem for us taxpaying folks. And it's growing. The calls were not from the IRS; they were made by scammers.

The IRS renewed its warning about an emerging phone scam that continues to target people across the nation, especially recent immigrants. Thieves pose as the IRS and make unsolicited calls to their targets. The caller tells victims that they owe taxes to the IRS. They demand that victims pay immediately with a pre-loaded debit card or wire transfer. They threaten victims with arrest, deportation, or suspension of driver's license. If they don't get what they want, they become hostile and insulting.

HOW TELEPHONE SCAMMERS WORK:

1. Scammers use fake names and IRS badge numbers.
2. They use common names and surnames to identify themselves.
3. Scammers recite the last four digits of your Social Security Number.
4. They rig caller ID to falsely show that the call is from the IRS.
5. Callers will tell you that you owe taxes and demand immediate payment.
6. They tell you that you must pay the bogus tax bill with a pre-loaded debit card or wire transfer.
7. The callers are often abusive and threaten arrest or deportation.
8. If you don't answer, they often leave an "urgent" callback request.
9. Scammers follow up with emails to support their prior bogus calls.
10. Victims hear background noise of other calls being conducted to mimic a call site.
11. After threatening victims with jail time or driver's license revocation, scammers hang up.
12. Others soon call back pretending to be from the local police or DMV (Department of Motor Vehicles).

MANY UNSUSPECTING TAXPAYERS HAVE FALLEN FOR THESE TACTICS:

The Treasury Inspector General for Tax Administration has received about 100,000 complaints about these scams. Thieves have stolen an estimated $5 million from about 1,100 victims as of mid-year. There will be a lot more. You could be one of them if you are not prepared to react when a scammer calls.

WHAT TO DO IF YOU GET AN UNEXPECTED PHONE CALL FROM SOMEONE CLAIMING TO BE THE IRS:

1. Ask for a call back number and an employee badge number.
2. If you think you may owe taxes, call the IRS at 800-829-1040 (be prepared for a long wait).
3. If you don't owe taxes or have no reason to think that you do, call the Treasury Inspector General for Tax Administration at 800-366-4484 to report the incident.
4. Report it to the Federal Trade Commission by using their "FTC Complaint Assistant" on FTC.gov and add "IRS Telephone Scam" to the comments of your complaint.
5. Put caller on hold, on hold, on hold...

IRS ALERT 5 – PHISHING

"Phishing" is a scam carried out by thieves via unsolicited email and websites that pose as legitimate sites. Thieves lure unsuspecting victims to divulge personal and financial information. Phishing rhymes with "fishing" because criminals use the IRS as lure you in with a big refund as *bait.* They also set up a phony website that looks like the real McCoy—complete with the IRS seal and impressive graphics to make them appear official. Their goal is to steal your money or use your name and social security number to file returns and get refunds from the IRS.

Remember that IRS does not contact you by email about your tax account. IRS does not use email, social media, text, or fax to initiate contact or ask for personal or financial information. If you get an email, do not click on a link or open attachments. Forward it to the *IRS at phishing@irs.gov.* Visit IRS.gov and select a *'Reporting Phishing'* link at the bottom of the page.

If you experience monetary losses due to an IRS-related incident, file a complaint with the Federal Trade Commission through their Complaint Assistant to make that information available to investigators. Use their "FTC Complaint Assistant" at *FTC.gov.* Add "IRS Telephone Scam" to your comments.

HOW TO AVOID BECOMING A VICTIM OF IDENTITY THEFT:

1. Be aware that the IRS does not initiate contact with taxpayers by email.
2. The IRS does not send emails stating you are being electronically audited.
3. The IRS does not use emails to notify you that you are getting a refund.
4. The IRS does not use social media channels to notify you of an audit or tax refund.
5. If you receive a scam email claiming to be from the IRS, *forward* it to the IRS at *phishing@irs.gov.*

HERE ARE MORE TIPS TO PROTECT YOU FROM BECOMING A VICTIM:

1. Be vigilant of any unexpected communication purportedly from the IRS.
2. Don't fall for phone and email phishing scams that use the IRS as a lure.
3. Don't fall for refund schemes especially if you owe taxes to the government.
4. Thieves often pose as the IRS using bogus warnings to pay past-due taxes.
5. The IRS does not initiate contact with taxpayers by email to request personal data.
6. This includes emails, text messages, and social media channels.
7. The IRS does not ask for passwords, PINs, credit card, bank or other accounts.
8. If you get an unexpected email, don't open any attachments or click on any links'
9. Instead, forward the email to *phishing@irs.gov.*
10. Go to *report phishing scams* at the genuine IRS website of IRS.gov.

"JUNIOR, CAN YOU HACK INTO THE I.R.S. COMPUTER AND GET ME A BIGGER REFUND?"

CHAPTER

HOW TO CHOOSE THE RIGHT ENTITY FOR YOUR BUSINESS

I have always been an advocate of asset protection planning. I look for kinks in my client's armor should some unfortunate event happen. You see, we spend our lives accumulating assets to provide for our families and retirement, but it takes only one lawsuit or one IRS examination to take us down. Part of asset protection is choosing the right entity for your business to shield your assets. An entity exposes you; another one protects you. Let's discuss which entity shelters you from harm.

One of the first decisions a business owner must make in setting up a business is choosing a legal entity to operate the business enterprise. The basic and most commonly used business entities are sole proprietorship, general partnership, limited partnership, C corporation, S corporation, limited liability company, and limited liability partnership. The entity must match the owners' assets, finances, temperament, and requirements with the particular characteristics and needs of the business. The federal tax consequences of each type of entity play a major role, especially in closely held entities where the parties' combined tax liabilities should be analyzed instead of just the individual or business separately.

SHOULD YOU RUN YOUR BUSINESS AS A SOLE PROPRIETORSHIP?

Should you operate as a sole proprietorship, partnership, corporation, LLC, or LLP? Which entity is most beneficial for you? Choosing the wrong form could cause unnecessary taxes, increased liability, and unnecessary exposure to lawsuits. What you should *not* do is listen to your neighbor or friend because each one has a different set of circumstances calling for a different set of strategies, a different form of entity. What you should do is seek professional advice to help you understand the attributes of each form and evaluate a whole multitude of confusing tax, legal and personal issues. The objective here is to set *you* up with a form that is tailored to your particular needs, *your* particular industry, and *your* particular business. Let me describe for you the nature, advantages, and disadvantages of each form of entity. We start with sole proprietorships in the article and move to corporations, partnerships, and LLCs in succeeding articles.

Sole Proprietorship is the simplest form of doing business. The business is your own alter ego. It does not require any legal filing with the California and most other states... It does not file a separate return. You merely include form Schedule C with your individual income tax return. This is often referred as a DBA (Doing Business As) that is rather inaccurate because a partnership or corporation can also have a DBA. The need for a DBA occurs when you decide not to use your name and instead opt to use a fictitious name to hold your business out to the public. For example, John Smith decides to run his auto parts retail business as Acme Auto Parts. This name has to be registered in the county where the business is located. Caveat: The most common error of sole proprietors that I have encountered over 23 years of practice is the commingling of personal and business assets, income, and expenses. You need to open a business checking account to which all business revenues are deposited and from which all business expenses are paid. Take a periodic draw. Deposit a check from the business account to your personal account from which you pay mortgage, grocery and other personal expenses. Read on to review the pluses and minuses of being a sole proprietor.

ADVANTAGES:
1. *It's simple.* Administration and organizational needs are less complicated.

2. It's *less expensive to organize* because there are no legal papers except minimal DBA filing costs.

3. Federal and state taxes are usually lower (no double taxation for regular corporations).

4. You save on FICA (Social Security tax) on the wages of your children under 18 years old.

5. You save on FUTA (unemployment tax) on the wages of your children under 21 years old.

DISADVANTAGES:
1. You are *exposed* to personal liabilities from business-related lawsuits. So is your business from personal-related lawsuits. A successful plaintiff against the business can come after your personal assets; so can a plaintiff against you go after your business assets.

2. You have a *high risk of being audited by the IRS.* Schedule Cs are a prime target for audits.

3. You have to pay self-employment tax (social security tax) of about 15%.

4. Your fringe benefits are limited (compared to other forms of entity).

5. Business dies when owner dies.

PARTNERSHIPS

A Partnership is an association of two or more persons as co-owners who intend to carry on a business for profit. Each person must contribute money, property, labor, or skill. Mere co-ownership of property that is leased or rented is not a partnership. Spouses carrying on a business together and sharing profits are partners. The burden of filing partnership returns may be alleviated by having one spouse work for the entity. Here are benefits and drawbacks of using partnerships.

ADVANTAGES:

1. The partnership *avoids double taxation* as any net income is passed through to the partners.

2. Losses are also passed through to your personal income tax.

3. Such *losses may be used to offset other forms of income* in your personal income tax.

4. Partnerships are allowed to specially allocate Income and expenses.

5. Partnerships are *not* subject to the accumulated earnings tax.

6. Partnerships are *not* subject to or personal holding company tax.

7. A special election allows a *step-up in the basis of assets upon the death of a partner.*

8. This special step-up is also available on the sale or exchange of partnership interest or in certain partnership distributions.

9. A partner's basis includes the partner's share of partnership debts.

10. It has a *lower audit profile* than sole proprietors.

DISADVANTAGES:

1. General partners have unlimited liability.

2. Their situation is even worse than sole proprietors because they also have to worry about other partners' liabilities that can affect business operations as well their own personal assets.

3. Partner fringe benefits are not excludable from their income. This includes 100% health insurance deductibility, meals and lodging, and group term insurance.

4. Partner earnings from a trade or business are subject to FICA even if earnings are not distributed.

5. Partnerships must use calendar years (December) in the absence of a business purpose to use a fiscal year end (January to December)

SHOULD YOU DO BUSINESS AS A REGULAR C CORPORATION?

A corporation is a legal fiction. It exists only in contemplation of law. It has a separate legal identity. That entity, not you, operates the business. It owns the business assets, owes business debts, collects business revenues, and pays business expenses. It possesses characteristics such as continuity of life, centralized management, free transferability of ownership, and that limited liability that we all look for in our business dealings.

THERE ARE TWO BASIC TYPES OF CORPORATION:

1. *C corporations* (regular corporations).
2. *S corporations* (corporations that elect to be taxed as "S' corporations).
The "C" and "S" refer to code sections of the Internal Revenue Code that govern taxation in the U.S.

Let's enumerate the benefits and drawbacks of regular C corporations in this article.

ADVANTAGES:

1. *Limited liability* – business problems can be kept in the corporation without exposing personal assets; likewise, personal problems do not have to put the business in jeopardy.
2. *Limited liability* – is enjoyed since it is a corporation, a separate entity.
3. It has a lower audit profile than sole proprietors.
4. *Income splitting* – between family members is possible as spouse and children can work for and get paid by the corporation.
5. *Passive activity losses* – can be deducted in full. Closely held C corporations may offset passive losses and credits against active business income (but not portfolio income).
6. *Exclusion of capital gain* – by investors who hold qualified business stock for five years are able to exclude 50% of gain from sale of stock.
7. *Dividend received exclusion* – of 80% from another domestic corporation.
8. *Multiple corporations* – can be used, subject to some limitations.
9. *Election of fiscal year* – can choose fiscal year ends from January to November.
10. *Trust Fund* – Discuss with your tax adviser how you can save on the employer's portion of problematic delinquent payroll taxes.

DISADVANTAGES:

1. *Double taxation* – Corporations pays tax on net income. Shareholders pay tax again later upon receipt of dividends. New law reduces this disadvantage by taxing dividends at a very low rate of 15%. Traditional tax planning ideas of "zeroing out" bottom lines should be re-examined to consider leaving net income that can be distributed later as dividends. Along the same lines, S corporations with accumulated earnings and profits from prior years of operating as regular C corporations should consider declaring and distributing dividends at the low rate of 15%.
2. *Constructive dividends* – can be asserted for personal use of assets in an IRS audit.
3. *Accumulated earnings tax* – 20% (15% through the year 2012) can be assessed on accumulated earnings in excess of reasonable needs. This is in addition to regular income tax.
4. *Personal holding company tax* – 20% (15% through the year 2012) applies to undistributed personal holding company income in addition to the regular income tax.
5. *Alternative minimum tax* – 20% applies to taxpayers who would otherwise escape taxation.
6. *Accrual method of accounting* – is generally required. The cash basis, of course, is easier to operate, as one does not have to account for receivables, payables and inventory.

SHOULD YOU RUN YOUR BUSINESS AS AN S CORPORATION?

S Corporation is a corporation that has elected to be taxed under Subchapter S of the Internal Revenue Code. But why elect S status? Well, this type of entity enjoys both the limited liability of corporations and absence of double taxation of sole proprietorships and partnerships. The corporation elects to pay *zero corporate federal tax!* Boy, this is a goodie, a real nice tax break for businesses that are aware of its existence. Other states have different rates. For example, it pays a *super-low California franchise tax of only 1 ½ %.* In general, S corporations enjoy the best of both worlds of sole proprietorships and corporations.

ADVANTAGES:

1. *Single tax* – The entity escapes taxation at the corporate level. There is only a one-time tax at the shareholder level. The net income is passed through a K-1 to the shareholder.
2. *Limited liability* – is enjoyed since it is a corporation, a separate entity.
   It has a lower audit profile than sole proprietors.
3. *Corporate net losses* – are also passed through and taken advantage by the shareholder to offset other income. For example, a shareholder's loss of $20,000 can offset the spouse' $30,000 wage leaving the couple with zero taxable income after deducting standard deduction and personal exemptions. Nice.
4. *Self-employment tax* – does not apply to the net income of S corporations. This savings can be substantial, as the shareholder does not have to pay FICA of about 15% on the net income passed through from the corporation. This savings in the first year alone can pay for incorporating costs.
5. *Accumulated earnings tax* – does not apply to S corporations.
6. *Personal holdings tax* – does not apply to S corporations.
7. *Alternative minimum tax* – also does not apply to S corporations.
8. *Trust Fund* – Discuss with your tax adviser how you can save on the employer's portion of problematic delinquent payroll taxes.
9. *Passive losses* – of passive S corporation shareholders can be offset against passive loss activities with their S corporate earnings.
10. *Deductible business interest* – S corporate shareholders who incurred debt to acquire company stock may deduct the expense as business interest if they materially participate (debts of sole proprietors are treated as investment interest that can only be offset against investment income).

DISADVANTAGES:

1. *Some fringe benefits* received by 2% shareholders are not excludable from shareholder income. These include $50,000 group term insurance, health insurance premiums, meals and lodging for the convenience of the employer, and the $5000 death benefit exclusion.
2. *Calendar year* – must be used generally.
3. *Pension plan borrowings* – prohibited for 5% shareholders.
4. *New shareholders* may miss to file S election documents or existing dissident shareholders may purposely cause trouble by making a disqualified transfer of stock.
5. *Higher marginal tax* – than a C corporation could result.
6. *Limitation on the use of cash basis* – an S corporation that has more than 35% of its losses allocated to shareholders who do not actively participate in the management of the company will be treated as a tax shelter and therefore will be required to use the accrual method of accounting.
7. *Tax liabilities* of an S corporation in trouble could end up with the shareholders (as opposed to being trapped inside a C corporation). You could enjoy the tax benefits of an S corp and switch to C corp as soon as problems are anticipated.

SHOULD YOU FORM A LIMITED LIABILITY COMPANY (LLC)?

LIMITED LIABILITY COMPANY (LLC) is a hybrid that combines the pass-through attributes of a partnership with the limited liability of a corporation. The owners are called "members" who hold "interests" and are governed by an "operating agreement." An LLC with more than one member is taxed as a partnership. This is a relatively new form of doing business.

Let's explore the plus and minuses of LLCs.

ADVANTAGES:

1. *Liabilities of members* are limited to their investments in the LLC.

2. *No double income tax.* No double tax on liquidation.

3. *A Limited Liability Partnership (LLP)* for professionals allows protection from claims involving the wrongful acts of other partners (vicarious liability).

4. *Can specially allocate* profits and losses.

5. *A member contributing* appreciated assets to an LLC in exchange for membership interest is not required to recognize gain on that exchange.

6. *Distributions of appreciated property* from an LLC are generally received without gain.

7. *Receipt of an interest* in an LLC for a profit interest is generally not taxable.

8. *It is not subject to accumulated earnings tax,* personal holdings tax, or alternative minimum tax.

9. *It is not required to maintain* certain formalities such as corporate minutes.

10. *The basis of a member's interest* can be increased by the member's share of LLC debts.

DISADVANTAGES:

1. *Each state has its own regulations.* For example, California LLCs pay additional annual fee based on gross receipts. This is the main reason why I seldom recommend LLCs for small estates. The annual fee increased every year and has doubled since its introduction until entities challenged the Golden State's anti-business stance. Others fled the state to other business-friendly neighboring states. It is now permanently set at $900/2,500/6,000/11,790 for gross receipts of $250K, $500K, $1M, and $5M.

2. *A member's net earnings* are subject to self-employment tax, whether distributed or not.

3. *Loss from the sale* of LLC interest is a capital loss (limited to $3000 per year).

4. *An LLC will be constructively terminated* if 50% or more of total interest is sold or exchanged within 12 months.

5. *Disassociation events* such as death, retirement or bankruptcy dissolve the LLC unless all remaining members consent to reinstate the entity.

"WELCOME ABOARD. YOU ARE NOW OUTSIDE THE JURISDICTION OF THE IRS."

SHOULD YOU FORM A NEVADA CORPORATION FOR YOUR BUSINESS?

Promoters selling Nevada corporations to entrepreneurs based in other states claim that such entities protect shareholders from liabilities and save state taxes. We agree that Nevada corporations offer liability protection and save taxes imposed by their state of residency. But do they save taxes?

The California Franchise Tax Board was alerted of this gimmick and the number of "Nevada" corporations actually doing business in California dwindled. Before you get carried away by seminars and ads into forming your own Nevada Corporation to avoid California taxation, read on:

1. A corporation is considered domiciled in California if its principal office or place of business is located in California.

2. It is also considered domiciled in California if its business is managed or controlled from within California.

3. Any corporation domiciled in California has to register in California.

4. The cost of registering a foreign (Nevada) corporation in California is exactly the same as that of forming a domestic corporation

5. The only difference is that in addition to the cost of registering in California, you also have to spend for incorporating in Nevada.

6. You also have to pay ongoing fees to pay an agent, maintain an address, forward telephone calls, forward mail, as well as all the hustles of making authorities believe that you do business in Nevada.

7. Then come penalties assessed on unregistered corporations doing business in California: $2,000 per year.

8. Then come legal issues related to the very reason for a Nevada corporation: lawsuit protection. An unregistered corporation does not have a legal standing and cannot defend itself in this state. A California corporation can.

9. It also cannot file a lawsuit to protect its interests in a California court of law. A California corporation can.

10. It may also have its contracts voided.

So why form a Nevada corporation to do *business in California?* Unless you really and actually conduct active business operations in Nevada, do *not* create one to run your business in California. It does not work. It does not save taxes. It merely creates more headaches, more expenses, and compromises your ability to defend yourselves against lawsuits.

NOTE: Prior article applies to LLCs for passive rentals while this one applies to corporations for *active business.*

SHOULD YOU FORM A NEVADA LLC FOR CALIFORNIA RENTALS?

I have been conducting trade seminars for real estate investors for decades. I wrote this article specifically for California apartment owners, but the principles apply to other states as well as other industries and sectors. Landlords who own and operate apartments and houses in states with state income taxes form an LLC in a state with no state income taxes to avoid state income taxes. California has state taxes while Nevada does not.

The early 90s saw a proliferation of Nevada entities. Promoters claimed that Nevada entities protect the members from liabilities and save California taxes. True—Nevada LLCs offer liability protection. True—Nevada LLCs save California taxes—but only if your rental property is located in Nevada and you are a Nevada resident, not if you are a California resident with rental property in California.

The California Franchise Tax Board has caught up with this gimmick and the number of "Nevada" entities doing business in California dwindled. Before you get carried away by seminars and ads to form your own Nevada Corporation to avoid California taxation, read on:

1. An LLC is considered domiciled in California if its principal office or place of business is located in California.

2. It is also considered domiciled in California if its business is managed or controlled from within California.

3. Any LLC domiciled in California has to register in California.

4. The cost of registering a foreign LLC (such as Nevada) in California is the same as that of forming a domestic LLC.

5. The only difference is that, in addition to the cost of registering in California, you also have to spend funds to form an entity in Nevada.

6. You also have to pay ongoing fees to pay an agent, maintain an address, forward telephone calls, forward mail, as well as all the hustle of making authorities believe that you do business in Nevada.

7. Then come penalties assessed on unregistered LLCs doing business in California: $2,000 per year.

8. Then come legal issues related to the very reason for a Nevada LLC: lawsuit protection. An unregistered entity does not have a legal standing and cannot defend itself in this state. A California LLC can.

9. It also cannot file a lawsuit to protect its interests in a California court of law. A California LLC can.

10. An unregistered Nevada LLC can also have its contracts voided.

So why form a Nevada corporation to do business in California? Let's just say that the California Franchise Tax Board knows what you are up to. They deal with this subject on a routine basis. This is probably your first try at a foreign corporation. My advice to you is, unless you real estate properties in Nevada, do *not* create one to run your rentals in California or other states. It does not work. It does not save taxes. It merely creates more headaches, more expenses, and compromises your ability to defend yourselves against lawsuits. Sorry.

NOTE: This article applies to LLCs with passive rentals while other articles apply to corporations with active business.

FOREIGN BANK ACCOUNTS & FINANCIAL ASSETS

If you have a financial interest in or signature authority over a foreign financial account, including a bank account, brokerage account, mutual fund, trust, or other type of foreign financial account, exceeding certain thresholds, the Bank Secrecy Act may require you to report the account yearly to the Department of Treasury.

What started as an investigation of Swiss banks has snared local folks like you and me. In recent years, the IRS has aggressively pursued taxpayers involved in abusive offshore transactions. Taxpayers have tried to avoid or evade U.S. income tax by hiding income in offshore banks, brokerage accounts or through the use of nominee entities. Taxpayers also evade taxes by using offshore debit cards, credit cards, wire transfers, foreign trusts, employee-leasing schemes, private annuities, or insurance plans. To help prevent such abuses, a Foreign Bank & Financial Account Report (FBAR) filing requirement was created. The FBAR is used as a tool to help IRS and Department of Treasury investigators trace funds used for illicit purposes or to identify unreported income maintained or generated abroad.

FBAR filings have risen dramatically in recent years as the Foreign Account Tax Compliance Act (FATCA) phases in and other international compliance efforts raise awareness among taxpayers with offshore assets.

The IRS encourages taxpayers with foreign assets, even relatively small amounts, to check if they have a filing requirement. First, consider whether your failing is only in taxes, only FBARs, or both. If your problem is only FBARs, the IRS wants you to file back FBARs and explain that you didn't know. There's no guarantee, but you will probably be OK. Besides, the alternative of doing nothing is probably much riskier. The IRS has made clear that non-compliant accounts—and there's no threshold for what accounts are too small to ignore—can be dealt with severely. Criminal penalties are even more frightening, including a fine of $250,000 and 5 years of imprisonment. If the FBAR violation occurs while violating another law (such as tax law, which it often will) the penalties are increased to $500,000 in fines and/or 10 years of imprisonment. A formal voluntary disclosure is probably safest.

However, if your problem is both unreported income and unfiled FBARs, be careful. IRS cautions people who try to fix it quietly without going into one of the IRS programs (the OVDP or Streamlined Programs).

The chapter ends with a list of banks that provide the IRS with data about their depositors.

THE ABCs OF FOREIGN BANK AND FINANCIAL ACCOUNTS (FBAR)

If you have offshore bank accounts, should you report the accounts to the U.S. government? Yes, if the aggregate balances exceed $10,000 at any time during the year. What if you had the accounts *before* you left for the U.S.? Yes, you should. There are reasons why our government wants to know: combat money laundering, fight terrorism, and avert tax evasion. If you are not guilty of any of these conducts, there is nothing to worry about. Filing the report causes no harm, no foul. But there are penalties if you don't. Read on and learn about FBAR.

WHAT IS FBAR:
It's a Foreign Bank & Financial Accounts Report on *FinCEN Form 114* (was Form TD F 90-22.1).

WHO MUST FILE THE FBAR: A United States person must e-file new FinCEN Form 114 if that person has financial interest in or signature authority over any financial accounts in a foreign country and the aggregate value of these accounts *exceeds* $10,000 at any time during the calendar year.

Definition of a United States Person:
• A citizen or resident of the United States.
• A domestic partnership, domestic corporation, domestic trust or estate.

Definition of Foreign Financial Accounts:
• Bank accounts such as savings accounts, checking accounts, and time deposits.
• Securities accounts such as mutual funds, brokerage accounts, and securities derivatives.
• Accounts where assets are held in a commingled fund that is a mutual fund.
• And are located outside the United States, District of Columbia, Guam, Puerto Rico, U.S. Virgin Islands, American Samoa, Northern Mariana Islands, Trust Territories of the Pacific Islands

Examples of Financial Interest:
• John, a U.S. citizen, left bank accounts of more than $10,000 in the Philippines. He must file FBAR.
• Same scenario as above except that John is a U.S. resident (not a U.S. citizen). He must file FBAR.

Reporting for Joint Accounts:
• If two persons jointly maintain an account, or if several persons each own a partial interest in an account, then each U.S. person has a financial interest in that account and each person must file an FBAR.
• A spouse having a joint financial interest in an account with the filing spouse should be included as a joint account owner and does not need to file a separate FBAR.
• If the filer's spouse has separate accounts, that spouse must file a separate FBAR for all of the accounts, including those owned jointly with the spouse.

Recordkeeping: FBAR records should be kept for five years from the due date of the report which is June 30 of the following calendar year. The records should contain the following:
• Name maintained on each account and number or other designation of the account.
• Name and address of the foreign bank.
• Name and address of other person with whom the account is maintained.
• Type of account and maximum value of each account during the reporting period.

PENALTIES FOR FAILURE TO REPORT FOREIGN ACCOUNTS:
• You may be subject to civil penalties, criminal penalties, or both if you do not comply with FBAR rules.
• The statutory civil penalty for failing to file an FBAR can be up to *$10,000* for non-willful violation.
• Penalty increases for *willful* failure to the greater of *$100,000 or 50%* of the total balance of the foreign account at the time of the violation. Ouch!

FOREIGN BANK AND FINANCIAL ACCOUNTS (FBAR) REPORTING REQUIREMENTS

FBAR UPDATE:
IRS no longer accepts paper filing of forms. *Online E-file* is now required through the BSA E-Filing System website.

If you own a foreign bank account, brokerage account, mutual fund, or other financial account, you may be required to report the account annually to the government. Let's get an understanding of what FBAR is, who must file new forms, and who do not have to file. I also included a few tips on filing requirements.

WHAT IS FBAR (REPORT OF FOREIGN BANK AND FINANCIAL ACCOUNTS)?
If you have a financial interest in or signature authority over a foreign financial account, including a bank account, brokerage account, mutual fund, trust, or other type of foreign financial account, the Bank Secrecy Act may require you to report the account yearly to the Internal Revenue Service by filing FinCEN Form 114, Report of Foreign Bank and Financial Accounts (FBAR). FBAR is required because foreign financial institutions may not be subject to the same reporting requirements as domestic financial institutions. The FBAR is a tool to help the United States government identify persons who may be using foreign financial accounts to circumvent United States law. Investigators use FBARs to help identify or trace funds used for illicit purposes or to identify unreported income maintained or generated abroad.

WHO MUST FILE AN FBAR?
United States persons are required to file an FBAR if:
- You had a *financial interest or signature authority* over at least one financial account located outside the U.S.
- The aggregate value of all foreign financial accounts *exceeded $10,000* at any time during the calendar year.
United States person means United States citizens; United States residents; entities, including but not limited to, corporations, partnerships, or limited liability companies created or organized in the United States; and trusts or estates formed under the laws of the United States.

WHO DO *NOT* HAVE TO FILE FBAR FORMS?
- Certain foreign financial accounts jointly owned by spouses.
- IRA owners and beneficiaries,
- Participants in and beneficiaries of tax-qualified retirement plans.
- Certain individuals with signature authority over but no financial interest in a foreign financial account.
- Trust beneficiaries.
- Foreign financial accounts maintained on a United States military banking facility.
- United States persons included in a consolidated FBAR.
- Correspondent accounts.
- Foreign financial accounts owned by a governmental entity.
- Foreign financial accounts owned by an international financial institution.

CAN YOU GIVE US SOME TIPS ON REPORTING AND FILING FBAR?
- You may have a reporting obligation even though the account produces no taxable income.
- You may be subject to civil penalties, criminal penalties, or both if you do not comply with FBAR rules.
- Do not file FBAR with your federal income tax return.
- An extension to file federal income tax returns does not extend the due date for FBAR filing.
- FBAR must be received by the IRS on or before June 30 of the year following the calendar year.
- You may not request an extension for filing the FBAR.

FREQUENTLY ASKED QUESTIONS (FAQ) #1 - FBAR BANK ACCOUNTS

Q. Am I required to report bank accounts in a foreign country?
A. Yes, if you have more than $10,000 at any time outside the U.S.

Q. Am I exempted from reporting if my accounts are in Euros, Chinese Yuan, Philippines pesos, or Mexican pesos?
A. No, you are not exempt from reporting foreign accounts just because they are not in U.S. dollars. Convert international denominations to U.S. dollars and report FBAR if the amount is more than $10,000.

Q. What is FBAR?
A. FBAR is a Report of Foreign Bank and Financial Accounts on FinCEN Form 114 (was Form TD F 90-22.1).

Q. Who must file an FBAR?
A. Any United States person who has a financial interest in or signature authority over any financial account in a foreign country, if the aggregate value exceeds $10,000 at any time during the calendar year.

Q. Who is a United States person?
A. "United States person" includes a citizen or resident of the United States, a domestic partnership, a domestic corporation, or a domestic estate or trust (the term "domestic" means formed in the U.S.)

Q. What is a foreign country?
A. "Foreign country" includes all geographical areas outside the United States, Puerto Rico, Northern Mariana Islands, Guam, American Samoa, and the United States Virgin Islands.

Q. What constitutes signature or other authority over an account?
A. A person has signature authority over an account if such person can control the disposition of money.

Q. When is FBAR due?
A. FBAR is due by June 30 of the year following. There is no extension of the due date. (TIP: If you do not have all the available information to file the return by June 30, file and amend later).

Q. How do you amend a previously filed FBAR?
A. *Make the corrections, staple it to a copy of the original FBAR, and attach a statement explaining the corrections.*

Q. Should I file FBAR with my income tax return?
A. No, the FBAR is a separate report and should not be filed with your Federal tax return.

Q. What happens if an account holder fails to file a required FBAR report?
A. Failure to file an FBAR may result in civil penalties, criminal penalties or both.

Q. Can cumulative FBAR penalties exceed the amount in a taxpayer's foreign account?
A. Yes, penalties can be assessed every year. Repeated penalties can exceed what is inside the bank accounts. Ouch!

FREQUENTLY ASKED QUESTIONS (FAQ) #2 – FINANCIAL ACCOUNTS

The IRS issued new guidance requiring individuals with an interest in a "specified foreign financial asset" to attach a disclosure statement to your income tax return for any year in which the aggregate value of all such assets exceeds $50,000. Use new form Form 8938 (Statement of Specified Foreign Financial Assets) starting in 2011.

Q. What is a financial account?
A. *A "financial account" includes:*
Bank, securities, securities derivatives or other financial instruments accounts.
Savings, demand, checking, deposit or any other account maintained with a financial institution.
Accounts in which the assets are held in a commingled fund including mutual funds

Q. Is an FBAR required for accounts maintained with financial institutions located in a foreign country if the accounts hold noncash assets, such as gold or silver?
A. *Yes. An account with a financial institution that is located in a foreign country is a financial account for FBAR purposes whether the account holds cash or non-monetary assets.*

Q. If you own three foreign financial accounts with maximum account balances of $100, $12,000 and $3,000. Do you have to file an FBAR? Do you have to report all three accounts?
A. *Yes, because the aggregate value of foreign financial accounts X, Y and Z is $15,100. You must report all three X, Y and Z even though two accounts have values below $10,000.*

Q. If you own two foreign financial accounts with account balances of $3,000 and $8,000, do you have to file an FBAR? Which accounts must be reported?
A. *All three accounts, even though no single account is over $10,000, because the aggregate value of accounts A, B and C is over $10,000.*

Q. Is an FBAR required if the account does not generate interest or dividend income?
A. *Yes, you must file FBAR whether or not the foreign account generates any income.*

Q. Does the term "other authority over a financial account" mean that a person, who has the power to direct how an account is invested but who cannot make disbursements to the accounts, has to file an FBAR?
A. *No, an FBAR is not required because the person has no power of disposition of money in the account.*

Q. What are the exceptions to the FBAR filing requirement?
A. *Accounts in U.S. military banking facilities and an officer or employee of a bank if the officer or employee has no personal financial interest in the account.*

Q. Does more than one FBAR form need to be filed for a husband and wife owning a joint account?
A. *No, one is enough provided that the names and Social Security numbers of the joint owners are fully disclosed.*

Q. How long should account holders retain records of the foreign accounts?
A. *Retain your records for a period of five years.*

REQUIREMENT TO REPORT FOREIGN FINANCIAL ASSETS

IRS issued rules requiring you to *attach a disclosure* statement to your income tax return if you have an interest in a **"specified foreign financial asset"** for any year when the *aggregate value* of such assets *exceeds $50,000*. If the total value is at or below $50,000 at the end of the tax year, there is no reporting requirement for the year, *unless* the total value was *more than $75,000 at any time* during the tax year. Use *Form 8938* (Statement of Specified Foreign Financial Assets) to report these assets.

WHAT ARE SPECIFIED FOREIGN FINANCIAL ASSETS?
* *Depository or custodial accounts at foreign financial institutions.*
* Assets held for investment to the extent not held in an account at a financial institution:
* *Stocks or securities* issued by foreign persons,
* Any other financial instrument or contract held for investment that is issued by or has a counterparty that is not a U.S. person, and
* Any interest in a foreign entity.

WHO MUST FILE FORM 8938?
* You are a specified person that has an interest in specified foreign financial assets.
* The value of those assets is more than the applicable reporting threshold.

WHAT IF I FAIL TO FILE FORM 8938?
You are subject to a *$10,000 penalty*. A failure continuing for more than 90 days after the day on which IRS mails a notice subjects the specified person to *an additional penalty of $10,000* for each 30-day period (or fraction thereof) during which the failure continues after the 90-day period has expired, up to a *maximum penalty of $50,000* for each such failure. No penalty applies if the failure was due to reasonable cause and not willful neglect.

INDIVIDUALS LIVING IN THE U.S:
The following reporting thresholds apply to taxpayers living in the U.S.:
* A single or married taxpayer filing a separate income tax return is required to file only if the total value of his specified foreign financial assets is more than $50,000 on the last day of the tax year or more than $75,000 at any time during the tax year.
* Married taxpayers filing a joint tax return are required only if the total value of their specified foreign financial assets is more than *$100,000 on the last day* of the tax year or more than *$150,000 any time* during the tax year.

INDIVIDUALS LIVING ABROAD:
The following reporting thresholds apply to a taxpayer living abroad and whose tax home is in a foreign country and who is (1) a U.S. citizen who has been a bona fide resident of a foreign country for an uninterrupted period that includes an entire tax year; or (2) a U.S. citizen or resident who is present in a foreign country at least 330 full days during any period of 12 consecutive months that ends in the tax year being reported:
* A single taxpayer is required to file only if the total value of his specified foreign financial assets is more than *$200,000 on the last day* of the tax year or more than *$300,000 at any time* during the tax year.
* A *married* taxpayer filing a separate income tax return is required to file only if the total value of his specified foreign financial assets is more than *$200,000 on the last day* of the tax year or more than *$300,000 at any time* during the tax year.
* A *married* taxpayer who files a joint income tax return satisfies the reporting threshold only if the total value of all specified foreign financial assets he or his spouse owns is more than *$400,000* on the last day of the tax year or more than *$600,000* at any time during the tax year.

EXAMPLES OF FILING FORM 8938 TO REPORT FOREIGN FINANCIAL ASSETS

We have a new set of bank secrecy rules that are quite complex. Let's get a grasp of these new rules with examples to illustrate how these new Foreign Accounts rules work.

Example 1: Mr. A sold his only specified foreign financial asset on October 15, when its value was $125,000. He isn't married and doesn't live abroad. Mr. A *has to file Form 8938*. He satisfies the reporting threshold even though he doesn't hold any specified foreign financial assets on the last day of the tax year because he owned specified foreign financial assets of *more than $75,000 at any time* during the tax year.

Example 2: Ms. B and an unrelated U.S. resident jointly own a specified foreign financial asset valued at $60,000. Ms. B isn't married and doesn't live abroad. Each has to file Form 8938 because each satisfies the reporting threshold of more than $50,000 on the last day of the tax year. (TIP: Married taxpayers filing a joint income tax return satisfy the reporting threshold only if the total value of their specified foreign financial assets is more than *$100,000 on the last day* of the tax year or more than *$150,000 any time* during the tax year).

Example 3: Mr. C and his wife file a joint income tax return and do not live abroad. They jointly own a single specified foreign financial asset valued at $60,000. They do *not* have to file Form 8938 because they do not satisfy the reporting threshold of more than $100,000 on the last day of the tax year or more than $150,000 at any time during the tax year.

Example 4: Mr. and Mrs. D file a joint income tax return, and jointly and individually own specified foreign financial assets. They do not live abroad. On the last day of the tax year, they jointly own a specified foreign financial asset with a value of $90,000. Mrs. D also has a separate interest in a specified foreign financial asset with a value of $10,000, while Mr. D has a separate interest in a specified foreign financial asset with a value of $1,000. Mr. D and Mrs. D *must file a combined Form 8938*. They have an interest in specified foreign financial assets in the amount of *$101,000 on the last day* of the tax year—i.e., ($90,000, the entire value of the specified foreign financial asset that they jointly own, + $10,000, the value of the asset that Mrs. D separately owns, + $1,000, the value of the asset that Mr. D separately owns). Mr. and Mrs. D satisfy the reporting threshold of more than $100,000 on the last day of the tax year. (TIP: A married taxpayer filing a separate income tax return satisfies the reporting threshold only if the total value of his specified foreign financial assets is more than $50,000 on the last day of the tax year or more than $75,000 at any time during the tax year).

Example 5: Mr. and Mrs. F file separate returns, and jointly own a specified foreign financial asset valued at $60,000 for the entire year. They do not live abroad. *Neithe*r has to file Form 8938. They each use one-half of the value of the asset, $30,000, to determine the total value of specified foreign financial assets that they each own. *Neither* satisfies the reporting threshold of more than $50,000 on the last day of the tax year or more than $75,000 at any time during the tax year.

Example 6: Mr. and Mrs. G file separate income tax returns. They live *abroad*. Mrs. G isn't a specified individual. On the last day of the tax year, Mr. G and Mrs. G jointly own a specified foreign financial asset with a value of $150,000. Mrs. G has a separate interest in a specified foreign financial asset with a value of $10,000, while Mr. G has a separate interest in a specified foreign financial asset with a value of $60,000. Mr. G has to file Form 8938 but Mrs. G, who isn't a specified individual, doesn't. Mr. G has an interest in specified foreign financial assets in the amount of $210,000 on the last day of the tax year—i.e., $150,000, the entire value of the asset that he jointly owns, + $60,000, the entire value of the asset that he separately owns). He satisfies the reporting threshold for a married individual living abroad and filing a separate return of more than $200,000 on the last day of the tax year. (TIP: A married taxpayer who files a joint income tax return satisfies the reporting threshold only if the total value of all specified foreign financial assets he or his spouse owns is more than $400,000 on the last day of the tax year or more than $600,000 at any time during the tax year).

REPORTS, TRANSACTIONS, & SANCTIONS UNDER THE BANK SECRECY ACT (BSA)

New Foreign bank account rules were designed to combat money laundering, terrorism, and tax evasion. Unfortunately, folks like you and me get snared in the process. We get penalized if we don't follow the new rules. I have written a series of simplified articles on this subject to help you understand the new rules and protect yourself from harsh penalties if you fail to report foreign assets. Here we go.

TYPES OF REPORTS:

- Cash Payments Over $10,000 Received in a Trade or Business Form 8300: Business receiving one or more related cash payments totaling $10,000 or more must file form 8300.
- Currency Transaction Report (CTR) Form 104: This form must be filed for each *deposit, withdrawal, exchange of currency, or other payment or transfer*, which involves a transaction in currency of more than $10,000 with a financial institution. Multiple currency transactions must be treated as a single transaction if the financial institution has knowledge that: (a) they are conducted by or on behalf of the same person; and, (b) they result in cash received or disbursed by the financial institution of more than $10,000.
- Currency or Monetary Instruments (CMIR) Form 105: Report of International Transportation of each person (including a bank) who *physically transports, mails or ships, or causes to be physically transported, mailed, shipped or received, currency, traveler's checks,* and certain other monetary instruments in an aggregate amount *exceeding $10,000 into or out of the United States* must file a CMIR.
- Foreign Bank and Financial Accounts (FBAR) New FinCEN Form 114 (used to be Form TD F 90-22.1): Report of each person (including a bank) subject to the jurisdiction of the United States having an *interest in, signature or other authority* over, one or more bank, securities, or other financial accounts in a foreign country must file an FBAR if the aggregate value of such accounts at any point in a calendar year *exceeds $10,000.*
- Suspicious Activity Report (SAR): Form 90-22.47 and OCC Form 8010-9, 8010-1: Banks must file a SAR for any *suspicious transaction* relevant to a possible violation of law or regulation.
- Exempt Person Designation Form 110: Banks must file this form to designate an *exempt* customer for the purpose of CTR reporting under the BSA. In addition, banks use this form biennially (every two years) to renew exemptions for eligible non-listed business and payroll customers.

AFFECTED TRANSACTIONS:

- Currency Transaction Report (CTR): The CTR must report cash transactions in excess of *$10,000* during the same business day. The amount over $10,000 can be either in one transaction or a combination of cash transactions. It is filed with the Internal Revenue Service.
- Monetary Instrument Log (MIL): The MIL must indicate cash purchases of monetary instruments, such as money orders, cashier's checks and traveler's checks, in value totaling *$3,000 to $10,000, inclusive.* This form is required to be kept on record at the financial institution, and produced at the request of examiners or audit to verify compliance. A financial institution must maintain a Monetary Instrument Log for 5 years.
- Suspicious Activity Report (SAR): The SAR must report any cash transaction where the customer seems to be *trying to avoid BSA reporting requirements* by not filing CTR or MIL, for example. A SAR must also be filed if the customer's actions suggest that he is laundering money or otherwise violating federal criminal laws and committing wire transfer fraud, check fraud or mysterious disappearances. The bank should not let the customer know that a SAR is being filed. These reports are filed with the Financial Crimes Enforcement Network ("FINCEN").

SANCTIONS:

There are *heavy penalties for individuals* and institutions that fail to file CTRs, MILs, or SARs. There are also *penalties for a bank which discloses to its client that it has filed a SAR* about the client. Caveat: Penalties include heavy fines and prison sentences.

PENALTIES FOR NONCOMPLIANT U.S. CITIZENS RESIDING ABROAD

If you are a U.S. citizen (or dual citizen) residing outside the U.S. but do not report your foreign accounts, you may be subject to harsh penalties—penalties that are more severe than you expect, penalties that can even exceed balances in your accounts. It is therefore critical that you learn the new rules for FBAR (Report of Foreign Bank and Financial Accounts) to determine if you should report your offshore accounts.

Background on FBARs. Each U.S. person who has a financial interest, signature, or other authority over any foreign financial accounts, including bank and securities accounts with an *aggregate value of more than $10,000* at any time during the calendar year, in a foreign country, must report in each calendar year by filing an FBAR Form FinCEN 114 with the Department of the Treasury on or before *June 30th* of the succeeding year.

Potential FBAR penalties.
- Generally, the civil penalty for *willfully* failing to file an FBAR can be up to the *greater of $100,000 or 50%* of the total balance of the foreign account at the time of the violation.
- Alternatively, non-willful violations that the IRS concludes are not due to reasonable cause are subject to a penalty of up to *$10,000 per violation*.
- In addition to the failure to file and failure to pay penalties, the IRS said that other civil penalties may arise, including the accuracy-related penalty, fraud penalty and the other information reporting penalties.
- No penalties are imposed if the IRS determines the violation was due to reasonable cause.

Reasonable Cause for Failure to File FBAR:
Factors weighing in *favor* of a determination that an FBAR violation was due to *reasonable cause* include:
- Reliance upon a professional tax advisor who was informed of the existence of the foreign account,
- That the unreported account was established for a legitimate purpose and there were no indications of efforts taken to intentionally conceal the reporting of income or assets, and
- That there was no tax deficiency (or there was a tax deficiency but the amount was de minimis).

Factors weighing against such a determination that an FBAR violation was due to reasonable cause include:
Whether the taxpayer's background and education indicate that he should have known of the FBAR reporting,
Whether there was a tax deficiency related to the unreported foreign account, and
Whether the taxpayer failed to disclose the existence of the account to the person preparing his tax return.

Generally, reasonable cause relief is granted when the taxpayer can demonstrate to the IRS that he/she exercised *ordinary business care and prudence* but nevertheless failed to meet the tax burden. Factors demonstrating whether or not ordinary business care and prudence were exercised include:
- Reasons provided for failing to meet the tax obligations;
- Taxpayer's compliance history;
- Length of time between the taxpayer's failure to meet the tax obligation and the subsequent compliance;
- Circumstances beyond the taxpayer's control.

What the IRS Considers as Facts and Circumstance that determine Reasonable Cause for Failure to File FBAR:
- The taxpayer's education;
- Whether the taxpayer has been previously subject to the tax;
- Whether the taxpayer has been penalized before;
- Whether there were recent changes in the tax law that the taxpayer could not reasonably be expected to know;
- Level of complexity of a tax or compliance issue.

PARTIAL LIST OF BANKS THAT SUBMIT DEPOSITOR DATA TO IRS
(AUSTRALIA)

108 Wickham Unit Trust
120 Collins St Levels 5-21 Trust
120 Collins St Pty Ltd
12-26 Franklin Street Property Trust
130 Stirling Street Trust
132 Arthur Street North Sydney Unit Trust
140 St Georges Terrace Pty Ltd
1940's Lifestage Fund - A
1950's Lifestage Fund - A
1960's Lifestage Fund - A
1970's Lifestage Fund - A
1980's Lifestage Fund - A
1990's Lifestage Fund - A
2 Park Street Trust
2000's Lifestage Fund - A
255 Finance Pty Ltd
309 George Street Pty Ltd
33 Bligh Street Trust
35 Ocean Keys Pty Ltd
360 Capital Group Ltd
360 Capital Investment Mgt Ltd
80 Pacific Highway Trust
90 West Asset Mgt Ltd
90 West Global Basic Materials Fund
A&K Australia Pty., Ltd
Abacus Funds Mgt Ltd
Abacus Storage Funds Mgt Ltd
Abbey Capital Properties NSW Pty Ltd
ABC 123 Ltd
Abel Funding Pty Ltd
Aberdeen Asset Mgt Ltd
Aberdeen Leaders Ltd
ABL Funds Mgt Pty Ltd
ABN AMRO Clearing Sydney Pty Ltd
ABN AMRO Clearing Sydney Nominees Pty L
Aboud Family Trust
Absolute Equity Performance Fund Ltd
Access eWrap Investment
Access eWrap Super/Pension
Accolade Wines Holdings Australia Pty Ltd
Acorn Capital Investment Fund Ltd
ACPA PTY LTD
ACPP Industrial Pty Ltd
ACPP Office Pty Ltd
ACPP Retail Pty Ltd
ACT Private Equity No. 1 Fund
ACT Private Equity No.2 Fund
ACT Private Equity No.3 Fund
Adam Smith MicroCap Fund

Adam Smith Small Company Fund
Adelaide Managed Funds Ltd
Adelaide Managed Funds Ltd
Admiral Markets PTY Ltd
Advance Asian Shares Multi-Blend Fund
Advance Asset Mgt Ltd
Advance Australian Equity Growth Fund
Advance Australian Fixed Interest Multi-Blend Fund
Advance Australian Property Securities Index Fund
Advance Australian Shares Index Fund
Advance Australian Shares Multi-Blend Fund
Advance Australian Smaller Companies Fund
Advance Balanced Multi-Blend Fund
Advance Cash Multi-Blend Fund
Advance Commodities Fund
Advance Concentrated Australian Share Fund
Advance Defensive Multi-Blend Fund
Advance Defensive Yield Multi-Blend Fund
Advance Fixed Term Pension
Advance Global Alpha Fund - Wholesale Units
Advance Global Property Fund - Wholesale Units
Advance Global Unlisted Property Fund
Advance Growth Multi-Blend Fund
Advance High Growth Multi-Blend Fund
Advance International Fixed Interest Index Fund
Advance International Fixed Interest Multi-Blend
Advance International Sharemarket
Advance International Shares Core Fund
Advance International Shares Index Fund
Advance International Shares Multi-Blend Fund
Advance Investment Fund No. 4
Advance Moderate Multi-Blend Fund
Advance Moderate Multi-Blend Fund
Advance Money Market Multi-Blend Fund
Advance Mortgage Fund
Advance Mortgage Fund - Wholesale Units
Advance Property Securities Fund
Advance Tradewinds Global Equities Fund
Advent CI Pty Ltd as trustee for Advent Lake Co
Adveq Almond Trust 2
Adyen Australia PTY Ltd
AE Capital Pty Ltd
AE Capital Pty Ltd
AET PAF Pty Ltd
AET SPV Mgt Pty Ltd
AET Structured Finance Services Pty Ltd
Affinia Financial Advisers Ltd
AFSH Nominees Pty Ltd
Aged Care Investment Services No. 2 Pty Ltd

Aged Care Investment Services No.1 Pty Ltd
Agricultural Bank of China Ltd - Branch
AIA AUSTRALIA Ltd
Aim Global High Conviction Fund
Aioi Nissay Dowa Insurance Co.,Ltd - Branch
Aircraft Portfolio Investments Trust No. 1
Airlie Funds Mgt Pty Ltd
AirTree Ventures, Partnership, LP
Aitken Investment Mgt Pty Ltd
Alceon Group Pty Ltd
Alceon Group Trust
ALE Property Mgt Ltd
Alfred Street Nominees Pty Ltd
Alice Street Kedron Trust
Aliom Pty Ltd
Allard Investment Fund
Allard Partners Australia Pty Ltd
Allegro Funds Pty Ltd
Alleron Investment Mgt Ltd
Allfine Holdings Pty Ltd
AllianceBernstein Australia Ltd
Allianz Australia Ltd
Alpha Beta Asian Fund
AMB (Global) Pty Ltd
AMCI QCoal Pty Ltd
AMCIL Ltd
American Express Australia Ltd
AMP Bank Ltd
AMP Capital AA Reit Investments Aust P/L
AMP Capital Bayfair Pty Ltd
AMP Capital Core Property Fund
AMP Capital Finance Ltd
AMP Capital Funds Mgt Ltd
AMP Capital Investors Intern Holdings Ltd
AMP Capital Investors Ltd
AMP Capital Palms Pty Ltd
AMP Capital Property Nominees Ltd
AMP Capital SA Schools No. 1 Pty Ltd
AMP Capital SA Schools No.2 Pty Ltd
AMP Capital Wholesale Plus Corp Bond Fund
AMP CMBS No 2. Pty Ltd
AMP CMBS No. 1 Pty Ltd
AMP Crossroads Pty Ltd
AMP Davidson Road Pty Ltd
AMP Financial Services Holdings Ltd
AMP Foundation Ltd
AMP Group Services Ltd
AMP Investment Services Pty Ltd
AMP Life Ltd
AMP Ltd
AMP Macquarie Holding Pty Ltd
AMP Macquarie Pty Ltd

AMP Pacific Fair Pty Ltd
AMP Riverside Plaza Pty Ltd
AMP Royal Randwick Pty Ltd
AMP Services Ltd
AMP Warringah Mall Pty Ltd
Amundi Asset Mgt Australia ltd
Amundi Asset Mgt Australia ltd
AMWIN Innovation Follow On Fund
AMWIN Innovation Fund Pty Ltd
AMWIN Mgt Pty Ltd
Analytic Global Managed Volatility Fund
Anchorage Capital Partners Fund II LP
Anchorage Capital Partners Fund LP
Anchorage Capital Partners Pty Ltd
Andrea Hughes Family Trust
Angus William Johnson Family Trust
Antares Capital Partners Ltd
Antares Capital Partners Ltd
Antipodes Asia Fund
Antipodes Global Fund
Antipodes Global Fund - Long Only
Antipodes Partners Ltd
ANU Enhanced Index Fund
ANZ Capital Hedging Pty Ltd
ANZ Capital No. 1 Pty Ltd
ANZ Equities (Nominees) Pty Ltd
ANZ ETFS Mgt (AUS) Ltd
ANZ ETFS Mgt (AUS) Ltd
ANZ Margin Services Pty. Ltd
ANZ Nominees Ltd Branch - New Zealand
ANZ Securities (Nominee) Pty Ltd
ANZ Securities Ltd
ANZ Specialist Asset Mgt Ltd
ANZ Specialist Asset Mgt Ltd
ANZ Underwriting Ltd
ANZ Wealth Alternative Investments
AP#1 Trust
APC I Pty Ltd as Trustee for Advent
APN AREIT Fund ARSN 134 361 229
APN Asian REIT Fund ARSN 162 658 200
APN Development Fund No 2 ARSN 125 786 227
APN Property For Income Fund
APN Regional Property Fund ARSN 110 488 821
APN Unlisted Property Fund ARSN 156 183 872
APN Wholesale Plus AREIT Fund
APNO Co-investment Trust
Apostle Funds Mgt Pty Ltd
APP SECURITIES PTY LTD
Arab Bank Australia Ltd
ARAGOST P/L
Archer Capital GF Trust 1A
Archer Capital Growth Funds Pty Ltd

DISCLOSURE: There are thousands of banks that provide depositor names, account numbers, amounts and other data per country which we cannot accommodate in this chapter; therefore, we encourage you to visit *www.irs.gov* or send me an email at *vicirsaudits@gmail.com* for the rest of the list.

PARTIAL LIST OF BANKS THAT SUBMIT DEPOSITOR DATA TO IRS
(BAHAMAS)

47N Litigation Fund Ltd
4K Equity Fund Ltd
A.J.K. corp Services Bahamas Ltd
AAJ Investments I Ltd
AAM Investment Fund Ltd
AAS Investment Fund Ltd
AAZ Investments Fund Ltd
AB Investment Fund Ltd
AB Moore ET Investments LP
AB Moore LP
Abaco Advisory Co
ABLX Bahamas LP
ACACIA Investment Fund Ltd
Accuvest Core Equity Fund Ltd
Accuvest CST FundLtd
Accuvest Global Opportunities Fund Ltd
Accuvest Liquid Alternatives Fund Ltd
Ace Global Fund Ltd SAC
ACG Global Investment Fund Ltd
Acqua Fund Ltd
Active Recovery Fund Ltd
Adi Dassler Intern Family Office Ltd
Advantage Class II Cred Fund Ltd
Advantage mgt Ltd
AF Investment Fund Ltd
AGacquisitions Global Markets Ltd
Agencia Central II Ltd
Agency Development Ltd
Agno Investment Ltd
Agricola National II Ltd
Agricultural Investment Ltd
Aguavida Ltd
Aguavida Ltd
Ahab Redemption Fund Ltd
AI Investment Fund Ltd
AJ Foundation Investments I Ltd
AL Investments Fund Ltd
Alagre Investment Fund Ltd
Albacore Investments, Ltd
ALDR Investment Fund Ltd
ALF Investment Fund Ltd SAC
ALGA Investment Fund Ltd
ALI Investments Fund Ltd
Allegheny Corp
Alliance Investment mgt Ltd
Alliance Partners Ltd
Alpha Alternative Fund Ltd
Alphubel Overseas Ltd
Alphubel Overseas Ltd
Alpine Investments Inc

Alton Ltd
Ambassador Directors Ltd
Ambassador Directors Ltd
Amber Bank & Trust Ltd
AMC Investment Fund Ltd
AMG Investment Fund Ltd
Amicorp Bahamas Ltd
&bank Bahamas Ltd
Annacha Ltd
Ansbacher (Bahamas) Ltd
Ansbacher (Bahamas) Ltd
Ansbacher Money Market Fund SAC Ltd
AOD Investment Fund Ltd
AOM Investment Fund Ltd
APL Investment Fund Ltd
APO Investments Fund Ltd
AQ Investment Fund Ltd
Aqua Mars Incorp
Argau Inc
ARGUS LTD
Arndilly Trust Co Ltd
Arner Bank & Trust Bahamas Ltd
Arolla Ltd
Arolla Ltd
Arrowwood Ltd
ASE Investment Fund Ltd
ASG Investment Fund Ltd
AT Series Fund Ltd SAC
Atlantic Medical Insurance Ltd
Atmos Fund Ltd
Axxets mgt Inc
AYAJ Investments Ltd
Ayat Investment Holdings Ltd
Azzura mgt Ltd
Azzura mgt Ltd
B Capital UK Coml Property Fund Ltd
Babco Holdings Ltd
Bach Trust
Back California Beach Fund Ltd
Bael Investments Inc
BAF Financial & Insurance (Bahamas) Ltd
Baleen Rock Fund Ltd
Bamont Trust Co Ltd
Banca del Sempione Overseas Ltd
Banco BBM SA - Branch
Banco BBM SA - Nassau Branch
Banco de Bogota Nassau Ltd
Banco Nacional de Mexico SA - Branch
Banco Sant&er Bahamas Intern Li
Banif Intern Bank Ltd

Bank J. Safra Sarasin -Bahamas- Ltd
Bank of Baroda - Branch
Bank of The Bahamas Ltd
Banque Havill& (Bahamas) Ltd
Bantiger Intern Ltd
Bantiger Intern Ltd
Baraterre Ltd
Baraterre Ltd
Basic Intern Ltd
Bayalag Fund Ltd
BBA Investment Fund Ltd
BBM Bank Ltd
BCC Investment Fund Ltd
Beach Waters Ltd
Bearbull Degroof Intern Ltd
Beechcourt Ltd
Benedek Foundation
Betax Ltd
BF Investment Fund Ltd
BFC Investment Fund Ltd
Biscayne Capital LTD
BiscayneAmericas Intercam Global
Black Isle mgt
BLK Intern Holdings Ltd
Blue Hope Ltd
Blue Ruby Development SA
Blue Sea Asset mgt Ltd
Blue Seas Administration Ltd
Bluefeld Str& Holdings Ltd
BlueMar Offshore Fund Bahamas Ltd
BNS (Colombia) Holdings Ltd
Boulder Entreprises Inc
BOVS Investment Fund Ltd
BP Investment Fund Ltd
Bramer Money Transfers Ltd
Brazil Holdings Inc. Ltd
BREEC Fund
Brentwood Agencies Ltd
Brigadoon Investments Ltd
British American Insurance Co Ltd
Brunel Properties Ltd
BSI Overseas Bahamas Ltd
BSI SA or BSI AG or BSI LTD
Bukit Merah Ltd
Burgundy Red Ltd
Burgundy Red Ltd
Burhou Ltd
Burhou Ltd
Butterfield Trust (Bahamas) Ltd
Butterfly Fund Ltd
BVC Services Ltd
CAA INVESTMENT FUND LTD

Cabec Investments I Ltd
Caduceus Investments Ltd
Calcot Investments Ltd
Campbell & Co Intern Bahamas
CAMS Bahamas Ltd
Cannon corp Services Ltd
Caoba Investments Ltd
Capital Life Ins Co Bahamas Ltd
Capital Quant Fund Ltd
Capital Union Bank Ltd
Carbine Master Fund LP
Caribbean Alliance Insurance Co Ltd
Carnoustie Ltd
Catalytic corp Services Ltd
Caystone Solutions Ltd
Caystone Solutions Ltd
CB Comm&er
CB Investment Fund Ltd
CB Securities Ltd
CBH Bahamas Ltd
CBS Investment Fund Ltd
CBT Nassau Ltd
CC Moore LP
CCL Moore LP
CCR Inc
CCS Investment Fund Ltd
Cerberus Institutional Overseas
Cerberus Intern Ltd
Cerchio Ltd
Cerejeira Fund Ltd
CFAL Global Bond Fund Ltd
CFAL Global Equity fund Ltd
CH Amiral
CH Twister PTC
Challenger Fund Ltd
Channalou Ltd
Chase Manhattan FT Ltd
Chester Asset Holdings Ltd
Chestnut Brown Ltd
Chestnut Brown Ltd
CHL Investment Fund Ltd
CI Investment Fund Ltd
CIBC Trust Co Bahamas Ltd
CIBC Trust Co Bahamas Ltd
Cineta Ltd
CIT Bahamas Holdings Ltd
CIT Founder Germany I Ltd
CIT Founder Ltd
CIT Germany Fund I Feeder GP Ltd
CIT Holdings Investments Ltd
CIT Holdings Ltd
CIT Real Estate Fund Conduit One Ltd

DISCLOSURE: There are thousands of banks that provide depositor names, account numbers, amounts and other data per country which we cannot accommodate in this chapter; therefore, we encourage you to visit *www.irs.gov* or send me an email at *vicirsaudits@gmail.com* for the rest of the list.

PARTIAL LIST OF BANKS THAT SUBMIT DEPOSITOR DATA TO IRS
(BARBADOS)

Adams Capital Ltd
AIC Caribbean Fund Barbados LP
AIC Investors LP
Alex&ria Trust Corp
Amergeris Wealth Mgt (Barbados) Ltd
Amicorp (Barbados) Ltd
Amicorp Bank & Trust Ltd
Amicorp Bank & Trust Ltd
Amicorp Fund Services N.V Barbados
Amphora Bank & Trust Corp
Amphora Bank & Trust Corp
Amphora Life Insurance Company Ltd
Apollo Nominees Incorporated
Balmoral Life Insurance Corp
Bank of Montreal Barbados Ltd
BARCO Assignments Ltd
BARCO Assignments Ltd
Barrow Capital Ltd
BBO FINANCIAL SERVICES INC
B'dos Public Workers' Co-op Credit Union
BGI Insurance Ltd
BHEP Investment Holdings SRL
BHEP Investment SRL
BHEP IV Investment Holdings SRL
BHEP IV Investment SRL
Birch Hill Equity Partners II (Barbados) LP
Blue Bank Intl & Trust Barbados Ltd
BNS International (Barbados) Ltd
Bottlers United Co-op Credit Union Ltd
British American Insurance Co Bdos Ltd
Brookfield International Bank Inc
Brookfield International Ltd
C&lewood Investment SRL
Capita Financial Services Inc
Caribbean Investment Bank Inc
CCG Trust Corp
CIBC Offshore Banking Services Corp
CIBC World Markets Japan Inc
Cidel Bank & Trust Inc
Cidel Bank & Trust Inc
Citicorp Merchant Bank Ltd
Clarity Life Insurance Ltd
CLICO Balanced Fund
Clico International Life Insurance
CMV SRL
Concorde Bank Ltd
Concordia Capital Ltd
Consolidated Finance Co Ltd
Continental Bank Corp

Co-operators General Insurance Co Ltd
Credit Suisse -Barbados- SRL
CSFB Vengrowth -Barbados- SRL
Cummins Capital Ltd
D. E. Shaw Comp Invest Asia 1 Barb SRL
DAC China SOS (Barbados) SRL
DB (Barbados) SRL
DGM Bank & Trust Inc
DGM Insurance Corp
DGM Trust Corp
Durham Capital Ltd
Erie Capital Ltd
Exterran Finance Company Ltd
Fairbay Investment SRL
FCIS Barbados Ltd
Financorp Funds SCC
FINLA SCC
First Caribbean Intl Bank Barbados Ltd
FirstCaribbean Intl Bank Ltd
FirstCaribbean Intl Trust & Merchant
FirstCaribbean Intl Wealth Mgmt Barbados
Focused Opportunities Offshore Ltd
Fortress Fund Managers Ltd
Fortress Fund Managers Ltd
Fortress Insurance Company Ltd
Front Street Corp Mgt Services Ltd
Frontenac Capital Ltd
Gasper Funding Corp
Globe Finance Inc
Grey Capital Ltd
Guardian Life of the Caribbean Ltd
Havelet Assignment Company Ltd
Highlake International Business Company
HSBC Bridgetown Investments (Barbados) LLC
HSBC Carlisle (Barbados) LP
HSBC Carlisle II (Barbados) LP
HSBC Trident capital (Barbados) Corp
IB Reinsurance Inc
IFC ALAC GHL Holding Company Ltd
Insurance Corp of Barbados Ltd
Ironbridge Capital Ltd
J&T Bank & Trust Inc
J.P. Morgan Indies SRL
JLT Trust Services (Barbados) Ltd
LGR Barbados SRL
Luxembourg Investment Company 31 SARL
Manulife Asset Mgt Intern Holdings Ltd
MBPI Inc
Memoria Ltd

Mercom Bank Ltd
Millbranch Investment SRL
Misty Point Investment SRL
Miura Financial Services Ltd
Morecann Inc
MPOF Mainl& Company 1 Ltd
MWM Investments Ltd
NCB Capital Markets (Barbados) Ltd
OurInterest Advisers Inc
Oxbridge Bank & Trust SCC
Paiton Shipping Inc
Pan-American International Insurance CO
POINT Joint Investments SCC
Portl& Caribbean Fund II LP Barbados
Preservation Capital Ltd
RBC Capital Markets (Japan) Ltd
RBC Life Insurance Company
Republic Bank Barbados Ltd
Republic Finance&Trust Barbados Corp
Republic Funds Barbados Corp
RepublicBankTrinidad&TobagoBarbadosLtd
Rock Creek Investment SRL
Royal Bank of Canada
Sagicor Asset Mgt Inc
Sagicor Financial Corp
Sagicor Funds Inc
Sagicor Life Inc
S&storm Gold Bank Ltd
SC China Growth I Holdings SRL
SC China II Holdings SRL

Scotiabank Caribbean Holdings Ltd
Seaco SRL
Sequoain Financial Group Ltd
Sequoya Holding Ltd
Seville Trading Company Ltd
Signia Financial Group Inc
Sklyon Mgt Services Inc
SLAC of Canada Barbados Ltd
Soutterham Bank Corp
Springwood Investment SRL
St. Lawrence Bank Inc
St. Michael Trust Corp
Starr Financial Barbados I Inc
Starr Financial Barbados Inc
Structured Assignments Inc
Summit International Bank Ltd
Sun Life of Canada International Assuran
Tenor KRY (Barbados) SRL
The Bank of Nova Scotia
The Beacon Insurance Company Ltd
The Manufacturers Life Insurance Co
Thomvest Ventures Ltd
Tishman Speyer China Fund (Barbados) SRL
Tishman Speyer China Fund II (Barbados) SRL
Topaz Investment SRL
TPSA Investments Corp
Transcom Bank Barbados Ltd
Universal Ventures Fund, SCC
VL Assurance Inc

"HERE'S ONE PIECE OF GOOD NEWS! I'VE BEEN CALLED IN FOR AN IRS AUDIT, AND I WON'T BE ABLE TO MAKE IT."

DISCLOSURE: There are thousands of banks that provide depositor names, account numbers, amounts and other data per country which we cannot accommodate in this chapter; therefore, we encourage you to visit *www.irs.gov* or send me an email at *vicirsaudits@gmail.com* for the rest of the list.

PARTIAL LIST OF BANKS THAT SUBMIT
DEPOSITOR DATA TO IRS
(CANADA)

0884232 B.C. Ltd
0944566 B.C. Ltd
0981746 B.C. Ltd
1143986 Ontario Ltd
1411779 Alberta ULC
1462594 ONTARIO Inc
1469635 ONTARIO Inc
1478831 Ontario Inc
1478831 Ontario Inc
1500939 Alberta ULC
1629514 Alberta ULC
1684181 Ontario Inc
1684182 Ontario GP, LP
1684182 Ontario Inc
1684182 Ontario Intern GP, LP
1684182 Ontario Intern LP
1684182 Ontario LP
1730944 Alberta ULC
1832 Asset Mgt LP
1832 Asset Mgt LP
1832 Asset Mgt U.S. Inc
1st Choice Savings & Credit Union Ltd
2001 RBCP Canadian GP Ltd
2005 (A) Ltd Pship
2010A Mezzanine Fund Ltd Pship
2010B Mezzanine Fund Ltd Pship
2010B Mezzanine Fund Ltd Pship
2012 Mezz Co-Invest Ltd Pship
2012 Mezzanine Fund Ltd Pship
2013 Mezz Co-Invest Ltd Pship
2013 Mezzanine Fund Ltd Pship
2449048 Ontario Inc
2490827 Nova Scotia Ltd
3060097 Nova Scotia Co
3160343 Canada Inc
3195992 Nova Scotia Co
3195993 Nova Scotia Co
32 Degrees Diversified Energy Fund GP Inc
3216952 Nova Scotia Ltd
35th Street Properties Inc
5000 Yonge Street Toronto Inc
54th Avenue Properties Inc
5Banc Split Inc
726 Modular Finance Canada, Ltd
726 Remote Accommodations, Ltd
7337655 Canada Inc
7584253 Canada, Inc
9192-2971 Quebec Inc
A&B Rail Services Holdings Ltd

ABC American-Value Fund
ABC Dirt-Cheap Stock Fund
ABC Fully-Managed Fund
ABC Fundamental-Value Fund
ABC North American Deep-Value Fund
Aberdeen Asset Mgt Canada Ltd
Acadian Core Intern Fund
Acadie Vie
Accent Credit Union
Access Credit Union Ltd
Acker Finley Asset Mgt Inc
Acker Finley Inc
Acker Finley Select Canada Focus Fund
Acker Finley Select US Value 50 Fund
ACLF Co-Investment Fund LP
ACM Advisors Ltd
ACON Latin America Opp. Fund IV-A LP
ACON Latin America Opportunities Fund IV
ACON Power Investors Holdings, LP
Acorn Disciplined Core Fund
Acorn Diversified Portfolio
Acorn Diversified Trust
Acorn Global Investments Inc
ACTIVEnergy Income Fund
Actra Fraternal Benefit Society
Acuity Investment Mgt Inc
Acumen Capital Finance Partners Ltd
Addenda Capital Inc
Adroit Investment Mgt Ltd
Advantage-Value General Partner Ltd
Advantage-Value Ltd Pship
Advent Calgary (Canada) Holding Ltd
Advent Calgary (Canada) Intermediate Ltd
Adyen Canada Ltd
Aegon Capital Mgt Inc
AEP IV Power AIV, L.P.
AEPF II-A (Canada) Feeder, LP
Aetna Life Insurance Co
Affinity Credit Union 2013
Affirm Financial Services Inc
AFINA Affinity Fund LP
AFINA Capital Mgt Inc
AFT Trivest Mgt Inc
AGAWA Fund Mgt Inc
AgeChem Financial Inc
Agellan Commercial REIT
AGF Investments America Inc
AGF Investments Inc
AGF Securites Canada Ltd

Agilith Capital Inc
AGWF LP
AHF Capital Partners Inc
AIC Associates Canada Holdings ULC
AIP Falconer RE AIV LP
AIP Phoenix RE AIV LP
Alamer SA Holdco LP
Alaris IGF corp
Alaris Income Growth Fund Pship
Alaris Royalty corp
Alberta Treasury Branches
Aldergrove Credit Union
Algonquin Capital Corp
Algonquin Capital Partners Inc
Algonquin Debt Strategies Fund LP
Aligned Capital Partners Inc
Alignvest Capital Mgt Inc
Alignvest Capital Mgt Inc
Alignvest Investment Mgt Corp
Alignvest Mgt Corp
Alignvest Mgt Corp
Alitis Growth Pool
Alitis Income & Growth Pool
Alitis Investment Counsel Inc
Alitis Mortgage Plus Pool
Alitis Strategic Income Pool
Alize Capital Inc
Alize Capital Inc
All Equity Fund
Allard, Allard & Associes Inc
Allexium assets Mgt Inc
Alliance Trust Co
AllianceBernstein Canada, Inc
AllianceBernstein Canada, Inc
Alloy Merchant Finance, LP
Ally Financial Inc
Almanac Realty Securities Canada I, LP
Alothon Cristal LP
AlphaFixe Capital Inc
AlphaFixe Return Plus Fund
AlphaNorth Asset Mgt
AlphaNorth Mutual Funds Ltd
AlphaNorth Partners Fund Inc
AlphaPro Mgt Inc
Alsis Latin America Fund II, LP
Alsis Mexico Hous. Opp. Fund, LP
AltaCorp Capital Inc
Altairis Long/Short Fund
Altairis Long/Short Levered Canada
Altas General Partner Corp
Altas General Partner Corp

Alterna Savings & Credit Union Ltd
Altervest Absolute Fund
Altervest Ltd
Altimum Mutuals Inc
Altium Wealth Architecture Inc
Altum Mexico LP
Altus Securities Inc
AM Capital LP
AM Holdings LP
American Core Sectors Dividend Fund
American Hotel Income Properties REIT
American Income Life Insurance Co
Amethyst Arbitrage Fund
Amex Bank of Canada
AMG/FAMI Investment Corp
AmorChem Financial Inc
Amundi Canada inc
Analytic Global Low Volatility Equity Fu
Analytic US Low Volatility Equity Fund
Annapolis Capital Ltd
Annapolis Capital Ltd
Annapolis Investment (US) Ltd Pship
Annemasse Boisbri& Holdings LP
Antares Investment mgt Inc
Antares Investment mgt Inc
Antworthy Investment Mgt Ltd
Apex Trust
Apollo Intern Mgt Canada ULC
Apollo TR Emerging Markets (Can.) LP
ARC Equity Mgt (Fund) Ltd
ARC Financial corp
Arcano KRS Fund LP
Arcano Select Fund A LP
Argosy Securities Inc
Arias Resource Capital Fund II Mexico LP
Arlon Latin America Partners
Armstrong & Quaile Associates Inc
Arrow Capital Mgt Inc
Arrowstreet (Canada) Global All
Artemis Investment Mgt Ltd
Artis Real Estate Investment Trust
ARX CAPITAL Inc
Ashley Park Financial Services corp
Ashley Park Operations corp f/k/a 09604
Ashmore &ean Fund II, LP
Assante Capital Mgt Ltd
Assante Financial Mgt Ltd
Associated Electric & Gas Insurance
Aston Hill Asset Mgt Inc
Aston Hill Capital Markets Inc
Aston Hill Energy 2014 GP Inc

DISCLOSURE: There are thousands of banks that provide depositor names, account numbers, amounts and other data per country which we cannot accommodate in this chapter; therefore, we encourage you to visit *www.irs.gov* or send me an email at *vicirsaudits@gmail.com* for the rest of the list.

PARTIAL LIST OF BANKS THAT SUBMIT DEPOSITOR DATA TO IRS
(CHINA)

ABC Energy Investment Fund Mgt Co Ltd
ABC Int'l Hunan Investment Mgt Co Ltd
ABC Suzhou Investment Mgt Corp Ltd
ABCI China Investment Corp Ltd
ABCI Enterprise Mgt Corp Ltd
ABCI Guangde Investment Mgt Corp Ltd
ABCI Guolian Wuxi Investment Mgt Co Ltd
ABCI Wuxi Investment Consulting Corp Ltd
ABCI ZhuhaiHengqin Inv Fund Mgt Corp Ltd
Aberdeen Asset Mgt (Shanghai) Co Ltd
Adveq Investm. Mgmt. Beijing Co Ltd
Adveq Shanghai Eqt. Inv. Mgmt. Co Ltd
Aetna Life Insurance Co
Agricultural Bank of China Ltd
Agricultural Development Bank of China
AIA Co Ltd
AIA Group Ltd
Allianz China Life Insurance Co Ltd
ALLIED Coml BANK
Anbang Annuity Insurance Co Ltd
AnBang Life Insurance Co Ltd
Anfu BOC Fullerton CB
Anhui Fanchang Jianxin Rural Bank Co Ltd
Anyi Rongxing Village & Township Bank Co Ltd
Ardian Beijing Consulting Co Ltd
Ashmore Beijing Investment Consulting
Ashmore-CCSC Fund Mgt Co Ltd
Asset Mgt of Crush
Australia & New Zeal& Bank (China) Co Ltd
AXA SPDB Investment Managers Co Ltd
AXA SPDB Investment Managers Co Ltd
AXIS BANK Ltd
Baiquan Rongxing Village & Township Bank Co Ltd
Banca Monte dei Paschi di Siena S.p.A.
Banco do Brasil S/A Shanghai
Banco do Brasil SA
Banco Sant&er SA
Bangkok Bank China Co Ltd
Bank M&iri
Bank of America National Asso
Bank of Baroda
Bank of Beijing Co Ltd
Bank of Chengdu
Bank of China Investment Mgt
Bank of China Investment Mgt
Bank of China Ltd
Bank of Communications Co Ltd
Bank of Dalian CoLtd
Bank of Deyang CoLTD
Bank of Gravity

Bank of Guangzhou Co Ltd
Bank of Inner Mongolia Co Ltd
BANK OF JIANGSU Co Ltd
Bank of Jiaxing Co Ltd
BANK OF JILIN Co LTD
Bank of Jilin Co Ltd
Bank of Jinhua Co Ltd
bank of jinzhou CoLtd
Bank of Montreal China Co Ltd
Bank oF Nanchang
Bank of Nanjing Co Ltd
Bank of Ningbo Co Ltd
bank of ningxia Co Ltd
Bank of Qingdao Co Ltd
Bank of Ruifeng
Bank of Shanghai Co Ltd
Bank of Suzhou Co Ltd
Bank of Taiwan
Bank of Tokyo-Mitsubishi UFJ (China) Ltd
BANK OF WEIFANG Co Ltd
Bank of Wenzhou Co Ltd
Bank of Xi'an Co Ltd
BANK OF YINGKOU Co Ltd
Bank of Zhengzhou Co Ltd
Bank SinoPac China Ltd
Barclays Bank plc
Bayan Rongxing Village & Township Bank Co Ltd
Beijing Aozhan Education Tech Srvs Co Ltd
Beijing Benqingqingyuan Inv Consulting
Beijing Chuangyingshiji Inv Mgt LLP
Beijing Fenghuizhengrong Inv Mgt LP
Beijing Hua Ao Ya Invest Consult Co Ltd
Beijing Jinanchuangxin Inv Mgt Ltd
Beijing Jinwanzhi Mgt Advisory Co Ltd
Beijing Jinwanzhi Mgt Consulting Co Ltd
Beijing Kail Assets Servicing Co Ltd
Beijing Miyun HSBC Rural Bank Co Ltd
Beijing Redbud Huarong Entity Investment Co Ltd
Beijing Rongkunhoude Inv Consulting Ltd
Beijing Rural Coml Bank Co Ltd
Beijing SBI&BDJB Investment Advisors Ltd
Beijing Shiyinghuifu Inv Consulting Ltd
Bike Trading Shanghai Co Ltd
Biketwo Trading Shanghai Co Ltd
BitBays Ltd
BlackRock Overseas Investment Fund Mgt (Shanghai) Co Ltd
Blackstone (China) Equity Investment Mgt Co Ltd
BOC Global Strategic Fund(FOF)
BOC International Futures Ltd
BoCom Guoxin Asset Mgt Co Ltd

Bocom International Trust Co Ltd
Bocom Schroders Asset Mgt Co Ltd
BOCOM Schroders Fund Mgt Co Ltd
BoCommLife Insurance Co Ltd
Bohai Industrial Investment Fund Mgt Co
Bosera Asset Mgt Co Ltd
Bosera Asset Mgt Co Ltd
Bosera Capital Co Ltd
Bosera Capital Co Ltd
Caixa Geral de Depositos SA
Canara Bank
Caoxian BOC Fullerton CB
Cathay Advisory (Beijing) Co Ltd
Cathay Capital (Labuan) Co Ltd
Cathay United Bank Co Ltd
CCB Capital Mgt Co Ltd
CCB Financial Leasing Co Ltd
CCB Futures Co Ltd
CCB International China Ltd
CCB Life Insurance Co Ltd
CCB Principal Asset Mgt Co Ltd
CCB Principal Asset Mgt Co Ltd
CCB Principal Capital Mgt Co Ltd
CCBI Capital Mgt Tianjin Ltd
CCBI Chengtou Cleantech Fund Mgt Co
CCBI Chengtou Cleantech Fund Mgt Co
CCBI Chuangxin Inv Mgt Beijing Co Ltd
CCBI Cultural Industry Inv Fund Tianjin
CCBI Dingteng (Shanghai) Inv Mgt Co Ltd
CCBI Financial Advisory Shenzhen Co Ltd
CCBI Healthcare Investment Mgt Ltd
CCBI Investment Shenzhen Co Ltd
CCBI Jinding Investment Tianjin Ltd
CCBI Private Equity Fund Mgt Inc
CCBI Shanghai Equity Inv Mgt Ltd
CCBI Shanghai Venture Capital Co Ltd
CCBI Shenzhen Asset Mgt Co Ltd
CCBI Shenzhen Co Ltd
CCBI Venture Capital Shenzhen Co Ltd
CCBI Wealth Mgt Tianjin Ltd
CCBI Yiheng Investment Mgt Tianjin
CDH Shanghai Dinghui Bai Fu Wealth Mgt Co Ltd
CDH Shanghai Dinghui Bai Fu Wealth Mgt Co Ltd
CDIB International Leasing Corp
CEL BeiJing AnRong Inv Ctr LP
CEL ChengDu AnCheng Inv Ctr LP
CEL ChengDu &e Inv Ctr LP
CEL ChengDu AnXin Eq Inv Fund Mgmt Co Ltd
CEL ChengDu Ctry HC Venture Inv Co Ltd
CEL ChengDu HC Venture Inv Mgmt Co Ltd
CEL ChengDu Western Venture Inv Co Ltd
CEL ChongQing Equity Inv Mgmt Co Ltd

CEL GuangYu Investment Shanghai LP
CEL Haimen Venture Inv Co Ltd
CEL Huiling Inv Shanghai Co Ltd
CEL Huiyiweiye Inv Mgmt BJ Co Ltd
CEL Mgt Shanghai Co Ltd
CEL New Asset Venture Inv Co Ltd
CEL New Energy Inv Mgmt SH Co Ltd
CEL New EnergyVentureInv Jiangsu CoLtd
CEL QingDao AnBo Inv Center LP
CEL QingDao LowCarbonNewEn Eqty Inv Ltd
CEL QingDao New Asset Eqty Mgmt Ltd
CEL Shanghai Equity Inv Mgmt Co Ltd
CEL Shanghai JiaXin Eqty Inv Mgmt Co Ltd
CEL Shanghai Mgmt & Adv Service Co Ltd
CEL Shanghai Properties Co Ltd
CEL Venture Capital Shenzhen Ltd
Chang Xin Asset Mgt Corp Ltd
Chang'an International Trust Co Ltd
Changchun Development Rural Coml Bank
Changchun New Century Spearhead Inv Ltd
Changsheng Fund Mgt Co Ltd
Changzhou GSR Equity Investment Pship
CHC Fund
China ABC Security
China Asset Mgt Co Ltd
China Bohai Bank Co Ltd
China Capital Mgt Coltd
China CITIC Bank Corp
China Construction Bank Corp
China Culture Fund LP
China Culture Industrial Investment Fund
China Development Bank Corp
China Everbright Bank Co Ltd
China Galaxy Securities Co Ltd
China Giant Merchants Bank
China Guangfa Bank Co Ltd
China Huirong Financial Holdings Ltd
China Industrial International Trust Ltd
China International Capital Corp Ltd
China International Fund Mgt Co Ltd
China International Fund Mgt Co Ltd
China Life Insurance (Group) Co
China Life Insurance Co Ltd
China Merchants Bank Co Ltd
China Merchants Fund Mgt Co Ltd
China Merchants Fund Mgt Co Ltd
China Merchants Securities Asset Mgt Co Ltd
China Merchants Wealth Asset Mgt Co Ltd
China Minsheng Banking Corp Ltd
China New Enterprise Investment Co
China New Enterprise Investment Fund II

DISCLOSURE: There are thousands of banks that provide depositor names, account numbers, amounts and other data per country which we cannot accommodate in this chapter; therefore, we encourage you to visit *www.irs.gov* or send me an email at *vicirsaudits@gmail.com* for the rest of the list.

PARTIAL LIST OF BANKS THAT SUBMIT
DEPOSITOR DATA TO IRS
(COLUMBIA)

AdCap Colombia S.A. Comisionista de Bolsa
Administradora de Inversion Colseguros SA
Administradora SA
Alianza Fiduciaria
Alianza Fiduciaria SA
Alianza Fiduciaria SA
Allianz Colombia SA
Allianz Seguros de Vida SA
Ashmore Management Colombia SAS
Avenida Colombia PEF
Axa Colpatria Capitalizadora SA
Axa Colpatria Seguros de Vida SA
Bancapa I
Banco Caja Social SA
Banco Colpatria Multibanca Colpatria SA
Banco Davivienda SA
Banco de Bogota SA
Banco de las Microfinanzas Bancamia SA
Banco Falabella SA
Banco May
Banco Multibank SA
Banco Pichincha SA
Banco ProCredit SA
Banco Santander de Negocios Colombia
Bancoldex
Bancolombia SA
Black River Colombia SAS
Black River Colombia SAS
BTG Pactual Commodities Colombia SAS
BTG Pactual RE Income SAS
BTG Pactual S.A. Comisionista de Bolsa
BTGP SA
Capital Management Insight SAS
Capitalizadora Bolivar SA
Capitalizadora Colmena SA
Cia Aseguradora de Fianzas Confianza SA
Citibank-Colombia SA
Cititrust Colombia SA Sociedad
Cititrust Colombia SA Sociedad
Citivalores SA Comisionista de Bolsa
Colfondos SA Pensiones y Cesantias
Colfondos SA Pensiones y Cesantias
Compania de Financiamiento Tuya SA
Compania de Seguros Bolivar SA
Compass Group SA Comisionista de Bolsa
Compass Group SA Comisionista Bolsa
Cooperativa de Trabajadores de Medellin
Cooperativa Financiera John F Kennedy
Corpbanca Investment Trust Colombia SA

Corpbanca Investment Trust Colombia SA
Corredores Davivienda SA Comisionista de Bolsa
Corredores Davivienda SA Comisionista de Bolsa
Credicorp Capital Colombia SA
Credicorp Capital Colombia SA
Credicorp Capital Fiduciaria SA
Credicorp Capital Fiduciaria SA
Davivalores SA
Deceval SA
Deutsche Colombia SA
ETF Colombia Select
Factoring Bancolombia SA
Fidecomiso Acciones Ocensa
Fiduciaria Bancolombia SA
Fiduciaria Bancolombia SA
Fiduciaria Bancolombia SA
Fiduciaria Colmena SA
Fiduciaria Colmena SA Patrimonios Autonomos
Fiduciaria Colpatria SA
Fiduciaria Davivienda SA
Fiduciaria Davivienda SA
Fiduciaria Davivienda SA
Fiducoldex SA
Fiducoldex SA
Financiera Dann Regional Compania de Financiamiento SA
Fondo BBP Real FCP
Fondo de Capital Privado TRG FCP LA I
Fondo de Cesantias Proteccion
Fondo de Pensiones Obligatorias Conserva
Fondo de Pensiones Obligatorias Retiro
Fondo de Pensiones Proteccion
Fondo de Pensiones Smurfit de Colombia
Fondo Nacional de Garantias
Fondo Transandino Colombia FCP
Gestion Fiduciaria SA
Girosyfinanzas Compania de Financiamient
Global Seguros de Vida SA
GMAC Financiera de Colombia SA
Helm Comisionista de Bolsa SA
Helm Comisionista de Bolsa SA
Helm Fiduciaria SA
Helm Fiduciaria SA
Helm Fiduciaria SA
ICAP Colombia Holdings SAS
ICAP Securities Colombia SA
Inversiones Falabella de colombia SA
Istmo Compania de Reaseguros Inc - Branch
JPMorgan Colombia Ltda
JPMorgan Corporacion Financiera SA

La Equidad Seguros OC
Larrain Vial Colombia SA Com de Bolsa
Larrain Vial SA - Branch
Larrain Vial SA Corredora de Bolsa - Branch
Leasing Bancolombia SA
Leasing Bolivar SA
Liberty Seguros de Vida SA
Liberty Seguros SA
MAS Colombia LATAM FCP
MetLife Colombia Seguros de Vida SA
Multiacciones SA
Multiactivos SA-STANH
Old Mutual Administradora de Fondos de Pensiones y Cesantias SA
Old Mutual Administradora de Fondos de Pensiones y Cesantias SA
Old Mutual Compania de Seguros de Vida SA
Old Mutual Holding de Colombia SA
Old Mutual Sociedad Fiduciaria SA
Old Mutual Sociedad Fiduciaria SA
Opportunity International Colombia SA CF
Pali-Trocha SAS
Pan-American Life de Colombia, Compania de Seguros SA
Pasivos Pensionales Proteccion
Patrimonio Autonomo macondo
Promotora PalVal SAS

Proteccion SA
RF Encore SAS (Colombia)
Ripley Colombia Inversiones SA
Ripley Compania de Financiamiento SA
Scotia Securities Columbia SA Sociedad
SEAF Colombia SA
Seguridad Cia Administradora de Fondos
Seguros de Vida Suramericana SA
SERFINCO S.A. Comisionistas de Bolsa
SERFINCO S.A., Comisionistas de bolsa
Severance Pay (GM Colmotores/Zoficol)
Sociedad Adm Planes AutoCom ChevyPlan SA
Tecsefin SA
Titularizadora Colombiana SA
Tradition Colombia SA
Ultrabursatiles SA Carteras Colectivas
Ultraserfinco SA
Valores Bancolombia SA
Valores Bancolombia SA
Vectormex Colombia SAS
Whitewater Emerging Mkt Colombia SAS
Whitewater Inversiones SAS
Woodgate SA

DISCLOSURE: There are thousands of banks that provide depositor names, account numbers, amounts and other data per country which we cannot accommodate in this chapter; therefore, we encourage you to visit *www.irs.gov* or send me an email at *vicirsaudits@gmail.com* for the rest of the list.

PARTIAL LIST OF BANKS THAT SUBMIT DEPOSITOR DATA TO IRS
(GERMANY)

A8 GP GmbH
A8 MLP GmbH & Co KG
AAB Leasing GmbH
Aachener Bank eG
AachenMunchener Lebensversicherung AG
Aareal Bank AG
ABC International Bank plc
abcbank GmbH
abcfinance GmbH
Aberdeen Asset Mgt Deutschland AG
ABG SUNDAL COLLIER ASA
ABJ Beteiligung EIF IV GbR
ABJ Beteiligungsgesellschaft mbH & Co KG
ABJ US Funds GbR
ABJ Vermoegensverwaltung GmbH & Co KG
ABN AMRO Bank NV
ABN AMRO Clearing Bank NV
ABN AMRO Lease NV
Abtsgmuender Bank -Raiffeisen-eG
AC VERMOGENSANLAGEN GBR NR. III 1998
AC VI Initiatoren GmbH & Co KG
AC VI Initiatoren GmbH & Co KG
AC VII Beteiligungsgesellschaft mbH
AC VII Privatkunden GmbH & Co KG
Access Secondary Bridge Fund GmbH & Co KG
ACF III MMBO GmbH & Co KG
ACF Infrastructure GmbH & Co KG
ACF IV Growth Buy-out Europe GmbH & Co KG
ACF V Growth Buy-Out Europe GmbH & Co KG
Achte MPC Global Equity GmbH & Co KG
ACIF Buy-Out Europe GmbH & Co KG
ACIF Infrastructure GmbH & Co KG
ACON Actienbank AG
ACP Vermoegensverwaltung GmbH & Co KG N
ACP Vermoegensverwaltung GmbH Nr 4 d 1
ACT 2001 Venture Capital GmbH & Co KG
ACT Grundstucksverwaltungs Mgt Gm
Actium Leasobjekt Gesellschaft mbH
Acton GmbH & Co Heureka II KG
Acton GmbH & Co Heureka KG
ADCURAM Beteiligungen GmbH & Co KG
ADCURAM Construction Techn Holding GmbH
ADCURAM Development Holding GmbH
ADCURAM Fertigbautechnik Holding AG
Add One GmbH and Co KG
ADURAMA Verwaltung und Treuhand GmbH
Advent Chestnut V Beteiligungsverwaltungs GmbH
Advent Chestnut V GbR
Advent Chestnut VI GmbH & Co KG
Advent Chestnut VII GmbH & Co KG

Adveq Asia I GmbH
Adveq Asia II Erste GmbH
Adveq Europe II GmbH
Adveq Mgt Deutschland GmbH
Adveq Opportunity I GmbH
Adveq Technology III GmbH
Adyen GmbH
AEA Investors Germany GmbH
Aegon Ireland Plc
Aenova Holding GmbH
AEW Europe
AFA Private Equity Ger Feeder GmbH & CoKG
AFA Private Equity German GP GmbH
AGP 1 Investitions GmbH
AGP Advisor Global Partners Fund I GmbH & Co KG
Agricultural Bank of China Ltd
AI Beauty Mgt Beteiligungs GmbH
AI Beauty Mgt Verwaltungs GmbH
AI Chem GP GmbH
AIOF GP GmbH
AIOF Managing GmbH & Co KG
AIOF MLP GmbH
Aioi Nissay Dowa Life Insurance of Europe AG
Airbus Group Bank GmbH
AKBANK AG
AKERA Verwaltung und Treuhand GmbH
akf bank GmbH & Co KG
AKTIVBANK AG
AKTIVBANK AG
ALACRITAS Verwaltungs- und Treuhand GmbH
Alaska Beteiligungs GmbH
Alaska II Mgtbeteiligungs GmbH & Co KG
Alaska Mgtbeteiligungs GmbH & Co KG
Alaska Verwaltungs GmbH
ALBELLA Verwaltung und Treuhand GmbH
ALBOLA Verwaltung und Treuhand GmbH
Alcentra Ltd
ALDINGA Verwaltung und Treuhand GmbH
ALDULA Verwaltung und Treuhand GmbH
ALEMONA Verwaltung und Treuhand GmbH
ALINDA CAPITAL PARTNERS GMBH
ALINDA GROUP LP
Allgaeuer Volksbank eG Kempten Sonthofen
Allgemeine Beamten Kasse Kreditbank AG
Allgemeine Rentenanstalt Pensionskasse AG
Allianz Global Investors GmbH
Aloco Mgtbeteiligungs GmbH & Co KG
Aloco MPC Beteiligungs GmbH
Aloco MPC Verwaltungs GmbH
aloga der Versicherungsmakler GmbH

Alstertor BV Capital GmbH & Co KG
ALTE LEIPZIGER Bauspar AG
Alte Leipziger Lebensversicherung aG
ALUBRA Verwaltung und Treuhand GmbH
Amadeus II 'D' GmbH & Co KG
AMALIA Verwaltung und Treuhand GmbH
AMC Deutschland Holding GmbH f/k/a GMAC-
AMERA Verwaltung und Treuhand GmbH
AMMS Komplementar GmbH
Ampega Investment GmbH
Amundi Asset Mgt
Angel Mgt Vermoegensverwaltungs GmbH & Co.KG
Angel MEP GmbH & Co KG
Angel Reserve GmbH
Angel Verwaltungs GmbH
Annington Investments GmbH
Anspar FLEX Fonds 1 GmbH & Co KG
Antin Agata Bidco GmbH
Antin Aude Bidco GmbH
Aon BeteiligungsMgt Deutschland GmbH & Co KG
Aon Deutschland Beteiligungs GmbH
Aon Holding Deutschland GmbH
Apax Europe IV-C GmbH & Co KG
APEP Dachfonds GmbH & Co KG
Apollo 5 GmbH
Apollo Verwaltungs V GmbH
aPriori Capital Gmbh
Aquila AgrarINVEST III GmbH & Co KG
Aquila HydropowerINVEST IV GmbH & Co KG
Aquila Private Equity Investment GmbH & Co KG
Aquila SolarINVEST III GmbH & Co KG
Aquila WaldINVEST GmbH & Co KG
ARAG Lebensversicherungs-AG
ARCADIA Beteiligungen BT GmbH & Co KG
Archelon Deutschland
Ardian Germany GmbH
Area of Sports mbh & Co KG
AREBA Verwaltung und Treuhand GmbH
Argon GmbH
ArtOffice GmbH
Artom VV GMBH
ARVINA Verwaltung und Treuhand GmbH
ASG Dynamo GmbH
Asia Pacific Beteiligungsverwaltung GmbH
Asia Pacific Capital II GbR
Asian RT GbR
ASPECTA Assurance International Lux SA
Aster Mgt Vermogensverwaltungs
Aster Reserve GmbH
Aster Verwaltungs GmbH
Astorius Capital PE Fonds I GmbH & Co KG

ASTUTIA Beteiligungsgesellschaft mbH
ATLANTICLUX Lebensversicherung SA
Atlas Venture Fund VI GmbH & Co KG
Atrium Finance GmbH
Attijariwafa Bank Europe
ATUNO Verwaltung und Treuhand GmbH
Atypical Silent Partnership
AUCTUS II A GmbH & Co KG
Auda Asian Growth Fund GmbH & Co KG
Auda DPPAM Initiatoren GmbH & Co KG
Auda EnBW MA Initiatoren GmbH & Co KG
Auda Treuhand Beteiligungsverwaltung GmbH
AUG. PRIEN Immobilien PE Verwaltung Brah
Augsburger Aktienbank AG
Augusta-Bank eG Raiffeisen-Volksbank
Auris Holding GmbH
Australia and New Zealand Banking Group Ltd
Austria Beteiligungsgesellschaft mbH
AutoBank AG
Automic Holding GmbH
Avalon Beteilgungs GmbH
Avalon Co-Invest Beteilgungs GmbH
Avalon GmbH & Co KG
Avenso Mgt Beteilgungs GmbH & Co KG
Avenso MPP Beteilgungs GmbH
Avenso MPP Verwaltungs GmbH (GP)
AXA Bank AG
AXA Deutschland
AXA Euro Aggregate D
AXA Euro Aggregate DBVL
AXA Euro Aggregate K
AXA Euro Dividend S
AXA Europa
AXA Immobilien GmbH
AXA Immoresidential
AXA Immoselect
AXA Immosolutions
AXA Lebensversicherung AG
AXA Life Europe
AXA Life Europe Germany
AXA Merkens Fonds GmbH
AXA Portfolio 5
AXA Real Invest Europa 1
AXA Renten Euro
AXA Ros Global Equities DBVL
AXA US Short Duration High Yield AKAG
AXA Versicherung AG
AXA Wachstum Invest
AXA Wachstum Spektrum
AXA Welt
AXA Zeitwertfonds I Special Fund

DISCLOSURE: There are thousands of banks that provide depositor names, account numbers, amounts and other data per country which we cannot accommodate in this chapter; therefore, we encourage you to visit *www.irs.gov* or send me an email at *vicirsaudits@gmail.com* for the rest of the list.

PARTIAL LIST OF BANKS THAT SUBMIT DEPOSITOR DATA TO IRS
(HONGKONG)

360ip-Guosen Mgt HK Co Ltd
3i Infocomm Ltd
3W Fund Mgt Ltd
8 Securities Ltd
A.H. Intl Ltd
ABC Intl Holdings Ltd
ABCI Asset Mgt Ltd
ABCI Investment Funds
ABCI RMB Income Fund
ABCI Securities Co Ltd
Able Agrima Ltd
Able Consmat Ltd
Able Cyberstan Ltd
Able Newtech Ltd
ABN Amro AM Asia Ltd HK Staff Pro Scheme
ABN AMRO Bank NV
ABN AMRO Clearing Hong Kong Ltd
ABN AMRO Financial Products Ltd
ABN AMRO Fund Services -Asia- Ltd
ABN AMRO Nominees Services Hong Kong Ltd
ABN AMRO Securities Asia Ltd
ABN AMRO Securities Holdings Asia Ltd
About Capital Mgt (HK) Co Ltd
ABRAX
Abraxas Ltd
Abundancia Global Asset Mgt (Hong Kong) Ltd
Access Investment Mgt H.K. Ltd
Access Investment Mgt H.K. Ltd
Ace Finance Ltd
ACE Life Insurance Co Ltd
Acheson Ltd
Acheson Ltd
ACNielsen Group Ltd
ACNielsen Holdings Ltd
ACR Trading Asia Ltd
Adamas Asset Mgt HK Ltd
ADMIS Hong Kong Ltd
Advance Manufacturing Holdings Ltd
Advantech Capital LP
Adyen Hong Kong Ltd
AEON Credit Service Asia Co Ltd
AERAPAY Ltd
Aether Corp Ltd
AFA Fiduciary Services Ltd
AFA Fiduciary Services Ltd
AFL Automotive Holding Co Ltd
AFP Corporate Services Ltd
AFP Corporate Services Ltd
AFP Corporate Services Ltd
AFP Corporate Services Ltd

AFP Fiduciary Services Ltd
AFP Fiduciary Services Ltd
AFP Fiduciary Services Ltd
Africa Service Ltd
Ageas Insurance Co (Asia) Ltd
Ageas Investment Mgt (Asia) Ltd
Ageas Nominees Ltd
Agostini Ltd
Agricultural Bank of China Ltd
AIA /B/ Retirement Fund Scheme
AIA Co /Trustee/ Ltd
AIA Co Ltd
AIA Co Ltd
AIA Group Ltd
AIA Intl Ltd
AIA Intl Ltd
AIA Intl Ltd HK Agents' Prov Fd
AIA Retirement Fund Scheme
AIA Trust Retirement Plan
AIG Financial Products Hong Kong Ltd
Akron Securities Ltd
Alaskan Luxembourg SCA
Alestra /Hong Kong/ Ltd
All Noble Investments Ltd
Allard Partners Ltd
AllianceBernstein Hong Kong Ltd
AllianceBernstein Hong Kong Ltd
Allianz Global Investors Asia Pacific Ltd
Allianz Global Investors GmbH
Allianz Global Investors HK Retirement
Allianz Global Investors Nominee Service
Allianz Selection European Equity Divide
Allianz Selection Income and Growth
Allianz Selection Total Return Asian Eq
Allianz Selection US High Yield
Allied Banking Corp HongKong Ltd
Allied Finance HK Ltd Hong Kong
All-Stars Investment Ltd
Ally Point Ltd
Alpha Achieve Ltd
AlphaGrep Technologies Ltd
Alphalex Capital Mgt (HK) Ltd
Alphalex Capital Mgt Ltd
Alpine Springs Investment Holdings Ltd
Alply Business Inc Ltd
Alter Domus Asia Nominees Ltd
Alyco Advisory Asia Ltd
Alyco Advisory Asia Ltd
Amber Investment (HK) Ltd
AMCIC China Coal Holdings Ltd

American Consulate General H K P F Sch
Amicorp Fiduciary Ltd
Amicorp Fiduciary Ltd
Amicorp Hong Kong Ltd
Amicorp Ltd
Amicorp TST HK Ltd
Amicorp TST HK Ltd
AMP Capital China Future Growth Fund
Ample Capital Ltd
AMTD Asset Mgt Ltd
AMTD Financial Planning Ltd
Amundi Asset Mgt
Amundi HK MPF Series
Amundi HK Portfolios
Amundi Hong Kong ltd
Amundi Hong Kong ltd
Anchor Equity Partners Fund II-B, LP
Anfu Global Ltd
Anglo-Eastern Ship Mgt Ltd Staff P Fund
Anli Financial Communications Ltd
ANLI HOLDINGS Ltd
ANLI SECURITIES Ltd
ANZ IPB Nominees (Hong Kong) Ltd
ANZ Securities (HK) Ltd
AON Asia Retirement Scheme
Aon Services Hong Kong Ltd
AP Investments (HK) Ltd
Apex Achieve Ltd
Apex Ally Investment Ltd
Apex Corporate Services HK Ltd
Apex Speed Holdings Ltd
Apollo Mgt Asia Pacific Ltd
Aptor Ltd
Arcadia Asset Mgt (Asia) Ltd
ARCM II Investments HK Ltd
ARCM Investments Ltd
Areion Asset Mgt Co Ltd
Ark One Ltd
Ark Trust (Hong Kong) Ltd
ARK Trust (Hong Kong) Ltd
Arkkan Capital Mgt Ltd
Ascalon Capital Managers -Asia Ltd
Ascendo Consulting Ltd
ASI Asia Ltd
Asia Bottles HK Co Ltd
Asia Bright Ltd
Asia Cosmos Ltd
Asia Infrastructure & Redevelopment Fund
Asia Investment Capital 1 Ltd
Asia Newstar Ltd
Asia Research and Capital Mgt Ltd
Asia Selection Growth Fund

Asiaciti Trust Hong Kong Corp Ltd
Asiaciti Trust Hong Kong Corp Ltd
Asiaciti Trust Hong Kong Corp Ltd
Asiaciti Trust Hong Kong Ltd
Asiaciti Trust Hong Kong Ltd
Asia-Germany Productivity Promotion Ltd
Asialink Securities Ltd
Asian Capital Investment Opportunities
Asian Develop Corp Ltd
Asian Financial Common Wealth PTC Ltd
Asian Financial Common Wealth PTC Ltd
Asia-Pac Securities Ltd
Asiya Investments Hong Kong Ltd
ASJ Consultants Ltd
Aspen Crest Partners HK Ltd
Aspen Investment Ltd
Assicurazioni Generali SpA
Astec Provident Fund
Astrum Capital Mgt Ltd
Astrum Capital Mgt Ltd
Asuka CITF Ltd
ATC Hong Kong Holding Ltd
ATG Fiduciary HK Ltd
ATG Fiduciary HK Ltd
Atlantis Investment Mgt Hong Kong
Audrey Chow Securities Ltd
Aurora Borealis Investment Services Ltd
Auspicious Capital Mgt Ltd
Austen Capital Mgt Ltd
Austen Multi-Strategy Fund Ltd
Australia & New Zealand Banking Group Ltd
Austrian Financial Investors (HK) Ltd
Avalona Services Ltd
Avant Capital Mgt (HK) Ltd
AVIC Healthcare Group Ltd
Aviva Life Ins Co Ltd Provident Fund
Aviva Life Insurance Co Ltd
AXA Balanced Fund
AXA Capital Growth Fund
AXA Capital Stable Fund
AXA China Region Insurance Co Ltd
AXA China Region Investment Services Ltd
AXA China Region Ltd
AXA Financial Planning (Hong Kong) Ltd
AXA Financial Services Holdings Ltd
AXA Financial Services Trustees Ltd
AXA Fixed Income Fund
AXA Growth Fund
AXA Hong Kong Life Insurance Co Ltd
AXA IM MPF Fund
AXA Institutional Hong Kong Fund
AXA INVESTMENT Mgt ASIA Ltd

DISCLOSURE: There are thousands of banks that provide depositor names, account numbers, amounts and other data per country which we cannot accommodate in this chapter; therefore, we encourage you to visit *www.irs.gov* or send me an email at *vicirsaudits@gmail.com* for the rest of the list.

PARTIAL LIST OF BANKS THAT SUBMIT DEPOSITOR DATA TO IRS
(JAPAN)

8 Securities Inc
AAA Sovereign Fund
Abashiri Gyogyo Kyodo Kumiai
Aberdeen Investment Mgt KK
ABN AMRO Clearing Tokyo Co Ltd
Abrraj Infrastructure & Growth Capital M
AbukumaishikawaNogyoKyodoKumiai
Aburandohagi Nogyo Kyodo Kumiai
ACA Asset Godo Kaisha
ACA Healthcare Inc
ACA Inc
ACA Inc
Accordia Golf Trust
ACE New Small Cap Growth Open
Ace Securities Co Ltd
Activia Properties Inc
AD Capital Co Ltd
AD Capital Co Ltd
AD Investment Mgt Co Ltd
AD Support LLC
Adachino Nogyo Kyodo Kumiai
ADIC Co Ltd
Admiral Capital Co Ltd
Admiral Capital Co Ltd
ADP-CE Investment LPS
ADP-PRISM Investment Partnership
Advance Residence Investment Corp
Advantage Partners IV, ILP
Advantage Partners IV-S, ILP
Advantage Partners MBI Fund III
Advantage Partners V, ILP
Advantage Partners LLP
AEGON Sony Life Insurance Co Ltd
AEON Bank Ltd
AEON Financial Service Co Ltd
AEON Financial Service Co Ltd
AEON REIT Investment Corp
AEON Reit Mgt Co Ltd
AFT Co Ltd
Agatsuma Nogyo Kyodo Kumiai
Agility Asset Advisers Inc
Agility Asset Advisers Inc
Agricultural Bank of China Ltd
Aichiama Nogyo Kyodo Kumiai
Aichibitou Nogyo Kyodo Kumiai
Aichichita Nogyo Kyodo Kumiai
Aichichuuou Nogyo Kyodo Kumiai
Aichihigashi Nogyo Kyodo Kumiai
Aichi-ken Shinyo Gyogyo Kyodo Kumiai Ren

Aichimikawa Nogyo Kyodo Kumiai
Aichiminami Nogyo Kyodo Kumiai
Aichinishi Nogyo Kyodo Kumiai
aichishinren nogyo kyodo kumiai rengokai
Aichitoyota Nogyo Kyodo Kumiai
AIG Fuji Life Insurance Co
AIG Japan Holdings KK
Ailand KK
Aioi Nissay Dowa Insurance Co Ltd
Aioi securities Co Ltd
Aioishi Nogyo Kyodo Kumiai
Aira Nogyo Kyodo Kumiai
Airaizu Nogyo Kyodo Kumiai
Aitikita Nogyo Kyodo Kumiai
AIU Insurance Co Ltd
Aizu Nogyo Kyodo Kumiai
Aizuiide Nogyo Kyodo Kumiai
Aizumidori Nogyo Kyodo Kumiai
Aizuminami Nogyo Kyodo Kumiai
Akagitachibana Nogyo Kyodo Kumiai
Akan Nogyo Kyodo Kumiai
Akashi Nogyo Kyodo Kumiai
Akatsuki Securities Inc
Aki Nogyo Kyodo Kumiai
Aki TMK
Akigawa Nogyo Kyodo Kumiai
Akitafurusato Nogyo Kyodo Kumiai
Akitahokuo Nogyo Kyodo Kumiai
Akitakita Nogyo Kyodo Kumiai
Akitakotoh Nogyo Kyodo Kumiai
Akitaminami Nogyo Kyodo Kumiai
Akitaobako Nogyo Kyoudou Kumiai
Akitashinsei Nogyo Kyodo Kumiai
Akitashirakami Nogyo Kyodo Kumiai
Akitayamamoto Nogyo Kyodo Kumiai
Alberich LLC
ALJ CENTRAL RE1 Tokutei Mokuteki Kaisha
Allardstown TK
AllianceBernstein (Luxembourg) S.a r.l.
AllianceBernstein Japan Ltd
AllianceBernstein Japan Ltd
AllianceBernstein Japan Ltd
Allianz Global Investors Japan Co Ltd
Allianz Life Insurance Japan Ltd
Alphix Coltd
Alps Nogyo Kyodo Kumiai
Alternative Investment Capital Ltd
Alternative Investment Capital Ltd
Altus GK

Always Capital Corp
Amahigashi Nogyo Kyodo Kumiai
Amakusa Gyogyo Kyodo Kumiai
Amakusa Nogyo Kyodo Kumiai
Amami Nogyo Kyodo Kumiai
Amarumemachi Nogyo Kyodo Kumiai
American Home Assurance Co Ltd
Amundi Japan holding Ltd
Amundi Japan Ltd
Amundi Japan Ltd
Amundi Japan securities Ltd
Anan Nogyo Kyodo Kumiai
Anchor Ship Capital LLC
Anchor Ship Investment Co Ltd
ANCHOR SHIP PARTNERS Co Ltd
Ando Securities Co Ltd
Aneto GK
Ant Capital Partners Co Ltd
Ant Capital Partners Co Ltd
Aoba Nogyo Kyodo Kumiai
Aomi Project TMK
Aomori Nogyo Kyodo Kumiai
Aoyama Sogo Accounting Firm Co Ltd
Aozora Bank Ltd
Aozora Investment Mgt Co Ltd
Aozora Investment Mgt Co Ltd
Aozora Nogyo Kyodo Kumiai
AOZORA SECURITIES Co Ltd
Aozora Trust Bank Ltd
AP IV GP Investment Partnership
AP IV-S GP Investment Partnership
AP MC Fund-J, ILP
AP RCT Fund, ILP
AP RCT Fund, ILP
AP RX Fund-J, ILP
AP V GP Partnership
APLUS CoLtd
APM
APT, ILP
APW, ILP
ARENA-FX CoLtd
Ariake Gamma Four Godo Kaisha
Arida Nogyo Kyodo Kumiai
Arigato Asset Mgt Inc
Arigato Asset Mgt Inc
Arima IBLP
Arima TMK
Ark Securities Co Ltd
Ark Totan Alternative Co Ltd
Arlo XIV Ltd
Arsenal Asset IBLP
Arsenal Asset IBLP GK

Arsnova Capital Co Ltd
Arsnova TK
Artemis Funding Corp
Arts Securities CoLtd
Asahi Fire & Marine Insurance Co Ltd
Asahi Life Asset Mgt Co Ltd
Asahi Life Asset Mgt Co Ltd
Asahi Mutual Life Insurance Co
Asahikawa Nogyo Kyodo Kumiai
Asahina Nogyo Kyodo Kumiai
Asakano Nogyo Kyodo Kumiai
Ashikaga Enterprise No2. Investment LPS
Ashikaga Holdings Co Ltd
Ashikagashi Nogyo Kyodo Kumiai
Ashikita Nogyo Kyodo Kumiai
Ashikita Nogyo Kyodo Kumiai
Ashin Nogyo Kyodo Kumiai
Ashmore Japan Co Ltd
ASM Broadcasting Co Ltd
Aso Nogyo Kyodo Kumiai
ASTEC Technology Incubation Fund I P
Astmax Asset Mgt Inc
Astmax Asset Mgt Inc
Astmax Energy Inc
Astmax Trading Inc
Astro Tokutei Mokuteki Kaisha
Asturias IBLP
Asturias TMK
Asuka Asset Mgt Co Ltd
Asuka Corporate Advisory Co Ltd
Asuka Credit Cooperative
Asuka DBJ Investment LPS
Asyorocho Nogyo Kyodo kumiai
Atena Ltd
ATF Corp
Atsugishi Nogyo Kyodo Kumiai
Australia and New Zealand Banking Group Ltd
Ava Trade Japan KK
Avalsec Co Ltd
Avalsec Co Ltd
AVWL Japan Real Estate 2 TMK
AVWL Japan Real Estate TMK
Awa Nogyo Kyodo Kumiai
Awa Securities Co Ltd
Awacho Nogyo Kyodo Kumiai
Awaguntobu Nogyo Kyodo Kumiai
Awajihinode Nogyo Kyodo Kumiai
Awajishima Nogyo Kyodo Kumiai
Awamiyoshi Nogyo Kyodo Kumiai
AXA Direct Life Insurance Co. Ltd
AXA IM Global ex Japan Equity Fund
AXA IM Global ex Japan Equity Mother Fund

DISCLOSURE: There are thousands of banks that provide depositor names, account numbers, amounts and other data per country which we cannot accommodate in this chapter; therefore, we encourage you to visit *www.irs.gov* or send me an email at *vicirsaudits@gmail.com* for the rest of the list.

PARTIAL LIST OF BANKS THAT SUBMIT DEPOSITOR DATA TO IRS
(PHILIPPINES)

14-678 Property Holdings Inc JV
18-2 Property Holdings Inc JV
19-1 Realty Corporation JV
6-24 Property Holdings Inc JV
6-3 Property Holdings Inc JV
AB Capital and Investment Corp
AB Capital Securities Inc
ABC Financial Institution
AFS Philippines Inc
Al Amanah Islamic Inv Bank of the Phils
Altus Capital Corp
Armstrong Securities Inc
Asia Outsourcing Philippines Hold Inc
Asia United Bank
AsianLife & General Assurance Corp
Asiasec Equities Inc
ATR Kimeng Asset Management Inc
AY Holdings Inc
Ayala Plans Inc
Bahay Financial Services Inc
Balikatan Housing Finance Inc
Bank of Commerce
Bank of the Philippine Islands
Bayan Delinquent Loan Recovery 1 (SPV-AMC) Inc
BDO Capital & Investment Corp
BDO Leasing and Finance Inc
BDO Private Bank Inc
BDO Securities Corp
BDO Unibank Inc
Beneficial Life Insurance Company Inc
BPI - Philam Life Assurance Corp
BPI Capital Corp
BPI Direct Savings Bank
BPI Family Savings Bank
BPI Globe BanKO Inc A Savings Bank
BPI Investment Management Inc
BPI Securities Corp
Cavite United Rural Bank
China Bank Savings Inc
China Banking Corp
Citibank Savings Inc
Citicorp Capital Philippines Inc
Citicorp Fin Svcs and Ins Brk Phl Inc
Citifinancial Corp
City Savings Bank Inc
CLSA (Philippines) Inc
CLSA Capital Partners (HK) Limited
CLSA Exchange Capital Inc
COL Financial Group Inc

Credit Suisse Securities PHL Inc
Crescent Park 14-678 Prpty Hldgs Inc JV
Crescent Park 18-2 Property Hldgs Inc JV
Crescent Park 19-1 Property Hldgs Inc JV
Crescent Park 6-24 Property Hldgs Inc JV
Crescent Park 6-3 Property Hldgs Inc JV
Crown Bank Inc
CTBC Bank Philippines Corp
Dauntless Holdings Inc
DB Strategic Advisors Inc
DBP-Daiwa Capital Markets Philippines Inc
DBS Vickers Securities Phil Inc
Deutsche Regis Partners Inc
Development Bank of the Philippines
Dover-Sherborn Corp
East West Banking Corp
East West Rural Bank Inc
Equicom Savings Bank Inc
Filipino Fund Inc
First Metro Asia Focus Equity Fund Inc
First Metro Asset Management Inc
First Metro Investment Corp
First Metro Philippine Equity Exchange Traded Fund
First Metro Save & Learn Dollar Bond Fund
First Metro Save & Learn Equity Fund Inc
First Metro Save and Learn Balanced Fund
First Metro Save and Learn Fixed Income Fund
First Metro Securities Brokerage Corp
Fivepalms Corp
FMIC Equities Inc
FWD Life Insurance Corp
Generali Pilipinas Holding Co Inc
Generali Pilipinas Life Assurance Co Inc
Globalinks Securities & Stocks Inc
GPL Holdings Inc
Great Life Financial Assurance Corp
Grepa Realty Holdings Corp
Grepalife Asset Management Corp
HSBC Savings Bank (Philippines) Inc
ICAP Philippines Inc
ICCP Venture Partners Inc
Investment & Capital Corp of the Phils
Investments 2234 Philippines Fund I SPV
J.P. Morgan Securities Philippines Inc
JPMorgan Chase Bank N.A. - Manila Branch
Land Bank of the Philippines
Legazpi Savings Bank Inc
Longmeadow Corporation
Macquarie Capital Securities Philippines

Macquarie Infrsture Advisory Philippines
Malayan Bank Savings and Mortgage Bank
Mandarin Securities Corp
Manulife Chinabank Life Assurance Corp
Manulife Financial Plans Inc
Maybank ATR Kim Eng Capital Partners Inc
Maybank ATR Kim Eng Securities Inc
Maybank Philippines Incorp
Merchant's Savings and Loan Assoc
Meridian SPV AMC Corp
Metrobank Card Corp
Metropolitan Bank & Trust Company
MSSFG SPV-AMC Inc
NCM Mutual Fund of the Phils Inc
Orix Metro Leasing and Finance Corp
Pag-Asa Ng Masang Pinoy Foundation
Pagasa Philippines Lending Company Inc
PAMI Asia Balanced Fund Inc
PAMI Equity Index Fund Inc
PAMI Global Bond Fund Inc
PAMI Global Equity Fund Inc
PAMI Horizon Fund Inc
Pan Malayan Mgt. and Investment Corp
PAPA Securities Corp
Paramount Life & General Insurance Corp
PBC Capital Investment Corp
PCIB Securities Inc
Philam Asset Management Inc
Philam Bond Fund Inc
Philam Dollar Bond Fund Inc
Philam Equitable Life Assurance Co Inc
Philam Fund Inc
Philam Managed Income Fund Inc
Philam Strategic Growth Fund Inc
Philippine Asset Investment (SPV-AMC) Inc
Philippine AXA Life Insurance Corp
Philippine Bank of Communications
Philippine Business Bank Inc
Philippine Depository & Trust Corp
Philippine Equity Partners Inc
Philippine National Bank
Philippine Opportunities for Growth and Income (SPV-AMC) Inc
Philippine Postal Savings Bank Inc
Philippine Savings Bank
Philippine Tank Storage Int Holdings Inc
Philippine Trust Company
Philippine Veterans Bank
Philplans First Inc
Pioneer Life Inc
Planters Development Bank

PNB Life Insurance Inc
PNB Savings Bank
PNB Securities Inc
Pru Life Insurance Corp of UK
Rampver Financials and Insurance Agency Inc
RCBC Capital Corp
RCBC Forex Brokers Corp
RCBC Leasing and Finance Corp
RCBC Rental Corp
RCBC Savings Bank Inc
RCBC Securities Inc
Resiliency SPC Inc
Rizal Commercial Banking Corp
Robinsons Bank Corp
Rural Bank of Angeles
Rural Bank of Brooke's Point (Palawan) Inc
Salisbury Bkt Securities Corp
Salisbury BKT Securities Corp
SB Capital Investment Corp
SB Cards Corp
SB Equities Inc
Security Bank Corp
Security Bank Savings Corp
Sithe Global Camaya Holdings Inc
Sithe Global GNPD Holdings Inc
Soldivo Bond Fund Inc
Soldivo Strategic Growth Fund Inc
Sterling Bank of Asia Inc (A Savings Bank)
STI Investments Inc
Sun Life Asset Management Company Inc
Sun Life Financial Plans Inc
Sun Life Grepa Financial Inc
Sun Life of Canada Philippines Inc
The Insular Life Assurance Company Ltd
The Manufacturers Life Insurance Co (Phils.) Inc
The Philippine American Life & General
Tongyang Savings Bank Inc
Tranche 1 SPV-AMC Inc
UBS Securities Philippines Inc
UCPB Leasing & Finance Corp
UCPB Savings Bank Inc
UCPB Securities Inc
UCPB-CIIF Finance & Dev't Corp
Unicapital Securities Inc
Unicapital Inc
Union Bank of the Philippines
United Coconut Planters Bank
United Overseas Bank Philippines
Vicsal Investment Inc
VSec.com Inc

DISCLOSURE: There are thousands of banks that provide depositor names, account numbers, amounts and other data per country which we cannot accommodate in this chapter; therefore, we encourage you to visit *www.irs.gov* or send me an email at *vicirsaudits@gmail.com* for the rest of the list.

PARTIAL LIST OF BANKS THAT SUBMIT DEPOSITOR DATA TO IRS
(SAUDI ARABIA)

Abdulrahman Saleh Al Rajhi & Partners Co Ltd
Adeem Capital
Ahmad Yousef Mohammad Ahmad
Al Dhawahi Real Estate Fund
Al Emaar Fund
Al Hadi Fund
Al Hadi Sharia Compliant Fund
Al Istithmar for Financial Securities & Brokerage Co
Al Manarah Conservative Growth Fund
Al Manarah High Growth Fund
Al Manarah Medium Growth Fund
Al Mokdam Fund
Al Mokdam Sharia Compliant Fund
AL -Nfaie Invesmrnt Group
Al Rabia Real Estate Fund
AL Rajhi Banking & Investment Corp
Al Rajhi Capital
Al Rajhi Capital
Al Rajhi Capital
Al Rajhi Commodities Mudaraba Fund - SAR
Al Rajhi Commodities Mudaraba Fund - USD
Al Rajhi GCC Equity Fund
Al Rajhi Global Equity Fund
Al Rajhi Local Share Fund
Al Rajhi MENA Dividend Grouth Fund
Al Rajhi Multi Asset Balanced Fund
Al Rajhi Multi Asset Conservative Fund
Al Rajhi Multi Asset Growth Fund
Al Rajhi Petrochemical & Cement Equity Fund
AL Rajhi Real Estate Income Fund
Al Rajhi Sukuk Fund
Al Shamekh Fund
Al Shamekh Sharia Compliant Fund
Al Shuja'a Fund
Al Shuja'a Sharia Compliant Fund
AlAhli AlKhayrat Capital Secure Fund
AlAhli AlKhayyal Residential Development Fund
AlAhli Asia Pacific Trading Equity Fund
AlAhli Diversified Saudi Riyal Trade Fund
AlAhli Diversified US Dollar Trade Fund
AlAhli Emerging Markets Trading Equity Fund
AlAhli Euro Murabaha Fund
AlAhli Europe Trading Equity Fund
AlAhli GCC Growth & Income Fund
AlAhli GCC Trading Equity Fund
AlAhli Global Growth & Income Fund
AlAhli Global Natural Resource Fund
AlAhli Global Real Estate Fund
AlAhli Global Trading Equity Fund
AlAhli Health Care Trading Equity Fund

AlAhli International Trade Fund
AlAhli National Investment Fund
AlAhli Residential Real Estate Development Fund
AlAhli Sadaqqat Fund
AlAhli Saudi Mid-Cap Equity Fund
AlAhli Saudi Riyal Trade Fund
AlAhli Saudi Trading Equity Fund
AlAhli Short Term Dollar Fund
AlAhli Small Cap Trading Equity Fund
AlAhli Takaful Co
AlAhli US Dollar Sukuk & Murabaha Fund
AlAhli US Trading Equity Fund
Al-Badr Murabaha Fund -SAR
Al-Badr Murabaha Fund -USD
Albilad Investment Co
Aldahyah Fund
Al-Danah GCC Equity Trading Fund
Al-Fursan (BRIC) Equity Trading Fund
Alinma Bank
Alinma Investment Co
Aljazira Capital Co
AlJazira Capital Co
AlJazira Dawawen Fund
Aljazira Residential Projects Fund
Aljazira Residential Projects Fund 2
Aljazira Takaful Ta'awuni
Alkhabeer Capital
Alkhabeer Liquidity Fund - Hasseen
Alkhair Capital Co for Securities business
Alkhair Capital Saudi Arabia
AL-Khair International Equities Fund
Allianz Saudi Fransi Cooperative Insurance Co
AL-Mashareq Japanese Equities Fund
Al-Murabih SAR Murabaha Fund
Al-Naqaa Asia Growth Fund
Al-Nefaie Investment Group
Aloula Geojit Capital
Al-Qasr GCC Real Estate & Construction Equity Trading Fund
AL-Qawafeel Commodities Trading Fund
Alrajhi Co for Cooperative insurance
Al-Saffa Saudi Equity Trading Fund
Al-Sagr Cooperative Insurance Co
AL-Taiyebat Saudi Equities Fund
AL-Thoraiya European Equities Fund
American Express (Saudi Arabia) Ltd
American Stock Fund
Anfaal Capital Co
Arab Investment Co S.A.A.
Arab National Bank
Arab National Investment Co

Arab National Investment Co
ARAB Petroleum Investment Corp
ARC Real Estate Income Fund
Ashmore Asian Equity Fund
Ashmore GCC Equity Fund
Ashmore IPO Fund
Ashmore Saudi Equity Fund
Audi Capital KSA cjsc
Bait Al Mal Al khaleeji
Balanced Income Fund
Bank AlBilad
Bank AlJazira
Bank Muscat S.A.O.G.
Banque Saudi Fransi
BLOMINVEST Saudi Arabia
BNP PARIBAS
BNP PARIBAS INVESTMENT CO KSA
British Stock Fund
Commodity Trading Fund (SAR)
Commodity Trading Fund (USD)
Credit Suisse Saudi Arabia
Derayah Financial
Deutsche Bank Aktiengesellschaft
Deutsche Securities Saudi Arabia LLC
Diaverum AB
EFG Hermes KSA
EFG-Hermes Hasaad Freestyle Saudi Equity Fund
EFG-Hermes KSA
EFG-Hermes Saudi Arabia Equity Fund
Emirates NBD Capital KSA LLC
Emirates NBD PJSC
European Stock Fund
Ewan Al Qayrawan Real Estate Fund
FALCOM Arab Markets Fund
FALCOM Financial Services
FALCOM IPO Fund
FALCOM Petrochemical ETF
FALCOM SAR Murabha Fund
FALCOM Saudi Equity ETF
FALCOM Saudi Equity Fund
Future Equity Fund
GCC Ithmar Fund
GCC Real-Estate Equity Fund (Aqaar)
GIB Capital LLC
GLOBAL EQUITY FUND
Global Investment Holdings Co Ltd
Global Investment House Saudi
GLOBAL PROPERTY FUND
GOF Industrial Services Holding Co LLC
GOLDMAN SACHS SAUDI ARABIA
Gulf Fifth Gemstone Holding Co LLC

Gulf Fourth Gemstone Holding Co LLC
Gulf International Bank BSC
Gulf Investors Asset Mgt Co
Gulf One Capital Co JSC
Gulf Opportunities Trading Co LLC
HSBC Saudi Arabia Ltd
Industrial & Commercial Bank of China Ltd
International Bond Fund
International Fund
Invest. Saud. Arab. Finan. Investments
Investor For Securities
Ithmar Sharia Compliant Saudi Equity Fund
Ithraa Capital Co
Itqan Capital
Jadwa Investment Co
Japan Stock Fund
JPMorgan Chase Bank NA - Riyadh Branc
King Abdullah University of Science & Technology Investment Co
KSB Capital Group
Kuwaiti Equity Fund (Alseef)
L azurde Holding Co LLC
Maceen Capital
Malaz Capital
ME & SA Sub-Regions Hub Enterprise-Saudi Arabia
Meddle East Finical Investment Co
Med-SI Real Estate Development Fund II
Merrill Lynch, Kingdom of Saudi Arabia C
MetLife - AIG - ANB Cooperative Insurance Co
Middle East Financial investment Co
Morgan Stanley Saudi Arabia
Morgan Stanley Saudi Equity Fund
Multi Strategy Relative Return Fund
Muscat Capital
Muscat Capital
Musharaka Capital Co
Musharaka IPO Fund
National Bank of Kuwait SAK
National Bank of Pakistan
National Commercial Bank
NCB Capital Co
Nomura Saudi Arabia
NOMW Capital
Northern Trust Co of Saudi Arabia
Osool & Bakheet Investment Co
Private Fund 40
Private Fund 42
Rana Investment Co
Real Estate Income fund
Riyad Bank

DISCLOSURE: There are thousands of banks that provide depositor names, account numbers, amounts and other data per country which we cannot accommodate in this chapter; therefore, we encourage you to visit *www.irs.gov* or send me an email at *vicirsaudits@gmail.com* for the rest of the list.

PARTIAL LIST OF BANKS THAT SUBMIT DEPOSITOR DATA TO IRS
(SWITZERLAND)

1 Beneco SA
1741 Equity Active Indexing World Moment
1741 Equity Active Indexing World Value
1741 Equity Dynamic Indexing World
1741 Equity Systematic World
1741 Fixed Income Active Bond
1741 Institutional Equity Active Indexin
1741 Switzerland Accounting Based Index
1741 Switzerland Cap Weighted Index Fond
1741 Switzerland Equal Weighted Index Fo
1741 Switzerland Minimum Volatility Inde
1741 Switzerland Momentum Index Fonds
1741 Switzerland Quality Index Fonds
1741 Switzerland Risk Parity Index Fonds
1741 Switzerland Value Index Fonds
1788 Capital Trust
1875 Finance SA
2DR SA
2invest AG
2pm Suisse SA
2SW Asset Mgt AG
2trade group ltd
2trust schweiz ag
2Xideas AG
3T Family Office ltd
7G Asset Mgt SA
A F McLoughlin Settlement
A&M Global Family Office SA
A&O Mgt GmbH
A.BERTOLI SA
A.J.K. Bureau of Consultants Schweiz AG
A.M. Family Office SA
A.M.&C. Finance SA
A.T. Holdings I SARL
A.T. Holdings II SARL
aa group financial consulting ag
Aamil SWISS SA
Aare Insti F - Aktien Emer Markets
Aare Insti F - Obli FW Global Aktiv
Aargauische Kantonalbank
AAS Asset Advisory Services SA
AAS Asset Advisory Services SA
Abacus Trust
ABANCA Corporacion Bancaria SA
Abaris Investment Advisory AG
Abaris Investment Mgt AG
ABBR Aktiengesellschaft
Abegg & Co ltd Zurich
Aberdeen Swiss Funds Europ Opp Eq Fund

Aberdeen Swiss Funds Glob Energy Eq Fund
Aberdeen Swiss Funds Glob Gold Eq Fund
Aberdeen Swiss Funds Glob HT Eq Fund
Aberdeen Swiss Funds Glob Opp Eq Fund
Aberdeen Swiss Funds Glob Pharma Eq Fund
Aberdeen -Swiss- Funds Tiger Equity Fund
Abilen AG
Abrias Investment Mgt AG
Absolute Capital Group AG
Absolute Invest AG
Absolute Private Equity ltd
Abyss Fund Research, Sarl
AC Conseils Sarl
AC Conseils Sarl
ACATIS Fair Value Investment AG
Accreda Mgt AG
Accreda Mgt AG
Accredio Swiss AG
Accresco Investment AG
ACE ltd
ACE Trustees SA
ACE Trustees SA
Acies Asset Mgt AG
Acla Handels AG
Aclon Finance SA
Acorma Beteiligungen AG
Acorma Holding AG
Acorma Investments AG
acrevis Bank AG
ACT Asset Mgt AG
ACT Currency Partner AG
Actieninvest AG
Action Finance SA
Active Asset Mgt SA
Active Niche Funds SA
Active Timing - Quanto CHF
Actus Capital SA
Adegus GmbH
Adegus GmbH
Adel Consulting GmbH
Ademaf SA
Adi Treuhand GmbH
Adingest SA
Adinvest AG
Adinvest Holding AG
Adonis Global Strategies Irrevoc Trust
Aduno Finance AG
Adveq Mgt AG
AEIS Insti F - Short Duration CHF h

AEIS Institutional Fund - Aktien Global

AEIS Institutional Fund - Aktien Schweiz

AEIS Institutional Fund - CHF Obli

AEIS Institutional Fund - Obli Global

AEK Bank 1826 Genossenschaft

aeris CAPITAL AG

AETERNUM Asset Mgt Ltd

AFAG Verwaltungs- und Treuhand AG

AFAG Verwaltungs- und Treuhand AG

AFB Anlagen AG

AFP Unilever Schweiz - WULP 1

AFSW GmbH

AG 2011 Trust

AG 2012 Trust

AG fuer Fondsverwaltung

AG fuer Organisation und Verwaltung

AG Insurance SA

AGA Finance AG

Agentur De Luca GmbH

AGFIF Intl AG

AGH SA

AGI Finance SA

AGI Finance SA

AGORA Capital SA

Agroprosperis Trade TG

Aguaverde Family Office SA

AIA Artha Invest AG

AIG Div. Strategies II Event Driven

AIG Div. Strategies II Long Short Equity

AIG Diversified Strategies Fund

AIG Diversified Strategies II CHF

AIG Diversified Strategies II EUR

AIG Diversified Strategies II GBP

AIG Diversified Strategies II USD

AIG Life Insurance Company Switzerland

AJ Capital Mgt SA

AKB Aktien Europa Top Sector

AKB Aktien Schweiz passiv

AKB Aktien USA Top Sector

AKB Immobilien Werte CHF

AKB Medium Term Bond CHF

AKB Obligationen CHF

AKB Portfoliofonds (EUR)

AKB Rohstoff Werte

AKB Short Term Bond CHF

AKB Unternehmensanleihen CHF

Akribia Vermoegensverwaltung AG

Akron Asset Mgt SA

AKTS & Partners SA

Alatus Capital SA

Alba Advisors SA

Alban Basel GmbH

Albatros Investment Partners AG

Albin Kistler AG

Albin Kistler Aktien Schweiz

Albin Kistler Aktien Welt

Albin Kistler Obligationen CHF

Albin Kistler Obligationen FW

Albion Capital Mgt ltd

Albion Capital Mgt ltd

Albula Advisors SA

Alchemy Capital AG

Aldrin Wealth Mgt SA

Alessana Trust

All Seasons Portfolio Fund

Alleedo Invest AG

Allevo Capital AG

Allevo Capital AG

Alley Group AG

Allfinanz Service AG

Alliance Boots Investments 3 GmbH

Allianz Global Investors (Schweiz) AG

Allianz Global Investors GmbH

Allianz Suisse Lebensversicherungs-G AG

Allianz Suisse Vorsorge

Allied Finance Services AG Zurich

Allied Finance Trust AG

Allied Finance Trust AG Zurich

All-In Finanz AG

Allina Family Office Sarl

Alltrust AG

Ally Financial Inc

Almina AG

Alpadis SA

Alpadis SA

Alpadis Trustees SA

Alpen Asset Mgt Trust

Alpenrose Wealth Mgt AG

Alpenrose Wealth Mgt Int AG

Alp-Gestion.ch SA

Alpha Associates AG

Alpha Capital AG

Alpha et Omega Global Investments sarl

Alpha Kappa Financial Services SA

Alpha Portfolio Mgt Sa

Alpha RHEINTAL Bank AG

Alphen Asset Mgt AG

Alphen Asset Mgt AG

Alphen Trust Company AG

Alphen Trust Company AG

Alpine Atlantic Global Asset Mgt

Alpine Select AG

DISCLOSURE: There are thousands of banks that provide depositor names, account numbers, amounts and other data per country which we cannot accommodate in this chapter; therefore, we encourage you to visit *www.irs.gov* or send me an email at *vicirsaudits@gmail.com* for the rest of the list.

CHAPTER

M

OTHER
RELEVANT
TOPICS

This chapter covers a variety of topics from foreign earned income exclusion to states with the highest and lowest income and sales tax rates. It ends with a law that's more pleasing to read than tax law – Murphy's Law.

FOREIGN EARNED INCOME EXCLUSION

Are you a U.S. citizen or resident working in a foreign country? Have you declared your foreign income? Have you even filed a tax return? Or are you hiding from the long and lovely arms of the IRS? Can the U.S. government reach you on the other side of the globe? Unfortunately, yes.
But is there a way not to pay federal income taxes on your earned income? Fortunately, yes!

Well, perhaps, there may not be a reason to hide. Perhaps, there's a reason to declare your foreign income and not pay federal income taxes. You see, there's this goodie called Foreign Earned Income Exclusion that allows you to earn $$$ and not pay federal income taxes. Too good to be true? Read on and learn.

1. You may exclude about $100,000 (up to $99,200 for 2014 and $100,800 for 2015) of foreign earned income. To qualify for the exclusion, your tax home must be in a foreign country and you must meet either one of the following tests:

    • **Bona fide residence test:** You must be a resident of a foreign country for an uninterrupted period covering a complete tax year. You must show intention to establish residence even if there are temporary absences for short trips back to the U.S.

    • **Physical presence test:** This test is met if you are physically present in a foreign country for at least 330 full days during any consecutive twelve-month period.

2. Both of these tests may be waived if you leave the foreign country on account of civil unrest or adverse conditions similar to the conditions in Iraq, Iran, Egypt, Afghanistan, Pakistan, or Ukraine.

3. In addition to the foreign income exclusion, you may also exclude housing amounts such as rent, fair rental value of housing provided by your employer and included in your income, insurance, rentals of furnishings, and utilities (but not telephone).

4. You may elect the exclusion by filing Form 2555 or 2555 EZ with your income tax return.

5. Is excluded Foreign Earned Income subject to self-employment tax? Yes, it is. Private Letter Ruling 8749061 states that foreign earned income is considered income from trade or business and is therefore subject to self-employment taxes (FICA and Medicare). Since then, IRS has issued regulations that income exempt from income tax are now subject to self-employment tax.

CAVEAT:
Some states, including California does not have a similar exclusion so you have to pay state income taxes on your foreign income. But here's a TIP: claim non-residency if you are abroad for 18 consecutive months and do not have an intention of returning to the State. Take advantage of a new Safe Harbor Rule that allows individuals domiciled in California but are outside the State on an employment-related contract, unless you have intangible income in excess of $200,000 in any taxable year when employments-related contract is in effect, or principal purpose of absence in California is to avoid tax.

TIPS:
If you were outside the United States on April 15, the due date is automatically extended to June 15 without the need to file an extension form.

STATES WITH THE LOWEST & HIGHEST INCOME TAX RATES

Individuals and businesses in all 50 states pay federal income tax. Residents in 41 states also pay state income tax while nine states have no state income taxes. Here are list of states with lowest and highest state income tax, sales tax, combination of both, as well as county, city, and school district taxes.

TOP TEN STATES WITH THE HIGHEST COMBINED TAX BURDEN FOR ALL STATE, COUNTY, AND CITY TAXES:

1. New York
2. New Jersey
3. Connecticut
4. California
5. Wisconsin
6. Rhode Island
7. Minnesota
8. Massachusetts
9. Maine
10. Pennsylvania

10 STATES WITH THE LOWEST COMBINED INCOME AND SALES TAX RATES:

1. New Hampshire
2. Alaska
3. South Dakota
4. Wyoming
5. Florida
6. Texas
7. Washington
8. Delaware
9. Montana
10. Colorado

10 STATES WITH THE HIGHEST COMBINED INCOME AND SALES TAX RATES:

1. New York
2. New Jersey
3. Connecticut
4. California
5. Wisconsin
6. Minnesota
7. Maryland
8. Rhode island
9. Vermont
10. Pennsylvania

STATES WITH NO INCOME TAX:

1. Alaska
2. Florida
3. Nevada
4. South Dakota
5. Texas
6. Washington
7. Wyoming.

FIVE STATES WITH LOWEST SALES TAX:

1. Alaska 1.69%
2. Oregon 0%
3. Delaware 0%
4. Montana 0%
5. New Hampshire 0%

FIVE STATES WITH HIGHEST SALES TAX:

1. Tennessee 9.45%
2. Arkansas 9.19%
3. Louisiana 8.89%
4. Washington 8.88%
5. Oklahoma 8.72%

TOP 10 STATES WITH THE LOWEST COMBINED TOTAL TAX BURDEN FOR ALL STATE, COUNTY, AND CITY TAXES:

1. Alaska
2. South Dakota
3. Tennessee
4. Louisiana
5. Wyoming
6. Texas
7. New Hampshire
8. Alabama
9. Nevada
10. South Carolina

10 STATES WITH HIGHEST INCOME TAX:

1. California 13.3%
2. Hawaii 11.0%
3. Oregon 9.9%
4. Minnesota 9.85%
5. Iowa 8.98%
6. New Jersey 8.97%
7. Vermont 8.95%
8. District of Columbia 8.95%
9. New York 8.82%
10. Maine 7.95%

MURPHY'S LAW 1 – A LIGHTER SIDE OF LIFE

How appropriate to end this chapter of relevant topics with an irrelevant topic—in Chapter 13. It's even more appropriate to move from an aggravating world of IRS audits to an even more aggravating idiom—Murphy's Law, courtesy of Captain Edward A. Murphy Jr. of the U.S. Air Force.

1. If something can go wrong, it will.............. at the worst possible time.

2. Friends come and go, but enemies accumulate.

3. Brain cells come and brain cells go, but fat cells live forever.

4. In any company, each worker rises to a level of incompetence. And remains there.

5. The fastest lane on the freeway screeches down to a halt as soon as you change lanes. Do not change lanes and your lane remains stuck.

6. That darn stuck elevator moves—as soon as you head for the stairs.

7. You will find it in the last place you look at, right at the bottom of the pile.

8. The item that has taken you so long to buy goes on sale right after you buy it.

9. A $3,000 computer will blow first to protect a 10¢ fuse.

10. If computer software rejects all bad inputs, an ingenious idiot will discover a way to accept it.

11. It works better if you plug it in.

12. When in doubt, mumble. When in trouble, delegate.

13. The lights at the end of the tunnel are the headlights of an oncoming train.

14. Beauty is skin deep, ugly goes *kilig* to (core of) the bones.

15. Anything good is either illegal or fattening.

16. If you circumvent what could go wrong in four different ways, a fifth way promptly develops.

17. If everything seems to be going well, you have obviously overlooked something.

18. Anything that begins well ends badly; anything that begins badly ....ends worse.

19. Left to themselves, things tend to go from bad to worse.

20. And after things have gone from bad to worse, the cycle repeats itself.

And if at first you don't succeed.............. **STOP!**

MURPHY'S LAW 2 – A SOMBER SIDE OF LIFE

While my newsletters usually focus on the serious subject of IRS audits, let's end this book with more somber versions of Murphy's Law:

LAW OF IRS AUDITS: If you are a rat pack who keeps lots of tax records, you get an IRS audit letter as soon as you discard your records. Keep your records and you won't receive a letter.

LAW OF DOCTOR APPOINTMENTS: If you don't feel well and make an appointment to see a doctor, you'll feel better by the time you get there. Don't make an appointment and you stay sick.

LAW OF THE ALIBI: If you tell the boss you were late for work because of a flat tire, you will have a flat tire the very next morning.

LAW OF CAFE: As soon as you sit down for a cup of hot coffee, your boss will ask you to do something which will last until the coffee is cold.

LAW OF RANDOM: If you dial a wrong number, you never get a busy signal and someone always answers.

LAW OF RESULT: When you try to prove to someone that a machine won't work, it will.

LAW OF PROBABILITY: The probability of being watched is directly proportional to the stupidity of your act.

LAW OF CLOSE ENCOUNTERS: The probability of meeting someone you know increases dramatically when you are with someone you don't want to be seen with.

LAW OF COMMERCIAL MARKETING: As soon as you find a product that you really like, they stop making it.

LAW OF GRAVITY: Any tool, nut, bolt, screw, when dropped, will roll to the least accessible corner.

LAW OF LOCKERS: If there are only two people in a changing room, they will have adjacent lockers.

LAW OF LOGICAL ARGUMENT: Anything is possible if you don't know what you are talking about.

LAW OF MECHANICAL REPAIR: After your hands become coated with grease, your nose will itch. And yes, you also have to pee.

LAW OF PHYSICAL APPEARANCE: If the clothes fit, they're ugly.

LAW OF BIOMECHANICS: The severity of the itch is inversely proportional to your reach.

LAW OF BATH: the probability of your telephone ringing is directly proportional to how deep your body is immersed in your bathtub.

LAW OF THEATER: At any event, the people whose seats are farthest from the aisle arrive last.

LAW OF OPTIMISM: Smile today – tomorrow will be worse!

SAMPLE IRS FORMS & NOTICES

This chapter presents images of IRS forms and letters including early versions of individual income tax Form 1040, audit bill, tax court petition, collection forms for Offer in Compromise and installment agreements, report of cash payments over $10,000 and report of foreign bank accounts and other financial assets.

1040 1913 EDITION

<table>
<tr><td>TO BE FILLED IN BY COLLECTOR.</td><td>Form 1040.</td><td>TO BE FILLED IN BY INTERNAL REVENUE BUREAU.</td></tr>
</table>

TO BE FILLED IN BY COLLECTOR.

List. No. ....

.... District of ....

Date received ....

Form 1040.

INCOME TAX.

THE PENALTY
FOR FAILURE TO HAVE THIS RETURN IN THE HANDS OF THE COLLECTOR OF INTERNAL REVENUE ON OR BEFORE MARCH 1 IS $20 TO $1,000.

(SEE INSTRUCTIONS ON PAGE 4.)

TO BE FILLED IN BY INTERNAL REVENUE BUREAU.

File No. ....

Assessment List ....

Page .... Line ....

UNITED STATES INTERNAL REVENUE.

RETURN OF ANNUAL NET INCOME OF INDIVIDUALS.

(As provided by Act of Congress, approved October 3, 1913.)

RETURN OF NET INCOME RECEIVED OR ACCRUED DURING THE YEAR ENDED DECEMBER 31, 191 ....*

(FOR THE YEAR 1913, FROM MARCH 1, TO DECEMBER 31.)

Filed by (or for) .... of ....

(Full name of individual.)   (Street and No.)

in the City, Town, or Post Office of .... State of ....

(Fill in pages 2 and 3 before making entries below.)

1. GROSS INCOME (see page 2, line 12) . . . . $ ....

2. GENERAL DEDUCTIONS (see page 3, line 7) . . . . . $ ....

3. NET INCOME . . . . $ ....

Deductions and exemptions allowed in computing income subject to the normal tax of 1 per cent.

4. Dividends and net earnings received or accrued, of corporations, etc., subject to like tax. (See page 2, line 11) . . . $ ....

5. Amount of income on which the normal tax has been deducted and withheld at the source. (See page 2, line 9, column A)

6. Specific exemption of $3,000 or $4,000, as the case may be. (See Instructions 3 and 19) . . . .

Total deductions and exemptions. (Items 4, 5, and 6) . . . . $ ....

7. TAXABLE INCOME on which the normal tax of 1 per cent is to be calculated. (See Instruction 3) . $ ....

8. When the net income shown above on line 3 exceeds $20,000, the additional tax thereon must be calculated as per schedule below:

						INCOME.			TAX.		
1	per cent on amount over $20,000 and not exceeding $50,000 . .	$				$					
2	"	"	50,000	"	"	75,000 .					
3	"	"	75,000	"	"	100,000 .					
4	"	"	100,000	"	"	250,000 .					
5	"	"	250,000	"	"	500,000 .					
6	"	"	500,000								

Total additional or super tax . . . . $ ....

Total normal tax (1 per cent of amount entered on line 7) . . $ ....

Total tax liability . . . . $ ....

2

GROSS INCOME.

This statement must show in the proper spaces the entire amount of gains, profits, and income received by or accrued to the individual from all sources during the year specified on page 1.

DESCRIPTION OF INCOME.	A. Amount of income on which tax has been deducted and withheld at the source.				B. Amount of income on which tax has NOT been deducted and withheld at the source.			
1. Total amount derived from salaries, wages, or compensation for personal service of whatever kind and in whatever form paid	$				$			
2. Total amount derived from professions, vocations, businesses, trade, commerce, or sales or dealings in property, whether real or personal, growing out of the ownership or use of interest in real or personal property, including bonds, stocks, etc.								
3. Total amount derived from rents and from interest on notes, mortgages, and securities (other than reported on lines 5 and 6)								
4. Total amount of gains and profits derived from partnership business, whether the same be divided and distributed or not								
5. Total amount of fixed and determinable annual gains, profits, and income derived from interest upon bonds and mortgages or deeds of trust, or other similar obligations of corporations, joint-stock companies or associations, and insurance companies, whether payable annually or at shorter or longer periods								
6. Total amount of income derived from coupons, checks, or bills of exchange for or in payment of interest upon bonds issued in *foreign countries* and upon *foreign mortgages* or like obligations (not payable in the United States), and also from coupons, checks, or bills of exchange for or in payment of any dividends upon the stock or interest upon the obligations of foreign corporations, associations, and insurance companies engaged in business in foreign countries								
7. Total amount of income received from fiduciaries								
8. Total amount of income derived from any source whatever, not specified or entered elsewhere on this page								
9. TOTALS								

NOTES.—Enter total of Column A on line 5 of first page.

10. AGGREGATE TOTALS OF COLUMNS A AND B	$				
11. Total amount of income derived from dividends on the stock or from the net earnings of corporations, joint-stock companies, associations, or insurance companies subject to like tax (To be entered on line 4 of first page.)	$				
12. TOTAL "Gross Income" (to be entered on line 1 of first page)	$				

1040 1913 EDITION

3

GENERAL DEDUCTIONS.

1. The amount of necessary expenses actually paid in carrying on business, but not including business expenses of partnerships, and not including personal, living, or family expenses .	$			
2. All interest paid within the year on personal indebtedness of taxpayer	....			
3. All national, State, county, school, and municipal taxes paid within the year (not including those assessed against local benefits)	....			
4. Losses actually sustained during the year incurred in trade or arising from fires, storms, or shipwreck, and not compensated for by insurance or otherwise	....			
5. Debts due which have been actually ascertained to be worthless and which have been charged off within the year	....			
6. Amount representing a reasonable allowance for the exhaustion, wear, and tear of property arising out of its use or employment in the business, not to exceed, in the case of mines, 5 per cent of the gross value at the mine of the output for the year for which the computation is made, but no deduction shall be made for any amount of expense of restoring property or making good the exhaustion thereof, for which an allowance is or has been made	....			
7. Total "GENERAL DEDUCTIONS" (to be entered on line 2 of first page)	....			

AFFIDAVIT TO BE EXECUTED BY INDIVIDUAL MAKING HIS OWN RETURN.

I solemnly swear (or affirm) that the foregoing return, to the best of my knowledge and belief, contains a true and complete statement of all gains, profits, and income received by or accrued to me during the year for which the return is made, and that I am entitled to all the deductions and exemptions entered or claimed therein, under the Federal Income-tax Law of October 3, 1913.

Sworn to and subscribed before me this ....

day of .... , 191   ....
                                                                        (Signature of individual.)

SEAL OF
OFFICER
TAKING
AFFIDAVIT.   ....

                   ....
                           (Official capacity.)

AFFIDAVIT TO BE EXECUTED BY DULY AUTHORIZED AGENT MAKING RETURN FOR INDIVIDUAL.

I solemnly swear (or affirm) that I have sufficient knowledge of the affairs and property of .... to enable me to make a full and complete return thereof, and that the foregoing return, to the best of my knowledge and belief, contains a true and complete statement of all gains, profits, and income received by or accrued to said individual during the year for which the return is made, and that the said individual is entitled, under the Federal Income-tax Law of October 3, 1913, to all the deductions and exemptions entered or claimed therein.

Sworn to and subscribed before me this ....

day of .... , 191   ....
                                                                        (Signature of agent.)

SEAL OF   ADDRESS   { ....
OFFICER   IN FULL
TAKING
AFFIDAVIT.   ....

                   ....
                           (Official capacity.)

[SEE INSTRUCTIONS ON BACK OF THIS PAGE.]

UNITED STATES TAX COURT
www.ustaxcourt.gov

FILE COPY

(FIRST)   (MIDDLE)   (LAST)

████████████████████

(PLEASE TYPE OR PRINT)   Petitioner(s)

v.   Docket No.

COMMISSIONER OF INTERNAL REVENUE,

                    Respondent

PETITION

1. Please check the appropriate box(es) to show which IRS NOTICE(s) you dispute:

☑ Notice of Deficiency   ☐ Notice of Determination Concerning Your Request for Relief
                                   From Joint and Several Liability. (If you requested relief from joint and
                                   several liability but the IRS has not made a determination, please see the
                                   Information for Persons Representing Themselves Before the U.S. Tax
                                   Court booklet or the Tax Court's Web site.)

☑ Notice of Determination
   Concerning Collection Action   ☐ Notice of Determination Concerning Worker Classification

2. Provide the date(s) the IRS issued the NOTICE(s) checked above and the city and State of the IRS office(s)
issuing the NOTICE(S): 9-17-2012 HOLTSVILLE, NY 11742-9002

3. Provide the year(s) of period(s) for which the NOTICE(S) was/were issued: _____ 2009 & 2010
4. SELECT ONE OF THE FOLLOWING:

   If you want your case conducted under small tax case procedures, check here: ☒   (CHECK
   If you want your case conducted under regular tax case procedures, check here: ☐   ONE BOX)

      NOTE: A decision in a "small tax case" cannot be appealed to a Court of Appeals by the taxpayer
      or the IRS. If you do not check either box, the Court will file your case as a regular tax case.

5. Explain why you disagree with the IRS determination in this case (please list each point separately):

SEE ATTACHED EXPLANATION #1

_____

_____

_____

_____

_____

_____

_____

                                                      T.C. FORM 2 (REV. 5/11)

IRS FORM 433-A COLLECTION INFORMATION STATEMENT FOR *WAGE EARNERS*

page 1

Form 433-A
(Rev. December 2012)

Department of the Treasury
Internal Revenue Service

Collection Information Statement for Wage Earners and Self-Employed Individuals

Wage Earners Complete Sections 1, 2, 3, 4, and 5 including the signature line on page 4. *Answer all questions or write N/A if the question is not applicable.*
Self-Employed Individuals Complete Sections 1, 3, 4, 5, 6 and 7 and the signature line on page 4. *Answer all questions or write N/A if the question is not applicable.*
For Additional Information, refer to Publication 1854, "How To Prepare a Collection Information Statement."
Include attachments if additional space is needed to respond completely to any question.

Name on Internal Revenue Service (IRS) Account	Social Security Number SSN on IRS Account	Employer Identification Number EIN

Section 1: Personal Information

1a Full Name of Taxpayer and Spouse (if applicable)	1c Home Phone ( )	1d Cell Phone ( )
1b Address (Street, City, State, ZIP code) (County of Residence)	1e Business Phone ( )	1f Business Cell Phone ( )
	2b Name, Age, and Relationship of dependent(s)	

2a Marital Status: ☐ Married ☐ Unmarried (Single, Divorced, Widowed)

	Social Security No. (SSN)	Date of Birth (mmddyyyy)	Driver's License Number and State
3a Taxpayer			
3b Spouse			

Section 2: Employment Information for Wage Earners

If you or your spouse have self-employment income instead of, or in addition to wage income, complete Business Information in Sections 6 and 7.

Taxpayer	Spouse
4a Taxpayer's Employer Name	5a Spouse's Employer Name
4b Address (Street, City, State, and ZIP code)	5b Address (Street, City, State, and ZIP code)

4c Work Telephone Number ( )	4d Does employer allow contact at work ☐ Yes ☐ No	5c Work Telephone Number ( )	5d Does employer allow contact at work ☐ Yes ☐ No
4e How long with this employer (years) (months)	4f Occupation	5e How long with this employer (years) (months)	5f Occupation
4g Number of withholding allowances claimed on Form W-4	4h Pay Period: ☐ Weekly ☐ Bi-weekly ☐ Monthly ☐ Other	5g Number of withholding allowances claimed on Form W-4	5h Pay Period: ☐ Weekly ☐ Bi-weekly ☐ Monthly ☐ Other

Section 3: Other Financial Information (Attach copies of applicable documentation)

6 Are you a party to a lawsuit (If yes, answer the following) ☐ Yes ☐ No

	Location of Filing	Represented by	Docket/Case No.
☐ Plaintiff ☐ Defendant			
Amount of Suit $	Possible Completion Date (mmddyyyy)	Subject of Suit	

7 Have you ever filed bankruptcy (If yes, answer the following) ☐ Yes ☐ No

Date Filed (mmddyyyy)	Date Dismissed (mmddyyyy)	Date Discharged (mmddyyyy)	Petition No.	Location Filed

8 In the past 10 years, have you lived outside of the U.S for 6 months or longer (If yes, answer the following) ☐ Yes ☐ No

Dates lived abroad: from (mmddyyyy)	To (mmddyyyy)

9a Are you the beneficiary of a trust, estate, or life insurance policy (If yes, answer the following) ☐ Yes ☐ No

Place where recorded:		EIN:
Name of the trust, estate, or policy	Anticipated amount to be received $	When will the amount be received

9b Are you a trustee, fiduciary, or contributor of a trust ☐ Yes ☐ No

Name of the trust:	EIN:

10 Do you have a safe deposit box (business or personal) (If yes, answer the following) ☐ Yes ☐ No

Location (Name, address and box number(s))	Contents	Value $

11 In the past 10 years, have you transferred any assets for less than their full value (If yes, answer the following) ☐ Yes ☐ No

List Asset(s)	Value at Time of Transfer $	Date Transferred (mmddyyyy)	To Whom or Where was it Transferred

www.irs.gov   Cat. No. 20312N   Form **433-A** (Rev. 12-2012)

IRS FORM 433-A COLLECTION INFORMATION STATEMENT FOR *WAGE EARNERS*

page 2

Form 433-A (Rev. 12-2012)   Page **2**

Section 4: Personal Asset Information for All Individuals

12 CASH ON HAND Include cash that is not in a bank   **Total Cash on Hand** $

PERSONAL BANK ACCOUNTS Include all checking, online and mobile (e.g., PayPal) accounts, money market accounts, savings accounts, and stored value cards (e.g., payroll cards, government benefit cards, etc.).

Type of Account	Full Name & Address (Street, City, State, ZIP code) of Bank, Savings & Loan, Credit Union, or Financial Institution	Account Number	Account Balance As of ___ mmddyyyy
13a			$
13b			$
13c			$

13d Total Cash (Add lines 13a through 13c, and amounts from any attachments) $

INVESTMENTS Include stocks, bonds, mutual funds, stock options, certificates of deposit, and retirement assets such as IRAs, Keogh, and 401(k) plans. Include all corporations, partnerships, limited liability companies, or other business entities in which you are an officer, director, owner, member, or otherwise have a financial interest.

Type of Investment or Financial Interest	Full Name & Address (Street, City, State, ZIP code) of Company	Current Value	Loan Balance (if applicable) As of ___ mmddyyyy	Equity Value minus Loan
14a	Phone	$	$	$
14b	Phone	$	$	$
14c	Phone	$	$	$

14d Total Equity (Add lines 14a through 14c and amounts from any attachments) $

AVAILABLE CREDIT Include all lines of credit and bank issued credit cards. Full Name & Address (Street, City, State, ZIP code) of Credit Institution	Credit Limit	Amount Owed As of ___ mmddyyyy	Available Credit As of ___ mmddyyyy
15a Acct. No	$	$	$
15b Acct. No	$	$	$

15c Total Available Credit (Add lines 15a, 15b and amounts from any attachments) $

16a LIFE INSURANCE Do you own or have any interest in any life insurance policies with cash value (Term Life insurance does not have a cash value)

☐ Yes   ☐ No   If yes, complete blocks 16b through 16f for each policy.

16b	Name and Address of Insurance Company(ies):			
16c	Policy Number(s)			
16d	Owner of Policy			
16e	Current Cash Value	$	$	$
16f	Outstanding Loan Balance	$	$	$

16g Total Available Cash (Subtract amounts on line 16f from line 16e and include amounts from any attachments) $

Form **433-A** (Rev. 12-2012)

IRS FORM 433-A COLLECTION INFORMATION STATEMENT FOR *WAGE EARNERS*

page 3

Form 433-A (Rev. 12-2012)   Page **3**

REAL PROPERTY Include all real property owned or being purchased

	Purchase Date (mmddyyyy)	Current Fair Market Value (FMV)	Current Loan Balance	Amount of Monthly Payment	Date of Final Payment (mmddyyyy)	**Equity** FMV Minus Loan
17a Property Description		$	$	$		$
Location (Street, City, State, ZIP code) and County			Lender/Contract Holder Name, Address (Street, City, State, ZIP code), and Phone			
				Phone		
17b Property Description		$	$	$		$
Location (Street, City, State, ZIP code) and County			Lender/Contract Holder Name, Address (Street, City, State, ZIP code), and Phone			
				Phone		

17c Total Equity (Add lines 17a, 17b and amounts from any attachments) $

PERSONAL VEHICLES LEASED AND PURCHASED Include boats, RVs, motorcycles, all-terrain and off-road vehicles, trailers, etc.

Description (Year, Mileage, Make/Model, Tag Number, Vehicle Identification Number)		Purchase/ Lease Date (mmddyyyy)	Current Fair Market Value (FMV)	Current Loan Balance	Amount of Monthly Payment	Date of Final Payment (mmddyyyy)	**Equity** FMV Minus Loan
18a Year	Make/Model		$	$	$		$
Mileage	License/Tag Number	Lender/Lessor Name, Address (Street, City, State, ZIP code), and Phone					
Vehicle Identification Number					Phone		
18b Year	Make/Model		$	$	$		$
Mileage	License/Tag Number	Lender/Lessor Name, Address (Street, City, State, ZIP code), and Phone					
Vehicle Identification Number					Phone		

18c Total Equity (Add lines 18a, 18b and amounts from any attachments) $

PERSONAL ASSETS Include all furniture, personal effects, artwork, jewelry, collections (coins, guns, etc.), antiques or other assets. Include intangible assets such as licenses, domain names, patents, copyrights, mining claims, etc.

	Purchase/ Lease Date (mmddyyyy)	Current Fair Market Value (FMV)	Current Loan Balance	Amount of Monthly Payment	Date of Final Payment (mmddyyyy)	**Equity** FMV Minus Loan
19a Property Description		$	$	$		$
Location (Street, City, State, ZIP code) and County			Lender/Lessor Name, Address (Street, City, State, ZIP code), and Phone			
				Phone		
19b Property Description		$	$	$		$
Location (Street, City, State, ZIP code) and County			Lender/Lessor Name, Address (Street, City, State, ZIP code), and Phone			
				Phone		

19c Total Equity (Add lines 19a, 19b and amounts from any attachments) $

Form **433-A** (Rev. 12-2012)

IRS FORM 433-A COLLECTION INFORMATION STATEMENT FOR *WAGE EARNERS*

page 4

Form 433-A (Rev. 12-2012)   Page **4**

If you are self-employed, sections 6 and 7 must be completed before continuing.

Section 5: Monthly Income and Expenses

Monthly Income/Expense Statement *(For additional information, refer to Publication 1854.)*

Total Income		Total Living Expenses		IRS USE ONLY
Source	Gross Monthly	Expense Items [6]	Actual Monthly	Allowable Expenses
20 Wages (Taxpayer) [1]	$	35 Food, Clothing and Misc. [7]	$	
21 Wages (Spouse) [1]	$	36 Housing and Utilities [8]	$	
22 Interest - Dividends	$	37 Vehicle Ownership Costs [9]	$	
23 Net Business Income [2]	$	38 Vehicle Operating Costs [10]	$	
24 Net Rental Income [3]	$	39 Public Transportation [11]	$	
25 Distributions (K-1, IRA, etc.) [4]	$	40 Health Insurance	$	
26 Pension (Taxpayer)	$	41 Out of Pocket Health Care Costs [12]	$	
27 Pension (Spouse)	$	42 Court Ordered Payments	$	
28 Social Security (Taxpayer)	$	43 Child/Dependent Care	$	
29 Social Security (Spouse)	$	44 Life Insurance	$	
30 Child Support	$	45 Current year taxes (Income/FICA) [13]	$	
31 Alimony	$	46 Secured Debts (Attach list)	$	
Other Income (Specify below) [5]		47 Delinquent State or Local Taxes	$	
32	$	48 Other Expenses (Attach list)	$	
33	$	49 Total Living Expenses (add lines 35-48)	$	
34 Total Income (add lines 20-33)	$	50 Net difference (Line 34 minus 49)	$	

1 **Wages, salaries, pensions, and social security:** Enter gross monthly wages and/or salaries. Do not deduct tax withholding or allotments taken out of pay, such as insurance payments, credit union deductions, car payments, etc. To calculate the gross monthly wages and/or salaries:

If paid weekly - multiply weekly gross wages by 4.3. Example: $425.89 x 4.3 = $1,831.33

If paid biweekly (every 2 weeks) - multiply biweekly gross wages by 2.17. Example: $972.45 x 2.17 = $2,110.22

If paid semimonthly (twice each month) - multiply semimonthly gross wages by 2. Example: $856.23 x 2 = $1,712.46

2 **Net Income from Business:** Enter monthly net business income. This is the amount earned after ordinary and necessary monthly business expenses are paid. **This figure is the amount from page 6, line 89.** If the net business income is a loss, enter "0". Do not enter a negative number. If this amount is more or less than previous years, attach an explanation.

3 **Net Rental Income:** Enter monthly net rental income. This is the amount earned after ordinary and necessary monthly rental expenses are paid. Do not include deductions for depreciation or depletion. If the net rental income is a loss, enter "0." Do not enter a negative number.

4 **Distributions:** Enter the total distributions from partnerships and subchapter S corporations reported on Schedule K-1, and from limited liability companies reported on Form 1040, Schedule C, D or E. Enter total distributions from IRAs if not included under pension income.

5 **Other Income:** Include agricultural subsidies, unemployment compensation, gambling income, oil credits, rent subsidies, etc.

6 **Expenses not generally allowed:** We generally do not allow tuition for private schools, public or private college expenses, charitable contributions, voluntary retirement contributions or payments on unsecured debts. However, we may allow the expenses if proven that they are necessary for the health and welfare of the individual or family or the production of income. See Publication 1854 for exceptions.

7 **Food, Clothing and Miscellaneous:** Total of food, clothing, housekeeping supplies, and personal care products for one month. The miscellaneous allowance is for expenses incurred that are not included in any other allowable living expense items. Examples are credit card payments, bank fees and charges, reading material, and school supplies.

8 **Housing and Utilities:** For principal residence: Total of rent or mortgage payment. Add the average monthly expenses for the following: property taxes, homeowner's or renter's insurance, maintenance, dues, fees, and utilities. Utilities include gas, electricity, water, fuel, oil, other fuels, trash collection, telephone, cell phone, cable television and internet services.

9 **Vehicle Ownership Costs:** Total of monthly lease or purchase/loan payments.

10 **Vehicle Operating Costs:** Total of maintenance, repairs, insurance, fuel, registrations, licenses, inspections, parking, and tolls for one month.

11 **Public Transportation:** Total of monthly fares for mass transit (e.g., bus, train, ferry, taxi, etc.)

12 **Out of Pocket Health Care Costs:** Monthly total of medical services, prescription drugs and medical supplies (e.g., eyeglasses, hearing aids, etc.)

13 **Current Year Taxes:** Include state and Federal taxes withheld from salary or wages, or paid as estimated taxes.

Certification: *Under penalties of perjury, I declare that to the best of my knowledge and belief this statement of assets, liabilities, and other information is true, correct, and complete.*

Taxpayer's Signature	Spouse's signature	Date

After we review the completed Form 433-A, you may be asked to provide verification for the assets, encumbrances, income and expenses reported. Documentation may include previously filed income tax returns, pay statements, self-employment records, bank and investment statements, loan statements, bills or statements for recurring expenses, etc.

IRS USE ONLY *(Notes)*

Form **433-A** (Rev. 12-2012)

IRS FORM 433-A COLLECTION INFORMATION STATEMENT FOR *WAGE EARNERS*

page 5

Form 433-A (Rev. 12-2012)   Page **5**

Sections 6 and 7 must be completed only if you are SELF-EMPLOYED.

Section 6: Business Information

51	Is the business a sole proprietorship *(filing Schedule C)*	☐ **Yes**, Continue with Sections 6 and 7.	☐ **No**, Complete Form 433-B.

All other business entities, including limited liability companies, partnerships or corporations, must complete Form 433-B.

52 Business Name & Address *(if different than 1b)*

53 Employer Identification Number	54 Type of Business	55 Is the business a Federal Contractor ☐ Yes ☐ No
56 Business Website (web address)	**57** Total Number of Employees	**58** Average Gross Monthly Payroll
59 Frequency of Tax Deposits	**60** Does the business engage in e-Commerce *(Internet sales)* If yes, complete lines 61a and 61b ☐ Yes ☐ No	

PAYMENT PROCESSOR *(e.g., PayPal, Authorize.net, Google Checkout, etc.)* Name & Address *(Street, City, State, ZIP code)*	Payment Processor Account Number
61a	
61b	

CREDIT CARDS ACCEPTED BY THE BUSINESS

	Credit Card	Merchant Account Number	Issuing Bank Name & Address *(Street, City, State, ZIP code)*
62a			
62b			
62c			

63	**BUSINESS CASH ON HAND** Include cash that is not in a bank.	**Total Cash on Hand** $

BUSINESS BANK ACCOUNTS Include checking accounts, online and mobile *(e.g., PayPal)* accounts, money market accounts, savings accounts, and stored value cards *(e.g., payroll cards, government benefit cards, etc.)*. Report Personal Accounts in Section 4.

Type of Account	Full name & Address *(Street, City, State, ZIP code)* of Bank, Savings & Loan, Credit Union or Financial Institution.	Account Number	Account Balance As of _____ *mmddyyyy*
64a			$
64b			$
64c Total Cash in Banks *(Add lines 64a, 64b and amounts from any attachments)*			$

ACCOUNTS/NOTES RECEIVABLE Include e-payment accounts receivable and factoring companies, and any bartering or online auction accounts. *(List all contracts separately, including contracts awarded, but not started.)* **Include Federal, state and local government grants and contracts.**

Accounts/Notes Receivable & Address *(Street, City, State, ZIP code)*	Status *(e.g., age, factored, other)*	Date Due *(mmddyyyy)*	Invoice Number or Government Grant or Contract Number	Amount Due
65a				$
65b				$
65c				$
65d				$
65e				$
65f Total Outstanding Balance *(Add lines 65a through 65e and amounts from any attachments)*				$

Form **433-A** (Rev. 12-2012)

page 6

Form 433-A (Rev. 12-2012)   Page **6**

BUSINESS ASSETS Include all tools, books, machinery, equipment, inventory or other assets used in trade or business. Include a list and show the value of all intangible assets such as licenses, patents, domain names, copyrights, trademarks, mining claims, etc.

	Purchase/ Lease Date (mmddyyyy)	Current Fair Market Value (FMV)	Current Loan Balance	Amount of Monthly Payment	Date of Final Payment (mmddyyyy)	Equity FMV Minus Loan
66a Property Description		$	$	$		$
Location (Street, City, State, ZIP code) and Country			Lender/Lessor/Landlord Name, Address (Street, City, State, ZIP code), and Phone			
			Phone			
66b Property Description		$	$	$		$
Location (Street, City, State, ZIP code) and Country			Lender/Lessor/Landlord Name, Address (Street, City, State, ZIP code), and Phone			
			Phone			

66c Total Equity (Add lines 66a, 66b and amounts from any attachments) $

Section 7 should be completed only if you are SELF-EMPLOYED

Section 7: Sole Proprietorship Information *(lines 67 through 87 should reconcile with business Profit and Loss Statement)*

Accounting Method Used: ☐ Cash   ☐ Accrual

Use the prior 3, 6, 9 or 12 month period to determine your typical business income and expenses.

Income and Expenses during the period *(mmddyyyy)* _____ to *(mmddyyyy)* _____

Provide a breakdown below of your average monthly income and expenses, based on the period of time used above.

Total Monthly Business Income		Total Monthly Business Expenses (Use attachments as needed)	
Source	Gross Monthly	Expense Items	Actual Monthly
67 Gross Receipts	$	**77** Materials Purchased [1]	$
68 Gross Rental Income	$	**78** Inventory Purchased [2]	$
69 Interest	$	**79** Gross Wages & Salaries	$
70 Dividends	$	**80** Rent	$
71 Cash Receipts not included in lines 67-70	$	**81** Supplies [3]	$
Other Income (Specify below)		**82** Utilities/Telephone [4]	$
72 _____	$	**83** Vehicle Gasoline/Oil	$
73 _____	$	**84** Repairs & Maintenance	$
74 _____	$	**85** Insurance	$
75 _____	$	**86** Current Taxes [5]	$
		87 Other Expenses, including installment payments (Specify)	$
76 Total Income (Add lines 67 through 75)	$	**88 Total Expenses** (Add lines 77 through 87)	$
		89 Net Business Income (Line 76 minus 88) [6]	$

Enter the monthly net income amount from line 89 on line 23, section 5. If line 89 is a loss, enter "0" on line 23, section 5.
Self-employed taxpayers must return to page 4 to sign the certification.

1 Materials Purchased: Materials are items directly related to the production of a product or service.

2 Inventory Purchased: Goods bought for resale.

3 Supplies: Supplies are items used in the business that are consumed or used up within one year. This could be the cost of books, office supplies, professional equipment, etc.

4 Utilities/Telephone: Utilities include gas, electricity, water, oil, other fuels, trash collection, telephone, cell phone and business internet.

5 Current Taxes: Real estate, excise, franchise, occupational, personal property, sales and employer's portion of employment taxes.

6 Net Business Income: Net profit from Form 1040, Schedule C may be used if duplicated deductions are eliminated (e.g., expenses for business use of home already included in housing and utility expenses on page 4). Deductions for depreciation and depletion on Schedule C are not cash expenses and must be added back to the net income figure. In addition, interest cannot be deducted if it is already included in any other installment payments allowed.

IRS USE ONLY *(Notes)*

IRS FORM 433-B COLLECTION INFORMATION STATEMENT FOR *BUSINESS*

page 1

Form 433-B

(Rev. December 2012)

Department of the Treasury
Internal Revenue Service

Collection Information Statement for Businesses

Note: *Complete all entry spaces with the current data available or "N/A" (not applicable). Failure to complete all entry spaces may result in rejection of your request or significant delay in account resolution. Include attachments if additional space is needed to respond completely to any question.*

Section 1: Business Information

1a	Business Name		2a	Employer Identification No. (EIN)

2b Type of entity *(Check appropriate box below)*
☐ Partnership ☐ Corporation ☐ Other
☐ Limited Liability Company (LLC) classified as a corporation
☐ Other LLC - Include number of members

1b Business Street Address

Mailing Address
City _____ State _____ ZIP _____
1c County

2c Date Incorporated/Established
mmddyyyy

1d Business Telephone ( )
1e Type of Business

3a Number of Employees
3b Monthly Gross Payroll
3c Frequency of Tax Deposits

1f Business Website (web address)

3d Is the business enrolled in Electronic Federal Tax Payment System (EFTPS)   ☐ Yes   ☐ No

4 Does the business engage in e-Commerce *(Internet sales)* If yes, complete 5a and 5b.   ☐ Yes   ☐ No

PAYMENT PROCESSOR *(e.g., PayPal, Authorize.net, Google Checkout, etc.)* Name and Address *(Street, City, State, ZIP code)*	Payment Processor Account Number
5a	
5b	

CREDIT CARDS ACCEPTED BY THE BUSINESS

Type of Credit Card *(e.g., Visa, Mastercard, etc.)*	Merchant Account Number	Issuing Bank Name and Address *(Street, City, State, ZIP code)*
6a		Phone
6b		Phone
6c		Phone

Section 2: Business Personnel and Contacts

PARTNERS, OFFICERS, LLC MEMBERS, MAJOR SHAREHOLDERS, ETC.

7a Full Name		Social Security Number
Title		Home Telephone ( )
Home Address		Work/Cell Phone ( )
City _____ State _____ ZIP		Ownership Percentage & Shares or Interest
Responsible for Depositing Payroll Taxes ☐ Yes ☐ No		Annual Salary/Draw

7b Full Name		Social Security Number
Title		Home Telephone ( )
Home Address		Work/Cell Phone ( )
City _____ State _____ ZIP		Ownership Percentage & Shares or Interest
Responsible for Depositing Payroll Taxes ☐ Yes ☐ No		Annual Salary/Draw

7c Full Name		Social Security Number
Title		Home Telephone ( )
Home Address		Work/Cell Phone ( )
City _____ State _____ ZIP		Ownership Percentage & Shares or Interest
Responsible for Depositing Payroll Taxes ☐ Yes ☐ No		Annual Salary/Draw

7d Full Name		Social Security Number
Title		Home Telephone ( )
Home Address		Work/Cell Phone ( )
City _____ State _____ ZIP		Ownership Percentage & Shares or Interest
Responsible for Depositing Payroll Taxes ☐ Yes ☐ No		Annual Salary/Draw

www.irs.gov   Cat. No. 16649P   Form **433-B** (Rev. 12-2012)

page 2

Form 433-B (Rev. 12-2012)   Page **2**

Section 3: Other Financial Information *(Attach copies of all applicable documents)*

8 Does the business use a Payroll Service Provider or Reporting Agent *(If yes, answer the following)*   ☐ Yes ☐ No

Name and Address (Street, City, State, ZIP code)	Effective dates *(mmddyyyy)*

9 Is the business a party to a lawsuit *(If yes, answer the following)*   ☐ Yes ☐ No

☐ Plaintiff ☐ Defendant	Location of Filing	Represented by	Docket/Case No.
Amount of Suit	Possible Completion Date *(mmddyyyy)*	Subject of Suit	
$			

10 Has the business ever filed bankruptcy *(If yes, answer the following)*   ☐ Yes ☐ No

Date Filed *(mmddyyyy)*	Date Dismissed *(mmddyyyy)*	Date Discharged *(mmddyyyy)*	Petition No.	District of Filing

11 Do any related parties (e.g., officers, partners, employees) have outstanding amounts owed to the business *(If yes, answer the following)*   ☐ Yes ☐ No

Name and Address (Street, City, State, ZIP code)	Date of Loan	Current Balance As of _____ mmddyyyy	Payment Date	Payment Amount
		$		$

12 Have any assets been transferred, in the last 10 years, from this business for less than full value *(If yes, answer the following)*   ☐ Yes ☐ No

List Asset	Value at Time of Transfer	Date Transferred *(mmddyyyy)*	To Whom or Where Transferred
	$		

13 Does this business have other business affiliations (e.g., **subsidiary or parent companies**) *(If yes, answer the following)*   ☐ Yes ☐ No

Related Business Name and Address (Street, City, State, ZIP code)	Related Business EIN:

14 Any increase/decrease in income anticipated *(If yes, answer the following)*   ☐ Yes ☐ No

Explain *(Use attachment if needed)*	How much will it increase/decrease	When will it increase/decrease
	$	

15 Is the business a Federal Government Contractor *(Include Federal Government contracts in #18, Accounts/Notes Receivable)*   ☐ Yes ☐ No

Section 4: Business Asset and Liability Information

16a **CASH ON HAND** *Include cash that is not in the bank*   **Total Cash on Hand** $ _____

16b Is there a safe on the business premises   ☐ Yes ☐ No   Contents _____

BUSINESS BANK ACOUNTS Include online and mobile accounts (e.g., PayPal), money market accounts, savings accounts, checking accounts and stored value cards (e.g., payroll cards, government benefit cards, etc.)
List safe deposit boxes including location, box number and value of contents. Attach list of contents.

Type of Account	Full Name and Address (Street, City, State, ZIP code) of Bank, Savings & Loan, Credit Union or Financial Institution	Account Number	Account Balance As of _____ mmddyyyy
17a			$
17b			$
17c			$
17d Total Cash in Banks *(Add lines 17a through 17c and amounts from any attachments)*			$

Form **433-B** (Rev. 12-2012)

IRS FORM 433-B COLLECTION INFORMATION STATEMENT FOR *BUSINESS*

page 3

Form 433-B (Rev. 12-2012)   Page **3**

ACCOUNTS/NOTES RECEIVABLE Include e-payment accounts receivable and factoring companies, and any bartering or online auction accounts. *(List all contracts separately including contracts awarded, but not started).* **Include Federal, state and local government grants and contracts.**

Name & Address *(Street, City, State, ZIP code)*	Status *(e.g., age, factored, other)*	Date Due *(mmddyyyy)*	Invoice Number or Government Grant or Contract Number	Amount Due
18a Contact Name Phone				$
18b Contact Name Phone				$
18c Contact Name Phone				$
18d Contact Name Phone				$
18e Contact Name Phone				$

18f Outstanding Balance *(Add lines 18a through 18e and amounts from any attachments)* $

INVESTMENTS List all investment assets below. Include stocks, bonds, mutual funds, stock options, certificates of deposit and commodities *(e.g., gold, silver, copper, etc.)*.

Name of Company & Address *(Street, City, State, ZIP code)*	Used as collateral on loan	Current Value	Loan Balance	Equity Value Minus Loan
19a Phone	☐ Yes ☐ No	$	$	$
19b Phone	☐ Yes ☐ No	$	$	$

19c Total Investments *(Add lines 19a, 19b, and amounts from any attachments)* $

AVAILABLE CREDIT Include all lines of credit and credit cards.

Full Name & Address *(Street, City, State, ZIP code)*	Credit Limit	Amount Owed As of ___ mmddyyyy	Available Credit As of ___ mmddyyyy
20a Account No.	$	$	$
20b Account No.	$	$	$

20c Total Credit Available *(Add lines 20a, 20b, and amounts from any attachments)* $

Form **433-B** (Rev. 12-2012)

IRS FORM 433-B COLLECTION INFORMATION STATEMENT FOR *BUSINESS*

page 4

Form 433-B (Rev. 12-2012)   Page **4**

REAL PROPERTY Include all real property and land contracts the business owns/leases/rents.

	Purchase/ Lease Date (mmddyyyy)	Current Fair Market Value (FMV)	Current Loan Balance	Amount of Monthly Payment	Date of Final Payment (mmddyyyy)	Equity FMV Minus Loan

21a Property Description
Location (Street, City, State, ZIP code) and County — Lender/Lessor/Landlord Name, Address, (Street, City, State, ZIP code) and Phone — Phone

21b Property Description
Location (Street, City, State, ZIP code) and County — Lender/Lessor/Landlord Name, Address, (Street, City, State, ZIP code) and Phone — Phone

21c Property Description
Location (Street, City, State, ZIP code) and County — Lender/Lessor/Landlord Name, Address, (Street, City, State, ZIP code) and Phone — Phone

21d Property Description
Location (Street, City, State, ZIP code) and County — Lender/Lessor/Landlord Name, Address, (Street, City, State, ZIP code) and Phone — Phone

21e Total Equity (Add lines 21a through 21d and amounts from any attachments)

VEHICLES, LEASED AND PURCHASED Include boats, RVs, motorcycles, all-terrain and off-road vehicles, trailers, mobile homes, etc.

	Purchase/ Lease Date (mmddyyyy)	Current Fair Market Value (FMV)	Current Loan Balance	Amount of Monthly Payment	Date of Final Payment (mmddyyyy)	Equity FMV Minus Loan

22a Year / Make/Model
Mileage / License/Tag Number — Lender/Lessor Name, Address, (Street, City, State, ZIP code) and Phone
Vehicle Identification Number (VIN) — Phone

22b Year / Make/Model
Mileage / License/Tag Number — Lender/Lessor Name, Address, (Street, City, State, ZIP code) and Phone
Vehicle Identification Number (VIN) — Phone

22c Year / Make/Model
Mileage / License/Tag Number — Lender/Lessor Name, Address, (Street, City, State, ZIP code) and Phone
Vehicle Identification Number (VIN) — Phone

22d Year / Make/Model
Mileage / License/Tag Number — Lender/Lessor Name, Address, (Street, City, State, ZIP code) and Phone
Vehicle Identification Number (VIN) — Phone

22e Total Equity (Add lines 22a through 22d and amounts from any attachments)

Form **433-B** (Rev. 12-2012)

IRS FORM 433-B COLLECTION INFORMATION STATEMENT FOR *BUSINESS*

page 5

Form 433-B (Rev. 12-2012)   Page **5**

BUSINESS EQUIPMENT AND INTANGIBLE ASSETS Include all machinery, equipment, merchandise inventory, and other assets in 23a through 23d. List intangible assets in 23e through 23g (licenses, patents, logos, domain names, trademarks, copyrights, software, mining claims, goodwill and trade secrets.)

	Purchase/ Lease Date (mmddyyyy)	Current Fair Market Value (FMV)	Current Loan Balance	Amount of Monthly Payment	Date of Final Payment (mmddyyyy)	**Equity** FMV Minus Loan
23a Asset Description		$	$	$		$
Location of asset (Street, City, State, ZIP code) and County			Lender/Lessor Name, Address, (Street, City, State, ZIP code) and Phone			
				Phone		
23b Asset Description		$	$	$		$
Location of asset (Street, City, State, ZIP code) and County			Lender/Lessor Name, Address, (Street, City, State, ZIP code) and Phone			
				Phone		
23c Asset Description		$	$	$		$
Location of asset (Street, City, State, ZIP code) and County			Lender/Lessor Name, Address, (Street, City, State, ZIP code) and Phone			
				Phone		
23d Asset Description		$	$	$		$
Location of asset (Street, City, State, ZIP code) and County			Lender/Lessor Name, Address, (Street, City, State, ZIP code) and Phone			
				Phone		
23e Intangible Asset Description						$
23f Intangible Asset Description						$
23g Intangible Asset Description						$

23h **Total Equity** *(Add lines 23a through 23g and amounts from any attachments)* $

BUSINESS LIABILITIES Include notes and judgements not listed previously on this form.

Business Liabilities	Secured/ Unsecured	Date Pledged (mmddyyyy)	Balance Owed	Date of Final Payment (mmddyyyy)	Payment Amount
24a Description:	☐ Secured ☐ Unsecured		$		$
Name Street Address City/State/ZIP code				Phone	
24b Description:	☐ Secured ☐ Unsecured		$		$
Name Street Address City/State/ZIP code				Phone	

24c **Total Payments** *(Add lines 24a and 24b and amounts from any attachments)* $

Form **433-B** (Rev. 12-2012)

IRS FORM 433-B COLLECTION INFORMATION STATEMENT FOR *BUSINESS*

page 6

Form 433-B (Rev. 12-2012)   Page **6**

Section 5: Monthly Income/Expenses Statement for Business

Accounting Method Used: ☐ Cash ☐ Accrual

Use the prior 3, 6, 9 or 12 month period to determine your typical business income and expenses.

Income and Expenses during the period *(mmddyyyy)* _____ to *(mmddyyyy)* _____

Provide a breakdown below of your average monthly income and expenses, based on the period of time used above.

Total Monthly Business Income		Total Monthly Business Expenses	
Income Source	Gross Monthly	Expense items	Actual Monthly
25 Gross Receipts from Sales/Services	$	36 Materials Purchased [1]	$
26 Gross Rental Income	$	37 Inventory Purchased [2]	$
27 Interest Income	$	38 Gross Wages & Salaries	$
28 Dividends	$	39 Rent	$
29 Cash Receipts (Not included in lines 25-28)	$	40 Supplies [3]	$
Other Income (Specify below)		41 Utilities/Telephone [4]	$
30	$	42 Vehicle Gasoline/Oil	$
31	$	43 Repairs & Maintenance	$
32	$	44 Insurance	$
33	$	45 Current Taxes [5]	$
34	$	46 Other Expenses (Specify)	$
35 **Total Income** (Add lines 25 through 34)	$	47 IRS Use Only-Allowable Installment Payments	$
		48 **Total Expenses** (Add lines 36 through 47)	$
		49 **Net Income** (Line 35 minus Line 48)	$

1 **Materials Purchased:** Materials are items directly related to the production of a product or service.

2 **Inventory Purchased:** Goods bought for resale.

3 **Supplies:** Supplies are items used to conduct business and are consumed or used up within one year. This could be the cost of books, office supplies, professional equipment, etc.

4 **Utilities/Telephone:** Utilities include gas, electricity, water, oil, other fuels, trash collection, telephone, cell phone and business internet.

5 **Current Taxes:** Real estate, state, and local income tax, excise, franchise, occupational, personal property, sales and the employer's portion of employment taxes.

Certification: *Under penalties of perjury, I declare that to the best of my knowledge and belief this statement of assets, liabilities, and other information is true, correct, and complete.*

Signature	Title	Date

Print Name of Officer, Partner or LLC Member

After we review the completed Form 433-B, you may be asked to provide verification for the assets, encumbrances, income and expenses reported. Documentation may include previously filed income tax returns, profit and loss statements, bank and investment statements, loan statements, financing statements, bills or statements for recurring expenses, etc.

IRS USE ONLY *(Notes)*

Form **433-B** (Rev. 12-2012)

IRS FORM 433-D
INSTALLMENT AGREEMENT

Form **433-D** (Rev. January 2015)	Department of the Treasury - Internal Revenue Service **Installment Agreement** *(See Instructions on the back of this page)*

Name and address of taxpayer(s)

Social Security or Employer Identification Number (SSN/EIN)
(Taxpayer) | *(Spouse)*

Your telephone numbers *(including area code)*
(Home) | *(Work, cell or business)*

For assistance, call: 1-800-829-0115 (Business), or
1-800-829-8374 (Individual – Self-Employed/Business Owners), or
1-800-829-0922 (Individuals – Wage Earners)

☐ Submit a new Form W-4 to your employer to increase your withholding.

Or write _____
(City, State, and ZIP Code)

Employer *(Name, address, and telephone number)*

Financial Institution *(Name and address)*

Kinds of taxes *(Form numbers)*	Tax periods	Amount owed as of _____ $

I / We agree to pay the federal taxes shown above, PLUS PENALTIES AND INTEREST PROVIDED BY LAW, as follows

$ _____ on _____ and $ _____ on the _____ of each month thereafter

I / We also agree to increase or decrease the above installment payments as follows:

Date of increase (or decrease)	Amount of increase (or decrease)	New installment payment amount

The terms of this agreement are provided on the back of this page. Please review them thoroughly.

☐ Please initial this box after you've reviewed all terms and any additional conditions.

Additional Conditions / Terms *(To be completed by IRS)*

Note: Internal Revenue Service employees may contact third parties in order to process and maintain this agreement.

DIRECT DEBIT — Attach a voided check or complete this part only if you choose to make payments by direct debit. Read the instructions on the back of this page.

a. Routing number

b. Account number

I authorize the U.S. Treasury and its designated Financial Agent to initiate a monthly ACH debit (electronic withdrawal) entry to the financial institution account indicated for payments of my federal taxes owed, and the financial institution to debit the entry to this account. This authorization is to remain in full force and effect until I notify the Internal Revenue Service to terminate the authorization. To revoke payment, I must contact the Internal Revenue Service at the applicable toll free number listed above no later than 14 business days prior to the payment (settlement) date. I also authorize the financial institutions involved in the processing of the electronic payments of taxes to receive confidential information necessary to answer inquiries and resolve issues related to the payments.

Your signature	Title (if Corporate Officer or Partner)	Date
Spouse's signature *(if a joint liability)*		Date

FOR IRS USE ONLY

AGREEMENT LOCATOR NUMBER: ▢ ▢ ▢ ▢

Check the appropriate boxes:

☐ RSI "1" no further review ☐ AI "0" Not a PPIA
☐ RSI "5" PPIA IMF 2 year review ☐ AI "1" Field Asset PPIA
☐ RSI "6" PPIA BMF 2 year review ☐ AI "2" All other PPIAs
Agreement Review Cycle ▢▢▢▢▢▢ Earliest CSED _____
☐ Check box if pre-assessed modules included
Originator's ID number _____ Originator Code _____
Name _____ Title _____

A NOTICE OF FEDERAL TAX LIEN (Check one box below)
☐ HAS ALREADY BEEN FILED
☐ WILL BE FILED IMMEDIATELY
☐ WILL BE FILED WHEN TAX IS ASSESSED
☐ MAY BE FILED IF THIS AGREEMENT DEFAULTS

NOTE: A NOTICE OF FEDERAL TAX LIEN WILL NOT BE FILED ON ANY PORTION OF YOUR LIABILITY WHICH REPRESENTS AN INDIVIDUAL SHARED RESPONSIBILITY PAYMENT UNDER THE AFFORDABLE CARE ACT.

Agreement examined or approved by (Signature, title, function)	Date

Catalog Number 16644M | www.irs.gov | Form **433-D** (Rev. 1-2015)
Part 2 — Taxpayer's Copy

FinCEN Form 105 REPORT OF
INTERNATIONAL TRANSPORT OF CURRENCY

OMB NO. 1506-0014

FinCEN Form **105**

March 2011

Department of the Treasury
FinCEN

▶ Please type or print.

DEPARTMENT OF THE TREASURY
FINANCIAL CRIMES ENFORCEMENT NETWORK

REPORT OF INTERNATIONAL
TRANSPORTATION OF CURRENCY
OR MONETARY INSTRUMENTS

▶ To be filed with the Bureau of Customs and Border Protection
▶ For Paperwork Reduction Act Notice and Privacy Act Notice, see back of form.

31 U.S.C. 5316; 31 CFR 1010.340 and 1010.306

PART I FOR A PERSON DEPARTING OR ENTERING THE UNITED STATES, OR A PERSON SHIPPING, MAILING, OR RECEIVING CURRENCY OR MONETARY INSTRUMENTS. (IF ACTING FOR ANYONE ELSE, ALSO COMPLETE PART II BELOW.)

1. NAME (Last or family, first, and middle)	2. IDENTIFICATION NO. (See Instructions)	3. DATE OF BIRTH (Mo./Day/Yr.)

4. PERMANENT ADDRESS IN UNITED STATES OR ABROAD	5. YOUR COUNTRY OR COUNTRIES OF CITIZENSHIP

6. ADDRESS WHILE IN THE UNITED STATES	7. PASSPORT NO. & COUNTRY

8. U.S. VISA DATE (Mo./Day/Yr.)	9. PLACE UNITED STATES VISA WAS ISSUED	10. IMMIGRATION ALIEN NO.

11. IF CURRENCY OR MONETARY INSTRUMENT IS ACCOMPANIED BY A PERSON, **COMPLETE 11a OR 11b, not both**

A. EXPORTED FROM THE UNITED STATES	COMPLETE "A" OR "B" NOT BOTH	B. IMPORTED INTO THE UNITED STATES	
Departed From: (U.S. Port/City in U.S.)	Arrived At: (Foreign City/Country)	Departed From: (Foreign City/Country)	Arrived At: (City in U.S.)

12. IF CURRENCY OR MONETARY INSTRUMENT WAS MAILED OR OTHERWISE SHIPPED, COMPLETE 12a THROUGH 12f

12a. DATE SHIPPED (Mo./Day/Yr.)	12b. DATE RECEIVED (Mo./Day/Yr.)	12c. METHOD OF SHIPMENT (e.g. u.s. Mail, Public Carrier, etc.)	12d. NAME OF CARRIER

12e. SHIPPED TO (Name and Address)

12f. RECEIVED FROM (Name and Address)

PART II INFORMATION ABOUT PERSON(S) OR BUSINESS ON WHOSE BEHALF IMPORTATION OR EXPORTATION WAS CONDUCTED

13. NAME (Last or family, first, and middle or Business Name)

14. PERMANENT ADDRESS IN UNITED STATES OR ABROAD

15. TYPE OF BUSINESS ACTIVITY, OCCUPATION, OR PROFESSION	15a. IS THE BUSINESS A BANK? ☐ Yes ☐ No

PART III CURRENCY AND MONETARY INSTRUMENT INFORMATION (SEE INSTRUCTIONS ON REVERSE)(To be completed by everyone)

16. TYPE AND AMOUNT OF CURRENCY/MONETARY INSTRUMENTS			17. IF OTHER THAN U.S. CURRENCY IS INVOLVED, PLEASE COMPLETE BLOCKS A AND B.
Currency and Coins	▶	$	A. Currency Name
Other Monetary Instruments (Specify type, issuing entity and date, and serial or other identifying number.)	▶	$	
(TOTAL)	▶	$	B. Country

PART IV SIGNATURE OF PERSON COMPLETING THIS REPORT

Under penalties of perjury, I declare that I have examined this report, and to the best of my knowledge and belief it is true, correct and complete.

18. NAME AND TITLE (Print)	19. SIGNATURE	20. DATE OF REPORT (Mo./Day/Yr.)

CUSTOMS AND BORDER PROTECTION USE ONLY

THIS SHIPMENT IS ☐ INBOUND ☐ OUTBOUND	PORT CODE	CBP QUERY? Yes ☐ No ☐	COUNT VERIFIED Yes ☐ No ☐	VOLUNTARY REPORT Yes ☐ No ☐
DATE	AIRLINE/FLIGHT/VESSEL	LICENSE PLATE STATE/COUNTRY NUMBER	INSPECTOR (Name and Badge Number)	

FinCEN FORM 105

IRS FORM 433-F
COLLECTION INFORMATION STATEMENT

page 1

Collection Information Statement

Name(s) and Address	Your Social Security Number or Individual Taxpayer Identification Number
	Your Spouse's Social Security Number or Individual Taxpayer Identification Number

☐ If address provided above is different than last return filed, please check here

County of Residence

Your Telephone Numbers	Spouse's Telephone Numbers
Home:	Home:
Work:	Work:
Cell:	Cell:

Enter the number of people in the household who can be claimed on this year's tax return including you and your spouse. Under 65 [ ] 65 and Over [ ]

If you or your spouse are self employed or have self employment income, provide the following information:

Name of Business	Business EIN	Type of Business	Number of Employees *(not counting owner)*

A. ACCOUNTS / LINES OF CREDIT Include checking, online, mobile (e.g., PayPal) and savings accounts, Certificates of Deposit, Trusts, Individual Retirement Accounts (IRAs), Keogh Plans, Simplified Employee Pensions, 401(k) Plans, Profit Sharing Plans, Mutual Funds, Stocks, Bonds and other investments. If applicable, include business accounts. *(Use additional sheets if necessary.)*

Name and Address of Institution	Account Number	Type of Account	Current Balance/Value	Check if Business Account
				☐
				☐
				☐
				☐
				☐
				☐
				☐

B. REAL ESTATE Include home, vacation property, timeshares, vacant land and other real estate. *(Use additional sheets if necessary.)*

Description/Location/County	Monthly Payment(s)	Financing		Current Value	Balance Owed	Equity
☐ Primary Residence ☐ Other		Year Purchased	Purchase Price			
		Year Refinanced	Refinance Amount			
☐ Primary Residence ☐ Other		Year Purchased	Purchase Price			
		Year Refinanced	Refinance Amount			

C. OTHER ASSETS Include cars, boats, recreational vehicles, whole life policies, etc. Include make, model and year of vehicles and name of Life Insurance company in Description. If applicable, include business assets such as tools, equipment, inventory, etc. *(Use additional sheets if necessary.)*

Description	Monthly Payment	Year Purchased	Final Payment (mo/yr)	Current Value	Balance Owed	Equity
			/			
			/			
			/			
			/			
			/			
			/			
			/			

NOTES *(For IRS Use Only)*

TURN PAGE TO CONTINUE

Form 433-F (Rev. 1-2013) Catalog 62053J Department of the Treasury Internal Revenue Service publish.no.irs.gov

page 2

D. CREDIT CARDS *(Visa, MasterCard, American Express, Department Stores, etc.)*

Type	Credit Limit	Balance Owed	Minimum Monthly Payment

E. BUSINESS INFORMATION Complete E1 for Accounts Receivable owed to you or your business. *(Use additional sheets if necessary.)* Complete E2 if you or your business accepts credit card payments.

E1. Accounts Receivable owed to you or your business

Name	Address	Amount Owed
	List total amount owed from additional sheets	
	Total amount of accounts receivable available to pay to IRS now	

E2. Name of individual or business on account

Credit Card *(Visa, Master Card, etc.)*	Issuing Bank Name and Address	Merchant Account Number

F. EMPLOYMENT INFORMATION If you have more than one employer, include the information on another sheet of paper. *(If attaching a copy of current pay stub, you do not need to complete this section.)*

Your current Employer *(name and address)*	Spouse's current Employer *(name and address)*

How often are you paid? *(Check one)*
☐ Weekly ☐ Biweekly ☐ Semi-monthly ☐ Monthly

How often are you paid? *(Check one)*
☐ Weekly ☐ Biweekly ☐ Semi-monthly ☐ Monthly

Gross per pay period

Gross per pay period

Taxes per pay period *(Fed)* *(State)* *(Local)*

Taxes per pay period *(Fed)* *(State)* *(Local)*

How long at current employer

How long at current employer

G. NON-WAGE HOUSEHOLD INCOME List monthly amounts. For Self-Employment and Rental Income, list the monthly amount received after expenses or taxes and attach a copy of your current year profit and loss statement.

Alimony Income	Net Rental Income	Interest/Dividends Income
Child Support Income	Unemployment Income	Social Security Income
Net Self Employment Income	Pension Income	Other:

H. MONTHLY NECESSARY LIVING EXPENSES List monthly amounts. (For expenses paid other than monthly, see instructions.)

1. Food / Personal Care *See instructions. If you do not spend more than the standard allowable amount for your family size, fill in the Total amount only.*
Food
Housekeeping Supplies
Clothing and Clothing Services
Personal Care Products & Services
Miscellaneous

Total

2. Transportation
Gas/Insurance/Licenses/Parking/ Maintenance etc.
Public Transportation

3. Housing & Utilities
Rent
Electric, Oil/Gas, Water/Trash
Telephone/Cell/Cable/Internet
Real Estate Taxes and Insurance *(If not included in B above)*
Maintenance and Repairs

Total

4. Medical
Health Insurance
Out of Pocket Health Care Expenses

5. Other
Child / Dependent Care
Estimated Tax Payments
Term Life Insurance
Retirement *(Employer Required)*
Retirement *(Voluntary)*
Union Dues
Delinquent State & Local Taxes *(minimum payment)*
Student Loans *(minimum payment)*
Court Ordered Child Support
Court Ordered Alimony
Other Court Ordered Payments
Other *(specify)*
Other *(specify)*
Other *(specify)*

Under penalty of perjury, I declare to the best of my knowledge and belief this statement of assets, liabilities and other information is true, correct and complete.

Your Signature	Spouse's Signature	Date

Form 433-F (Rev. 1-2013) Catalog 62053J Department of the Treasury Internal Revenue Service publish.no.irs.gov

IRS FORM 656 OFFER IN COMPROMISE OIC

page 1

Form **656** (Rev. March 2011)	Department of the Treasury — Internal Revenue Service **Offer in Compromise**

Attach Application Fee and Payment *(check or money order)* here.

Section 1	**Your Contact Information**	**IRS Received Date**

Your First Name, Middle Initial, Last Name

If a Joint Offer, Spouse's First Name, Middle Initial, Last Name

Your Physical Home Address *(Street, City, State, ZIP Code)*

Mailing Address *(if different from above or Post Office Box number)*

Business Name

Your Business Address *(Street, City, State, ZIP Code)*

Social Security Number (SSN) *(Primary)*	*(Secondary)*	Employer Identification Number *(EIN)*	*(EIN not included in offer)*

Section 2 — **Tax Periods**

▶ **To: Commissioner of Internal Revenue Service**

In the following agreement, the pronoun "we" may be assumed in place of "I" when there are joint liabilities and both parties are signing this agreement.

I submit this offer to compromise the tax liabilities plus any interest, penalties, additions to tax, and additional amounts required by law for the tax type and period(s) marked below:

☐ 1040 Income Tax-Year(s)

☐ 1120 Income Tax-Year(s)

☐ 941 Employer's Quarterly Federal Tax Return - Quarterly period(s)

☐ 940 Employer's Annual Federal Unemployment (FUTA) Tax Return - Year(s)

☐ Trust Fund Recovery Penalty as a responsible person of *(enter corporation name)*
for failure to pay withholding and Federal Insurance Contributions Act taxes (Social Security taxes), for period(s) ending

☐ Other Federal Tax(es) [specify type(s) and period(s)]

Note: If you need more space, use attachment and title it "Attachment to Form 656 dated _____." Make sure to sign and date the attachment.

Section 3 — **Reason for Offer**

☐ **Doubt as to Collectibility** - I have insufficient assets and income to pay the full amount.

☐ **Exceptional Circumstances (Effective Tax Administration)** - I owe this amount and have sufficient assets to pay the full amount, but due to my exceptional circumstances, requiring full payment would cause an economic hardship or would be unfair and inequitable. I am submitting a written narrative explaining my circumstances.

Catalog Number 16728N · www.irs.gov · Form **656** (Rev. 3-2011)

page 2

Section 3	Reason for Offer *(Continued)*

Explanation of Circumstances *(Add additional pages, if needed)*

The IRS understands that there are unplanned events or special circumstances, such as serious illness, where paying the full amount or the minimum offer amount might impair your ability to provide for yourself and your family. If this is the case and you can provide documentation to prove your situation, then your offer may be accepted despite your financial profile. Describe your situation below and attach appropriate documents to this offer application.

Section 4	Low Income Certification *(Individuals Only)*

Do you qualify for Low-Income Certification? You qualify if your gross monthly household income is less than or equal to the amount shown in the chart below based on your family size and where you live. If you qualify, you are not required to submit any payments during the consideration of your offer.

☐ Check here if you qualify for Low-Income Certification based on the monthly income guidelines below.

Size of family unit	48 contiguous states and D.C.	Hawaii	Alaska
1	$2,256	$2,596	$2,819
2	$3,035	$3,492	$3,794
3	$3,815	$4,388	$4,769
4	$4,594	$5,283	$5,744
5	$5,373	$6,179	$6,719
6	$6,152	$7,075	$7,694
7	$6,931	$7,971	$8,669
8	$7,710	$8,867	$9,644
For each additional person, add	$ 779	$ 896	$ 975

Section 5	Payment Terms

Enter the amount of your offer $ _____

Check one of the payment options below to indicate how long it will take you to pay your offer in full.

Payment Option 1

☐ Check here if you will pay your offer in five or fewer payments:

Enclose a check for 20% of the offer amount (waived if you are an individual and met the requirements for Low-Income certification) and fill in the amount(s) and date(s) of your future payment(s).

20% of the offer amount is $ _____ leaving a balance of $ _____ to be paid as follows after the acceptance of your offer:

Amount of payment 1 $ _____ date _____

Amount of payment 2 $ _____ date _____

Amount of payment 3 $ _____ date _____

Amount of payment 4 $ _____ date _____

Amount of payment 5 $ _____ date _____

Payment Option 2

☐ Check here if you will pay your offer in full in more than five months and pay in monthly installments

Enclose a check for one month's installment (waived if you are an individual and met the requirements for Low-Income certification)

$ _____ is being submitted with the Form 656 and then $ _____ on the _____ (day) of each month thereafter for a total of _____ months. Total payments must equal the total Offer Amount.

You must continue to make these monthly payments while the IRS is considering the offer. Failure to make regular monthly payments will cause your offer to be returned.

IRS FORM 656 OFFER IN COMPROMISE OIC

page 3

Section 6	Designation of Down Payment and Deposit *(Optional)*

If you want your payment to be applied to a specific tax year and a specific tax debt, please tell us the tax form _____ and Tax Year/Quarter _____ . If you do not designate a preference, we will apply any money you send in to the governments best interest.

If you are paying more than the required payment when you submit your offer and want any part of that payment treated as a deposit, check the box below and insert the amount.

☐ I am making a deposit of $ _____ with this offer.

Section 7	Source of Funds

Tell us where you will obtain the funds to pay your offer. You may consider borrowing from friends and/or family, taking out a loan, or selling assets.

Include separate checks for the payment and application fee.

Make payable to the "United States Treasury" and attach to the front of your Form 656, Offer in Compromise. Do not send cash. Send a separate application fee with each offer; do not combine it with any other tax payments, as this may delay processing of your offer. Your offer will be returned to you if the application fee and the required payments are not properly remitted, or if your check is returned for insufficient funds.

Section 8	Offer Terms

By submitting this offer, I/we have read, understand and agree to the following terms and conditions:

Terms, Conditions, and Legal Agreement	a) I request that the IRS accept the offer amount listed in this offer application as payment of my outstanding tax debt (including interest, penalties, and any additional amounts required by law) as of the date listed on this form. I authorize the IRS to amend Section 2 on page 1 in the event I failed to list any of my assessed tax debt.
IRS will keep my payments, fees, and some refunds.	b) I voluntarily submit the payments made on this offer and understand that they are not refundable even if I withdraw the offer or the IRS rejects or returns the offer. Unless I designated how to apply the required payment (page 3 of this application), the IRS will apply my payment in the best interest of the government, choosing which tax years and tax liabilities to pay off. The IRS will also keep my application fee unless the offer is not accepted for processing.
	c) The IRS will keep any refund, including interest, that I might be due for tax periods extending through the calendar year in which the IRS accepts my offer. I cannot designate that the refund be applied to estimated tax payments for the following year or the accepted offer amount. If I receive a refund after I submit this offer for any tax period extending through the calendar year in which the IRS accepts my offer, I will return the refund as soon as possible.
	d) The IRS will keep any monies it has collected prior to this offer and any payments that I make relating to this offer that I did not designate as a deposit. Only amounts that exceed the mandatory payments can be treated as a deposit. Such a deposit will be refundable if the offer is rejected or returned by the IRS or is withdrawn. I understand that the IRS will not pay interest on any deposit. The IRS may seize ("levy") my assets up to the time that the IRS official signs and accepts my offer as pending.
Pending status of an offer and right to appeal	e) Once an authorized IRS official signs this form, my offer is considered pending as of that signature date and it remains pending until the IRS accepts, rejects, returns, or terminates my offer or I withdraw my offer. An offer will be considered withdrawn when the IRS receives my written notification of withdrawal by personal delivery or certified mail or when I inform the IRS of my withdrawal by other means and the IRS acknowledges in writing my intent to withdraw the offer.
	f) I waive the right to an Appeals hearing if I do not request a hearing within 30 days of the date the IRS notifies me of the decision to reject the offer.
I must comply with my future tax obligations and understand I remain liable for the full amount of my tax debt until all terms and conditions of this offer have been met.	g) I will file tax returns and pay required taxes for the five year period beginning with the date of acceptance of this offer, or until my offer is paid in full, whichever is longer. If this is an offer being submitted for joint tax debt, and one of us does not comply with future obligations, only the non-compliant taxpayer will be in default of this agreement.
	h) The IRS will not remove the original amount of my tax debt from its records until I have met all the terms and conditions of this offer. Penalty and interest will continue to accrue until all payment terms of the offer have been met. If I file for bankruptcy before the terms are fully met, any claim the IRS files in the bankruptcy proceedings will be a tax claim.
	i) Once the IRS accepts my offer in writing, I have no right to contest, in court or otherwise, the amount of the tax debt.
I understand what will happen if I fail to meet the terms of my offer (e.g., default).	j) If I fail to meet any of the terms of this offer, the IRS may levy or sue me to collect any amount ranging from the unpaid balance of the offer to the original amount of the tax debt without further notice of any kind. The IRS will continue to add interest, as Section 6601 of the Internal Revenue Code requires, on the amount the IRS determines is due after default. The IRS will add interest from the date I default until I completely satisfy the amount owed.
I agree to waive time limits provided by law.	k) To have my offer considered, I agree to the extension of the time limit provided by law to assess my tax debt (statutory period of assessment). I agree that the date by which the IRS must assess my tax debt will now be the date by which my debt must currently be assessed plus the period of time my offer is pending plus one additional year if the IRS rejects, returns, or terminates my offer or I withdraw it. (Paragraph (e) of this section defines pending and withdrawal). I understand that I have the right not to waive the statutory period of assessment or to limit the waiver to a certain length or certain periods or issues. I understand, however, that the

page 4

Page 4 of 4

Section 8 - *(Continued)*

IRS may not consider my offer if I refuse to waive the statutory period of assessment or if I provide only a limited waiver. I also understand that the statutory period for collecting my tax debt will be suspended during the time my offer is pending with the IRS, for 30 days after any rejection of my offer by the IRS, and during the time that any rejection of my offer is being considered by the Appeals Office.

I understand the IRS may file a Notice of Federal Tax Lien on my property.	l) The IRS may file a Notice of Federal Tax Lien during the offer investigation. Generally, the IRS files a Notice of Federal Tax Lien to protect the Government's interest on offers that will be paid over time. This tax lien will be released when the payment terms of the accepted offer have been satisfied.
I authorize the IRS to contact relevant third parties in order to process my offer	m) By authorizing the IRS to contact third parties including credit bureaus, I understand that I will not be notified of which third parties the IRS contacts as part of the offer application process, as stated in section 7602(c) of the Internal Revenue Code.
I am submitting an offer as an individual for a joint liability	n) I understand if the liability sought to be compromised is the joint and individual liability of myself and my co-obligor(s) and I am submitting this offer to compromise my individual liability only, then if this offer is accepted, it does not release or discharge my co-obligor(s) from liability. The United States still reserves all rights of collection against the co-obligor(s).

Section 9 — Signatures

Under penalties of perjury, I declare that I have examined this offer, including accompanying schedules and statements, and to the best of my knowledge and belief, it is true, correct and complete.

▶ Signature of Taxpayer	Date *(mm/dd/yyyy)*
▶ Signature of Taxpayer	Date *(mm/dd/yyyy)*

Section 10 — Paid Preparer Use Only

Signature of Preparer

Name of Paid Preparer	Date *(mm/dd/yyyy)*	Preparer's CAF no. or PTIN

Firm's Name, Address, and ZIP Code

Include a valid, signed Form 2848 or 8821 with this application, if one is not on file.

Section 11 — Third Party Designee

Do you want to allow another person to discuss this offer with the IRS? ☐ Yes ☐ No

If yes, provide designee's name	Telephone Number ( )

IRS Use Only

I accept the waiver of the statutory period of limitations on assessment for the Internal Revenue Service, as described in Section 8 (k).

Signature of Authorized Internal Revenue Service Official	Title	Date *(mm/dd/yyyy)*

Privacy Act Statement

We ask for the information on this form to carry out the internal revenue laws of the United States. Our authority to request this information is Section 7801 of the Internal Revenue Code.

Our purpose for requesting the information is to determine if it is in the best interests of the IRS to accept an offer. You are not required to make an offer; however, if you choose to do so, you must provide all of the taxpayer information requested. Failure to provide all of the information may prevent us from processing your request.

If you are a paid preparer and you prepared the Form 656 for the taxpayer submitting an offer, we request that you complete and sign Section 10 on Form 656, and provide identifying information. Providing this information is voluntary. This information will be used to administer and enforce the internal revenue laws of the United States and may be used to regulate practice before the Internal Revenue Service for those persons subject to Treasury Department Circular No. 230, Regulations Governing the Practice of Attorneys, Certified Public Accountants, Enrolled Agents, Enrolled Actuaries, and Appraisers before the Internal Revenue Service. Information on this form may be disclosed to the Department of Justice for civil and criminal litigation.

We may also disclose this information to cities, states and the District of Columbia for use in administering their tax laws and to combat terrorism. Providing false or fraudulent information on this form may subject you to criminal prosecution and penalties.

Catalog Number 16728N   www.irs.gov   Form 656 (Rev. 3-2011)

FinCEN FORM 8300 REPORT OF
CASH PAYMENTS OVER $10,000

page 1

IRS Form **8300** (Rev. August 2014) Department of the Treasury Internal Revenue Service	**Report of Cash Payments Over $10,000 Received in a Trade or Business** ► See instructions for definition of cash. ► Use this form for transactions occurring after August 29, 2014. Do not use prior versions after this date. For Privacy Act and Paperwork Reduction Act Notice, see the last page.	FinCEN Form **8300** (Rev. August 2014) OMB No. 1506-0018 Department of the Treasury Financial Crimes Enforcement Network

1 Check appropriate box(es) if: **a** ☐ Amends prior report;   **b** ☐ Suspicious transaction.

Part I   Identity of Individual From Whom the Cash Was Received

2 If more than one individual is involved, check here and see instructions . . . . ► ☐

3 Last name		**4** First name	**5** M.I.	**6** Taxpayer identification number

7 Address (number, street, and apt. or suite no.)	**8** Date of birth . . ► (see instructions) M M D D Y Y Y Y

9 City	**10** State	**11** ZIP code	**12** Country (if not U.S.)	**13** Occupation, profession, or business

14 Identifying document (ID) ►	**a Describe ID** ► **c Number** ►	**b Issued by** ►

Part II   Person on Whose Behalf This Transaction Was Conducted

15 If this transaction was conducted on behalf of more than one person, check here and see instructions . . . . ► ☐

16 Individual's last name or organization's name	**17** First name	**18** M.I.	**19** Taxpayer identification number

20 Doing business as (DBA) name (see instructions)	Employer identification number

21 Address (number, street, and apt. or suite no.)	**22** Occupation, profession, or business

23 City	**24** State	**25** ZIP code	**26** Country (if not U.S.)

27 Alien identification (ID) ►	**a Describe ID** ► **c Number** ►	**b Issued by** ►

Part III   Description of Transaction and Method of Payment

28 Date cash received M M D D Y Y Y Y	**29** Total cash received $ .00	**30** If cash was received in more than one payment, check here . . . ► ☐	**31** Total price if different from item 29 $ .00

32 Amount of cash received (in U.S. dollar equivalent) (must equal item 29) (see instructions):

a U.S. currency $ _____ .00 (Amount in $100 bills or higher $ _____ .00)
b Foreign currency $ _____ .00 (Country ► _____)
c Cashier's check(s) $ _____ .00   Issuer's name(s) and serial number(s) of the monetary instrument(s) ►
d Money order(s) $ _____ .00
e Bank draft(s) $ _____ .00
f Traveler's check(s) $ _____ .00

33 Type of transaction
a ☐ Personal property purchased
b ☐ Real property purchased
c ☐ Personal services provided
d ☐ Business services provided
e ☐ Intangible property purchased
f ☐ Debt obligations paid
g ☐ Exchange of cash
h ☐ Escrow or trust funds
i ☐ Bail received by court clerks
j ☐ Other (specify in item 34) ►

34 Specific description of property or service shown in 33. Give serial or registration number, address, docket number, etc. ►

Part IV   Business That Received Cash

35 Name of business that received cash	**36** Employer identification number

37 Address (number, street, and apt. or suite no.)	Social security number

38 City	**39** State	**40** ZIP code	**41** Nature of your business

42 Under penalties of perjury, I declare that to the best of my knowledge the information I have furnished above is true, correct, and complete.

Signature ► _____ Authorized official   Title ► _____

43 Date of signature M M D D Y Y Y Y	**44** Type or print name of contact person	**45** Contact telephone number

IRS Form **8300** (Rev. 8-2014)   Cat. No. 62133S   FinCEN Form **8300** (Rev. 8-2014)

| IRS Form 8300 (Rev. 8-2014) | Page **2** | FinCEN Form 8300 (Rev. 8-2014) |

Multiple Parties
(Complete applicable parts below if box 2 or 15 on page 1 is checked.)

Part I   Continued—Complete if box 2 on page 1 is checked

3 Last name	4 First name	5 M.I.	6 Taxpayer identification number
7 Address (number, street, and apt. or suite no.)		8 Date of birth . . . ▶ (see instructions)	M M D D Y Y Y Y
9 City	10 State	11 ZIP code	12 Country (if not U.S.)	13 Occupation, profession, or business
14 Identifying document (ID)	a Describe ID ▶ / c Number ▶		b Issued by ▶

3 Last name	4 First name	5 M.I.	6 Taxpayer identification number
7 Address (number, street, and apt. or suite no.)		8 Date of birth . . . ▶ (see instructions)	M M D D Y Y Y Y
9 City	10 State	11 ZIP code	12 Country (if not U.S.)	13 Occupation, profession, or business
14 Identifying document (ID)	a Describe ID ▶ / c Number ▶		b Issued by ▶

Part II   Continued—Complete if box 15 on page 1 is checked

16 Individual's last name or organization's name	17 First name	18 M.I.	19 Taxpayer identification number
20 Doing business as (DBA) name (see instructions)			Employer identification number
21 Address (number, street, and apt. or suite no.)			22 Occupation, profession, or business
23 City	24 State	25 ZIP code	26 Country (if not U.S.)	
27 Alien identification (ID)	a Describe ID ▶ / c Number ▶		b Issued by ▶

16 Individual's last name or organization's name	17 First name	18 M.I.	19 Taxpayer identification number
20 Doing business as (DBA) name (see instructions)			Employer identification number
21 Address (number, street, and apt. or suite no.)			22 Occupation, profession, or business
23 City	24 State	25 ZIP code	26 Country (if not U.S.)	
27 Alien identification (ID)	a Describe ID ▶ / c Number ▶		b Issued by ▶

Comments – Please use the lines provided below to comment on or clarify any information you entered on any line in Parts I, II, III, and IV

| IRS Form 8300 (Rev. 8-2014) | | FinCEN Form 8300 (Rev. 8-2014) |

FORM 14039
IDENTITY THEFT AFFIDAVIT
page 1

Form 14039 Rev. February 2014	Department of the Treasury - Internal Revenue Service **Identity Theft Affidavit**	OMB Number 1545-2139

Complete and submit this form if you are an actual or potential victim of identity theft and would like the IRS to mark your account to identify questionable activity.

Check only one of the following two boxes if they apply to your specific situation. (Optional for all filers)

☐ I am submitting this form in response to a mailed notice or letter from the IRS.

☐ I am completing this form on behalf of another person, such as a deceased spouse or other deceased relative. You should provide information for the actual or potential victim in Sections A, B, & D.

Note to all filers: Failure to provide required information on **BOTH** sides of this form **AND** clear and legible documentation will delay processing.

THIS FORM MUST BE SIGNED ON THE REVERSE SIDE (SECTION F).

Section A – Reason For Filing This Form (Required for all filers)

Check only **ONE** of the following two boxes. You **MUST** provide the requested description or explanation in the lined area below.

1 ☐ I am a victim of identity theft **AND** it is affecting my federal tax records.

You should check this box if, for example, your attempt to file electronically was rejected because someone had already filed using your Social Security Number (SSN) or Individual Taxpayer Identification Number (ITIN), or if you received a notice or correspondence from the IRS indicating someone was otherwise using your number.

Provide a short explanation of the problem and how you were made aware of it.

2 ☐ I have experienced an event involving my personal information that may at some future time affect my federal tax records.

You should check this box if you are the victim of non-federal tax related identity theft, such as the misuse of your personal identity information to obtain credit. You should also check this box if no identity theft violation has occurred, but you have experienced an event that could result in identity theft, such as a lost/stolen purse or wallet, home robbery, etc.

Briefly describe the identity theft violation(s) and/or the event(s) of concern. Include the date(s) of the incident(s).

Section B – Taxpayer Information (Required for all filers)

Taxpayer's last name	First name	Middle initial	The last 4 digits of the taxpayer's SSN or the taxpayer's complete Individual Taxpayer Identification Number (ITIN)

Taxpayer's **current** mailing address (apt., suite no. and street, or P.O. Box)

City	State	ZIP code

Tax year(s) affected *(Required if you checked box 1 in Section A above)*	Last tax return filed (year) *(If you are not required to file a return, enter NRF and do not complete the next two lines)*

Address on last tax return filed *(If same as current address, write "same as above")*

City (on last tax return filed)	State	ZIP code

Section C – Telephone Contact Information (Required for all filers)

Telephone number *(include area code)* ☐ Home ☐ Work ☐ Cell	Best time(s) to call

I prefer to be contacted in *(select the appropriate language)* ☐ English ☐ Spanish ☐ Other _____

Section D – Required Documentation (Required for all filers)

Submit this completed form and a **clear and legible** photocopy of at least one of the following documents to verify your identity. If you are submitting this form on behalf of another person, the documentation should be for that person. If necessary, enlarge the photocopies so all information and pictures are clearly visible.

Check the box next to the document(s) you are submitting:

☐ Passport   ☐ Driver's license   ☐ Social Security Card   ☐ Other valid U.S. Federal or State government issued identification**

** Do not submit photocopies of federally issued identification where prohibited by 18 U.S.C. 701 (e.g., official badges designating federal employment).

Form **14039** (Rev. 2-2014) Catalog Number 52525A   www.irs.gov   Department of the Treasury - Internal Revenue Service

FORM 14039
IDENTITY THEFT AFFIDAVIT
page 2

N
09

Form 14039 Rev. February 2014	Department of the Treasury - Internal Revenue Service **Identity Theft Affidavit**	OMB Number 1545-2139

Section E – Representative Information (Required only if completing this form on someone else's behalf)

If you are completing this form on behalf of another person, you **must** complete this section and attach **clear and legible** photocopies of the documentation indicated.

Check only **ONE** of the following four boxes next to the reason why you are submitting this form

☐ The taxpayer is deceased and I am the surviving spouse. *(No attachments are required)*

☐ The taxpayer is deceased and I am the court-appointed or certified personal representative.
Attach a copy of the court certificate showing your appointment.

☐ The taxpayer is deceased and a court-appointed or certified personal representative has not been appointed.
Attach a copy of the death certificate or the formal notification from the appropriate government office informing the next of kin
of the decedent's death. Indicate your relationship to the decedent: _____

☐ The taxpayer is unable to complete this form and I have been appointed conservator or have Power of Attorney (POA) authorization.
Attach a copy of the documentation showing your appointment as conservator or your POA authorization.
If you are the POA and have been issued a CAF number by the IRS, enter it here: _____

Representative's name

Current mailing address

City	State	ZIP code

Section F – Penalty Of Perjury Statement and Signature (Required for all filers)

Under penalty of perjury, I declare that, to the best of my knowledge and belief, the information entered on this form is true, correct, complete, and made in good faith.

Signature of taxpayer or representative of taxpayer	Date signed

Instructions for Submitting this Form
Submit this form and **clear and legible** copies of required documentation using **ONE** of the following submission options.
Mailing **AND** faxing this form **WILL** result in a processing delay.

By Mail	By FAX
If you checked Box 1 in Section A and are unable to file your return electronically because the primary and/or secondary SSN was misused, attach this form and documentation to your paper return and submit to the IRS location where you normally file. If you have already filed your paper return, submit this form and documentation to the IRS location where you normally file. Refer to the "Where Do You File" section of your return instructions or visit IRS.gov and input the search term "Where to File". If you checked Box 1 in Section A and are submitting this form in response to a notice or letter received from the IRS, return this form and documentation with a copy of the notice or letter to the address contained in the notice or letter. If you checked Box 2 in Section A (you do not currently have a tax-related issue), mail this form and documentation to: **Internal Revenue Service** PO Box 9039 Andover MA 01810-0939	If you checked Box 1 in Section A and are submitting this form in response to a notice or letter received from the IRS that shows a reply FAX number, FAX this completed form and documentation with a copy of the notice or letter to that number. Include a cover sheet marked "Confidential." If no FAX number is shown, follow the mailing instructions on the notice or letter. If you checked Box 2 in Section A (you do not currently have a tax-related issue), FAX this form and documentation to: (855) 807-5720. **NOTE:** The IRS does not initiate contact with taxpayers by email, fax, or any social media tools to request personal or financial information. Report unsolicited email claiming to be from the IRS and bogus IRS websites to phishing@irs.gov. **NOTE:** For more information about questionable communications purportedly from the IRS, visit IRS.gov and input the search term "Fake IRS Communications".

Other helpful identity theft information may be found on www.irs.gov/uac/Identity-Protection. Additionally, locations and hours of operation for Taxpayer Assistance Centers can be found at www.irs.gov (search "Local Contacts").
Note: The Federal Trade Commission (FTC) is the central federal government agency responsible for identity theft awareness. The IRS does not share taxpayer information with the FTC. Refer to the FTC's website at www.identitytheft.gov for additional information, protection strategies, and resources.

Privacy Act and Paperwork Reduction Notice

Our legal authority to request the information is 26 U.S.C. 6001.
The primary purpose of the form is to provide a method of reporting identity theft issues to the IRS so that the IRS may document situations where individuals are or may be victims of identity theft. Additional purposes include the use in the determination of proper tax liability and to relieve taxpayer burden. The information may be disclosed only as provided by 26 U.S.C. 6103. Providing the information on this form is voluntary. However, if you do not provide the information it may be more difficult to assist you in resolving your identity theft issue. If you are a potential victim of identity theft and do not provide the required substantiation information, we may not be able to place a marker on your account to assist with future protection. If you are a victim of identity theft and do not provide the required information, it may be difficult for IRS to determine your correct tax liability. If you intentionally provide false information, you may be subject to criminal penalties.
You are not required to provide the information requested on a form that is subject to the Paperwork Reduction Act unless the form displays a valid OMB control number. Books or records relating to a form or its instructions must be retained as long as their contents may become material in the administration of any Internal Revenue law. Generally, tax returns and return information are confidential, as required by section 6103.
Public reporting burden for this collection of information is estimated to average 15 minutes per response, including the time for reviewing instructions, searching existing data sources, gathering and maintaining the data needed, and completing and reviewing the collection of information. If you have comments concerning the accuracy of these time estimates or suggestions for making this form simpler, we would be happy to hear from you. You can write to the Internal Revenue Service, Tax Products Coordinating Committee, SE:W:CAR:MP:T:T:SP, 1111 Constitution Ave. NW, IR-6526, Washington, DC 20224. Do not send this form to this address. Instead, see the form for filing instructions. Notwithstanding any other provision of the law, no person is required to respond to, nor shall any person be subject to a penalty for failure to comply with, a collection of information subject to the requirements of the Paperwork Reduction Act, unless that collection of information displays a currently valid OMB Control Number.

Form **14039** (Rev. 2-2014) Catalog Number 52525A   www.irs.gov   Department of the Treasury - Internal Revenue Service

IRS FORM 8938 SPECIFIED FOREIGN FINANCIAL ASSETS

page 1

Form 8938

Department of the Treasury
Internal Revenue Service

Statement of Specified Foreign Financial Assets

▶ Information about Form 8938 and its separate instructions is at www.irs.gov/form8938.
▶ Attach to your tax return.

For calendar year 20___ or tax year beginning ___ 20___ and ending ___ , 20___

OMB No. 1545-2195

2015

Attachment Sequence No. 175

If you have attached continuation statements, check here ☐   Number of continuation statements _____

Name(s) shown on return _____   TIN _____

Part I   Foreign Deposit and Custodial Accounts Summary

1	Number of Deposit Accounts (reported on Form 8938) . . . . ▶	
2	Maximum Value of All Deposit Accounts	$
3	Number of Custodial Accounts (reported on Form 8938) . . . . ▶	
4	Maximum Value of All Custodial Accounts	$
5	Were any foreign deposit or custodial accounts closed during the tax year?	☐ Yes ☐ No

Part II   Other Foreign Assets Summary

1	Number of Foreign Assets (reported on Form 8938) . . . . ▶	
2	Maximum Value of All Assets	$
3	Were any foreign assets acquired or sold during the tax year?	☐ Yes ☐ No

Part III   Summary of Tax Items Attributable to Specified Foreign Financial Assets (see instructions)

(a) Asset Category	(b) Tax Item	(c) Amount reported on form or schedule	Where reported	
			(d) Form and line	(e) Schedule and line
1 Foreign Deposit and Custodial Accounts	1a Interest	$		
	1b Dividends	$		
	1c Royalties	$		
	1d Other income	$		
	1e Gains (losses)	$		
	1f Deductions	$		
	1g Credits	$		
2 Other Foreign Assets	2a Interest	$		
	2b Dividends	$		
	2c Royalties	$		
	2d Other income	$		
	2e Gains (losses)	$		
	2f Deductions	$		
	2g Credits	$		

Part IV   Excepted Specified Foreign Financial Assets (see instructions)

If you reported specified foreign financial assets on one or more of the following forms, enter the number of such forms filed. You do not need to include these assets on Form 8938 for the tax year.

1. Number of Forms 3520 _____   2. Number of Forms 3520-A _____   3. Number of Forms 5471 _____
4. Number of Forms 8621 _____   5. Number of Forms 8865 _____

Part V   Detailed Information for Each Foreign Deposit and Custodial Account Included in the Part I Summary (see instructions)

If you have more than one account to report, attach a continuation statement for each additional account (see instructions).

1	Type of account ☐ Deposit ☐ Custodial	2 Account number or other designation

3 Check all that apply   a ☐ Account opened during tax year   b ☐ Account closed during tax year
c ☐ Account jointly owned with spouse   d ☐ No tax item reported in Part III with respect to this asset

4	Maximum value of account during tax year	$
5	Did you use a foreign currency exchange rate to convert the value of the account into U.S. dollars? . .	☐ Yes ☐ No
6	If you answered "Yes" to line 5, complete all that apply.	

(a) Foreign currency in which account is maintained	(b) Foreign currency exchange rate used to convert to U.S. dollars	(c) Source of exchange rate used if not from U.S. Treasury Department's Bureau of the Fiscal Service

For Paperwork Reduction Act Notice, see the separate instructions.   Cat. No. 37753A   Form **8938** (2015)

page 2

Part V   **Detailed Information for Each Foreign Deposit and Custodial Account Included in the Part I Summary** (see instructions) (continued)

7 a	Name of financial institution in which account is maintained	**b** Reserved

8   Mailing address of financial institution in which account is maintained. Number, street, and room or suite no.

9   City or town, state or province, and country (including postal code)

Part VI   **Detailed Information for Each "Other Foreign Asset" Included in the Part II Summary** (see instructions)

Note. If you reported specified foreign financial assets on Forms 3520, 3520-A, 5471, 8621, or 8865, you do not have to include the assets on Form 8938. You must complete Part IV. See instructions.

If you have more than one asset to report, attach a continuation statement for each additional asset (see instructions).

1	Description of asset	**2** Identifying number or other designation

3   Complete all that apply. See instructions for reporting of multiple acquisition or disposition dates.
a   Date asset acquired during tax year, if applicable . . . .
b   Date asset disposed of during tax year, if applicable . . . .
c   ☐ Check if asset jointly owned with spouse   **d** ☐ Check if no tax item reported in Part III with respect to this asset

4   Maximum value of asset during tax year (check box that applies)
a ☐ $0 - $50,000   **b** ☐ $50,001 - $100,000   **c** ☐ $100,001 - $150,000   **d** ☐ $150,001 - $200,000
e   If more than $200,000, list value . . . . $

5   Did you use a foreign currency exchange rate to convert the value of the asset into U.S. dollars? . . . ☐ Yes   ☐ No
6   If you answered "Yes" to line 5, complete all that apply.

(a) Foreign currency in which asset is denominated	**(b)** Foreign currency exchange rate used to convert to U.S. dollars	**(c)** Source of exchange rate used if not from U.S. Treasury Department's Bureau of the Fiscal Service

7   If asset reported on line 1 is stock of a foreign entity or an interest in a foreign entity, enter the following information for the asset.
a   Name of foreign entity   **b** Reserved
c   Type of foreign entity   **(1)** ☐ Partnership   **(2)** ☐ Corporation   **(3)** ☐ Trust   **(4)** ☐ Estate
d   Mailing address of foreign entity. Number, street, and room or suite no.

e   City or town, state or province, and country (including postal code)

8   If asset reported on line 1 is not stock of a foreign entity or an interest in a foreign entity, enter the following information for the asset.
   Note. If this asset has more than one issuer or counterparty, attach a continuation statement with the same information for each additional issuer or counterparty (see instructions).

a   Name of issuer or counterparty
   Check if information is for   ☐ Issuer   ☐ Counterparty

b   Type of issuer or counterparty
   (1) ☐ Individual   **(2)** ☐ Partnership   **(3)** ☐ Corporation   **(4)** ☐ Trust   **(5)** ☐ Estate

c   Check if issuer or counterparty is a   ☐ U.S. person   ☐ Foreign person
d   Mailing address of issuer or counterparty. Number, street, and room or suite no.

e   City or town, state or province, and country (including postal code)

Form **8938** (2015)

IRS FORM 8938 SPECIFIED FOREIGN FINANCIAL ASSETS

page 3

Form 8938 (2015)   Page

(Continuation Statement)

Name(s) shown on return	TIN

Part V Detailed Information for Each Foreign Deposit and Custodial Account Included in the Part I Summary (see instructions)

1 Type of account ☐ Deposit ☐ Custodial   **2** Account number or other designation

3 Check all that apply   a ☐ Account opened during tax year   b ☐ Account closed during tax year
                              c ☐ Account jointly owned with spouse   d ☐ No tax item reported in Part III with respect to this asset

4 Maximum value of account during tax year . . . . $

5 Did you use a foreign currency exchange rate to convert the value of the account into U.S. dollars? . . ☐ Yes ☐ No

6 If you answered "Yes" to line 5, complete all that apply.

(a) Foreign currency in which account is maintained	**(b)** Foreign currency exchange rate used to convert to U.S. dollars	**(c)** Source of exchange rate used if not from U.S. Treasury Department's Bureau of the Fiscal Service

7 a Name of financial institution in which account is maintained   **b** Reserved

8 Mailing address of financial institution in which account is maintained. Number, street, and room or suite no.

9 City or town, state or province, and country (including postal code)

Part VI Detailed Information for Each "Other Foreign Asset" Included in the Part II Summary (see instructions)

1 Description of asset   **2** Identifying number or other designation

3 Complete all that apply. See instructions for reporting of multiple acquisition or disposition dates.
 a Date asset acquired during tax year, if applicable . . . .
 b Date asset disposed of during tax year, if applicable . . . .
 c ☐ Check if asset jointly owned with spouse   **d** ☐ Check if no tax item reported in Part III with respect to this asset

4 Maximum value of asset during tax year (check box that applies)
 a ☐ $0 - $50,000   **b** ☐ $50,001 - $100,000   **c** ☐ $100,001 - $150,000   **d** ☐ $150,001 - $200,000
 e If more than $200,000, list value . . . . $

5 Did you use a foreign currency exchange rate to convert the value of the asset into U.S. dollars? . . . ☐ Yes ☐ No

6 If you answered "Yes" to line 5, complete all that apply.

(a) Foreign currency in which asset is denominated	**(b)** Foreign currency exchange rate used to convert to U.S. dollars	**(c)** Source of exchange rate used if not from U.S. Treasury Department's Bureau of the Fiscal Service

7 If asset reported on line 1 is stock of a foreign entity or an interest in a foreign entity, enter the following information for the asset.
 a Name of foreign entity   **b** Reserved
 c Type of foreign entity   **(1)** ☐ Partnership   **(2)** ☐ Corporation   **(3)** ☐ Trust   **(4)** ☐ Estate
 d Mailing address of foreign entity. Number, street, and room or suite no.

 e City or town, state or province, and country (including postal code)

8 If asset reported on line 1 is not stock of a foreign entity or an interest in a foreign entity, enter the following information for the asset.
 a Name of issuer or counterparty
    Check if information is for   ☐ Issuer   ☐ Counterparty

 b Type of issuer or counterparty
    (1) ☐ Individual   **(2)** ☐ Partnership   **(3)** ☐ Corporation   **(4)** ☐ Trust   **(5)** ☐ Estate

 c Check if issuer or counterparty is a   ☐ U.S. person   ☐ Foreign person
 d Mailing address of issuer or counterparty. Number, street, and room or suite no.

 e City or town, state or province, and country (including postal code)

Form **8938** (2015)

Made in the USA
Las Vegas, NV
30 January 2022

42662573R00109